Indian Accents

D1569970

THE ASIAN AMERICAN EXPERIENCE

Series Editors
Eiichiro Azuma
Jigna Desai
Martin F. Manalansan IV
Lisa Sun-Hee Park
David K. Yoo

Roger Daniels, Founding Series Editor

Indian Accents

Brown Voice and Racial Performance
in American Television and Film

SHILPA S. DAVÉ

UNIVERSITY OF ILLINOIS PRESS

Urbana, Chicago, and Springfield

Contents

Illustrations

Acknowledgments

I owe many thanks to the people who have helped support and develop this project. When I was a graduate student at the University of Michigan, Stephen Sumida and Simon Gikandi encouraged my early approaches to the intersection of Asian American literature and postcolonial narratives. Gail Nomura, Andrea Press, and Patricia Yaeger introduced me to new theories in history, communications and media, and women's studies. They set me on the path that would eventually expand my study from literature to ethnic studies and comparative American studies and popular culture. My special thanks goes to the UM group of scholars with whom I explored the borders of Asian American studies, including Linda Bachman, Nancy Cho, Larry Hashima, Stewart Ikeda, Daryl Maeda, LeiLani Nishime, Grace Pang, Cristine Paschild, and Morris Young.

I have been privileged to have a wide circle of colleagues who have enriched my life personally and intellectually over the years—I thank all of you. I acknowledge my colleagues who have especially motivated and encouraged me: Mary Beltrán, Rick Bonus, Jennifer Chan, Kenyon Chan, Floyd Cheung, Lavina Dhingra, Pawan Dhingra, Hien Duc Do, Augusto Espiritu, Jennifer Ho, Evelyn Hu-Du Hart, Pensri Ho, Emily Ignacio, Bill Imada, Jane Iwamura, Victor Jew, Moon-Ho Jung, L. S. Kim, Madulikha Khadelwal, Rebecca King, Robert Lee, Shirley Lim, Sunaina Maira, Martin Manalansan, Sucheta Mazumdar, Karen Naransaki, Franklin Odo, Gary Okihiro, Kent Ono, Edward Park, Jane Park, Vijay Prasad, Gita Rajan, Maria Sanchez, Jack Tchen, K. Scott Wong, Sau-ling Wong, Jeff Yang, and David Yoo.

Tasha Oren and LeiLani Nishime have been generous academic partners, the best coeditors I could wish for, and friends who have been there from the beginning of our academic careers. Rajini Srikanth is a warm generous mentor and adviser who has introduced me into a thriving intellectual and academic home for me in the Boston area. Mary Danico is a good friend who has inspired me with her active engagement for the future of Asian American Studies. Linda Vo is a veritable rock of professional support and a valued friend.

The staff of the Multicultural Resource Center at Oberlin College, especially Adrian Bautista, Joe DiChristina, Kenneth Holmes, Narges Kakalia, and Michelle Shim, as well as David Kamitsuka and the faculty, staff, and students inspired me and taught me about Asian American Studies and Comparative American Studies on the student-life side and in academia. My thanks to Amy Ling, Nellie McKay, Hemant Shah, and Susan Friedman for their support while I was a visiting professor in Asian American Studies and in the English department at the University of Wisconsin–Madison. I am especially indebted to my UW-Madison writing group, who saw the kernels of this project and propelled me to do a full study: Victor Bascara, Leslie Bow, Grace Hong, Lisa Nakamura, and Michael Peterson. A heartfelt appreciation goes to Anita Affeldt, Maria Christina Garcia, Viranjini Munasinghe, and Shelley Wong at Cornell University and to Patricia Hill, Allan Isaacs, Indira Karamcheti, J. Kehaulani Kauanui, Anita Mannur, Sean McCann, and William Stowe of Wesleyan University, where I was a visiting assistant professor. I have benefitted from knowing all my colleagues in the American Studies program at Brandeis University, especially Joyce Antler, Jerry Cohen, Tom Doherty, Maura Farrelly Angie Simeone, Cheryl Sweeney, and Melanie Zoltan. In addition, I have learned much from Anita Hill, Thomas King, Sarah Lamb, Susan Lanser, James Mandrell, Eileen McNamara, Laura Miller, Faith Smith, Harleen Singh, and Elaine Wong. Finally, I thank the students in all my courses, who inspire me and teach me new ideas on a daily basis.

The writing and research of this manuscript were done with the aid of a one-semester research sabbatical from Brandeis University and financial grants from the Dean of Arts and Sciences office, the Norman Grant for Research, and the Tomberg Fund for junior faculty. I also thank the staff at the Reading Room of the Margaret Herrick Library of the Academy of Motion Picture Arts and Sciences in Los Angeles for their generous comments and suggestions.

I have a sincere appreciation for my colleagues in the Boston area who provided a stimulating and intellectually vibrant community and inspired my best work. Thanks to Vivek Bald, Stella Chin, Monica Chiu, Peggy Leavitt, Min Song, Rajini Srikanth, Linnell Yugawa, and Jean Wu. Also I am indebted to my writing-group members Kimberly C. Davis and Lori Harrison-Kahan, who meticulously read and commented on almost every sentence (and version) of this book.

My thanks to University of Illinois Press editor Vijay Shah, who has been working with me on this project every step of the way. I am especially grateful to series editor Jigna Desai, whose enthusiasm and insightful comments helped me push the theoretical boundaries of my argument and reorganize my ideas. I appreciate the efforts of all the staff at University of Illinois Press in the production of this book.

Thanks to New York University Press for allowing me to include in this book sections of a chapter that appeared in an earlier publication: "Apu's Brown Voice: Cultural Inflection and South Asian Accents," in *East Main Street: Asian American Popular Culture*, edited by Shilpa Davé, LeiLani Nishime, and Tasha Oren (New York: New York University Press, 2005), 313–36.

Thank you to my friends and family for their patience and understanding as I completed this project. I owe my interest in popular culture to my late father, Suryakant J. Davé, who introduced me to his love of film and television. This book is the result of the support of my extended family of aunts, uncles, and cousins, who have been waiting to see this book, and of my late uncle Bhal Bhatt, who would have read every word. This book is for my brother Raj and his wife, Anita, and my nephew Evan and niece Emily, who have sat through and engaged with my musings on TV and film and will probably continue to do so. My sincere thanks to Elise Beltrami, Cathy Kaufmann, and Terri Cramer for their friendship, and my genuine gratitude to my lifetime friend Polly Mohs, who is the most generous person I know.

This book would not be possible without my mother, Hansa S. Davé, whose faith in and support of me and my work have never flagged and whose love, compassion, curiosity, humor, and understanding have sustained and inspired me through the ups and downs of my life.

Rethinking Accents
in America

Apu: Oh, you are just noticing
the way I am talking to you *now*.

"Much Apu about Nothing,"
The Simpsons, airdate May 5,
1996 (my emphasis)

In 1990, the animated Indian immigrant character Apu Nahas-apeemapetilon made his first extended appearance on the Fox network prime-time series *The Simpsons*. One of his signature characteristics was his distinct Indian accent. In the episode "Much Apu about Nothing," Apu feels compelled to change the Indian accent he has been speaking on the show for the previous six years because his position is threatened by the imminent passage of Springfield political legislation Proposition 24 to deport undocumented immigrants.[1] Apu tries to solve his citizenship problem by obtaining an illegal identification that proclaims him to be an American citizen, but as a result, he feels he has to deny his own ethnic identity. He proceeds to prove his American citizenship by donning new clothes and imitating behavior he thinks are culturally American: sporting a cowboy hat, wearing a New York Mets baseball shirt, and speaking in an accent that sounds like John Wayne. His garment exchange does not really alter his identity because he looks like Apu dressed up in a costume.

Apu's transformative moment hinges on changing his vocal accent to one of an undisputed movie icon of American culture. When he says to Homer Simpson, "You are noticing the way I am talking to you now," he emphasizes both the absence of his Indian accent and his "new" manner of speech. It is Apu's use of an iconic American accent rather than his visual façade that causes Homer to do a physical double take because hearing a different accent come from Apu defies conventional expectations about how Apu and South Asians in the United States are supposed to talk. When he changes his accent, he changes his racialized position as a foreigner and noncitizen to a (differently racialized) citizen: "It turns out that I am an American citizen after all. Apparently, I just plumb forgot about it." His Indian accent may allow him to live in the United States, but it does not award him the privileges of American identity that include belonging to or being associated with American culture. His use of American colloquialisms, such as "plumb," and the effort he makes to sound "American" show that in fact he cannot "forget" about his relationship to issues of citizenship. He is under pressure to constantly prove it. The emphasis on "the way" that he talks exposes the vocal performance of racial identity in the United States and emphasizes accent as a specific racializing trope for South Asian Americans.

In the broadest sense, *Indian Accents: Brown Voice and Racial Performance in American Television and Film* examines the representations and stereotypes of South Asian Americans in relation to immigrant narratives of assimilation in American film and television. In this book, I theorize the performance of accent as a means of representing race and particularly national origin beyond visual identification. For South Asians, accent simultaneously connotes difference and privilege. To focus on an Indian vocal accent is to reconsider racialization predicated on visual recognition. One of the primary definitions of accent is the manner of pronunciation. An accent involves verbal intonations that stress particular syllables so the manner of speaking is just as significant as what is being said. As an animated figure what makes Apu recognizable as an Indian immigrant is the way he talks: He speaks in understandable English (privilege), but he speaks with an accent (difference). Accent not only includes tonal qualities but also involves word choice, arrangement of words, and cultural expressions that are rooted in national (and regional) expressions of identity. By saying "plumb," Apu evokes an American expression affiliated with John Wayne and an American cowboy. A Southern accent might emphasize slower speech patterns or expressions, such as "y'all." Examining Apu's accent sets the foundation for how accents work beyond spoken language in the process of racialization.

The definition of accent is not limited to sound. In reference to decoration or fashion, an accent operates as an accessory or minor piece that highlights the dominant look or feature. An Indian accent therefore also becomes a cultural object, such as a hairstyle or a piece of clothing or a sidekick character, that adds to the overall picture. It is a contrasting detail. An accent piece, for example, suggests something that is minor but also significant in its contrast to what is the main feature. Indian accents can embellish or add to an already established identity and thus operate as a type of cultural formation. Representations of South Asians as immigrants, naturalized citizens, and second-generation Americans, contribute to the formation of American ideas of citizenship and immigration. Following Raymond Williams, I believe that Indian accents in popular culture are not only singular aesthetic works performed in the public eye but also are intertwined with social and political relations and part of larger cultural formations.[2]

Indian vocal accents and other kinds of cultural "accents" offer an alternative approach to discussing American racial and ethnic performances, because the notion of an accent is also inherently comparative. Accents appear only in comparison to "normal" or standard speech. An accent can mark or distinguish someone or something in relation to something else. An accent can create contrast by its very difference. Hence, in addition to focusing on vocal accents, I argue, for example, that the roles of South Asian American sidekicks in television and film also operate as accents because they are minor characters who are unique in their own right but also support the dominant narrative of the American Dream. In an era of media-saturated images, concentrating on how accent operates in the process of "othering" allows for an expanded definition of how we think about race, national origins, and American identity.

Indian Accents asks, "What is the relation among power, accent, and the media?" The book focuses on the representation of South Asians in American film and television to explore this relationship. A South Asian accent is an amalgamation of the practice of *brown voice* (the performance of Indian vocal accent) and *brownface* (wearing clothing and makeup to look Indian). It is associated with an English-speaking identity that offers some cultural privileges of assimilating into American culture because of the capability to speak English. The ability to fit in and depict South Asian racial difference (i.e., Apu) as "not too different" as opposed to the contrast emphasized in the black-white racial paradigm in the United States offers an opportunity for the "not too different" to qualify for citizenship and, hence, gain access to political, economic, and social power. It is the manner and expression rather than the words themselves that allow Apu and minorities in general to become part of dominant culture.[3] This book utilizes Stuart Hall's definitions of popular culture as the site of power relations that are often representative of social systems and indicative of American national and individual experiences. Ethnicity, according to Stuart Hall, "acknowledges the place of history, language and culture in the construction of subjectivity and identity."[4] I look at how popular culture and performances of Indian cultural accents comment on and influence political and social issues related to racial identity and American cultural citizenship. In some cases, an accent is a vocal inflection, but in others, Indian accents act as means to subvert the dominant narrative, such as when the Indian sidekick figure becomes the main character in the Harold and Kumar comedies. Asian American actors John Cho and Kal Penn are able to introduce their racial and cultural background into the films and offer an alternative vision of the American Dream.

An investigation into how vocal and cultural accents are used in racial and ethnic performances opens up new lines of inquiry that link the use of accent and performance to a larger discussion about the allocation of power and national belonging. In *Unthinking Eurocentrism: Multiculturalism and the Media*, Ella Shohat and Robert Stam discuss the struggle over representation of stereotypes of marginalized groups who have been powerless to represent themselves. They introduce the idea of *cultural syncretism*—the notion that cultural communities move within and between national borders. The performance of an Indian accent is representative of a kind of cultural syncretism, because the racialization of South Asian Americans falls between Orientalist discourses of the East and Asia and American racial representations of differences.[5] In critical race studies, Claire Jean Kim proposes that Asian Americans are "racially triangulated" with black and white racial dynamics where Asians are simultaneously "valorized" as assimilated immigrants and "civically ostracized" from public and national expressions of identity as foreigners.[6] Performances of Indian accents operate in a similarly dual manner where South Asian Americans are racialized as foreign and a reminder of a global connection outside of the United States but are also valorized as an idealized American immigrant because they speak English and are able to assimilate into mainstream culture.

Vocal Accents and Racial Hierarchies

Sociolinguists, anthropologists, and legal scholars have discussed the reception of vocal accents in U.S. culture, documenting racial bias and discrimination on the basis of national origin. Most scholars identify two different types of accents, the foreign accent and the regional accent. According to sociolinguists, such as Rosina Lippi-Green, when an individual is identified as having an "accent," s/he is designated as an outsider to the dominant culture. Vocal accents open up another way to discuss power hierarchies in the United States. An American accent is a "socially constructed reality" similar to the idea of race as a socially constructed system of difference and hierarchy.[7]

Although regional dialects in the United States are distinct, such as the southern accent or the nasal Midwestern accent, they are embraced as an integral component of American culture with specific regional mannerisms.[8] The accents are recognized as American English, and this recognition is reinforced by media stereotypes and portrayals. John Wayne's manner of speaking English is accented, but there is no doubt that he is speaking American English, and his citizenship would not be questioned. With regards to immigrant culture, accents are identified as foreign because the manner of speaking English is identified as not recognizably American. For the foreign-born and immigrant culture, the emphasis on accent is not only used as a means of "othering" within the community but also as a means to solidify a singular notion of American identity.

For Asian Americans, accent is another way of pointing out that difference is a socially nuanced and a socially constructed reality. While accent is something that an individual can change, the fact that we notice accents or ask people to change them does recognize that listeners have vocal bias and certain voices can have attached cultural meaning. Some accents are considered pleasing, and others are irritating; hence "good accents" and "bad accents" contribute to how we understand and treat people from different national origins.[9] The introduction of a foreign accent implies that even though someone may live in America, they are in fact not fully American. This is the case with Apu: His attempt to speak in an American accent indicates that he is not American. Even though he has the correct intonation, his pronunciation is so exaggerated that the racial impersonation becomes obvious. However, when he speaks in his Indian accent, it is not obvious that his accent is a brown-voice performance but instead reads as "authentic" in that it matches our expectations of how an Indian immigrant speaks English.

Accent, as a racializing trope that shows both difference and privilege, is related to the historical ambiguity of South Asian American ethnic and racial classification in the United States. The changing criteria and nomenclature of American racial categories that occurred in the early twentieth century put Indian Americans in the middle of a legal controversy about how to define "whiteness." Indian Americans (also called Hindus and Asian Indians) were the only Asian group to be granted naturalization on the basis of "being white" and then subsequently stripped of citizenship rights and relegated to a nonwhite position.[10] It was not until the 1980 U.S. Census that South Asians were documented as a minority group in the racial category of Asian American. However, this legal categorization does not necessarily reflect how South Asians and other groups identify as an ethnic and racial group. Similar to Vijay Prasad, who discusses South Asians as "brown folk,"

I use "brown" to evoke how South Asians (like Latinos and Filipinos) are racial anomalies in the black-white racial paradigms of the United States.[11] Each group has a different relationship to American identity that challenges American cultural notions of language, religion, colonization, and national history.[12] Even though South Asian Americans' experience with and use of the English language does offer an advantage in the process of assimilation, the privilege of the position is often trumped by the notion that South Asian immigrants retain foreign cultural traits that prohibit complete assimilation into American culture.[13] Ultimately, the practice of an Indian accent is a form of cultural inflection: a variation on cultural citizenship that depicts South Asian Americans as racialized foreigners regardless of their status or occupation in the United States. Hence, accent racializes a group that has been historically difficult to categorize.

Many of the themes present and associated with South Asian Americans in contemporary popular culture are rooted in how South Asians were written or not written into legal and measurable categories in U.S. law in the twentieth century. Historian Mae Ngai points out that immigration law dating from the 1882 Chinese Exclusion Act to the 1924 Johnson Reed Act racialized Asians in relation to the established categories of black and white. The racial category of "Asian [was] a peculiarly American racial category."[14] Like Mexicans, Filipinos, and Syrians, the Indian skin tone of brown coupled with Indians' status as members of the British Empire puts into question how whiteness was being defined in the United States and as a result who was allowed to become a citizen of the United States.[15] Citizenship also is complicated, because even though one may be a legal citizen, the law can change that status through the courts, as in the 1922 *Ozawa v. the United States* case and the 1923 *United States v. Bhagat Singh Thind* case, which denied Japanese immigrants and South Asian immigrants the right to naturalize by recategorizing their racial status as nonwhite, respectively.[16] Consequently, many Asian Indians (as South Asians were named at the time) who were granted citizenship years before the ruling were deprived of their American citizenship and their property rights during the early twentieth century.

From 1924 to 1947, U.S. legal restrictions on citizenship barred natives from South Asia from immigrating to the United States. After World War II, Indians and other South Asian nationalities went from being racially unclassified or in the position of "other" to being granted naturalization privileges and being counted as "white."[17] South Asians once again held special status as either "other" or white because of their ability to become citizens. It was not until the Immigration and Nationality Act of 1965 (also known as the

Hart-Cellar Immigration Act) that the United States eliminated quotas based on national origins and allowed unprecedented numbers from Asia to immigrate to the United States.[18] The current legal language of the U.S. federal government classifies South Asian identity as a minority under the racial category of Asian Pacific American. Since the 1980 U.S. Census, the short phrase "including the Indian subcontinent" hovers just below the explanatory notes for the Asian racial category in formal applications and documents, but the popular understanding of South Asian identity belies this fact.[19] For the 2010 census, different South Asian groups, including Indian, Pakistani, and Bangladeshi, were listed separately as national origin under the Asian American category. Clearly, South Asian American identity has a complex legal and administrative history that leaves South Asian American identity ambiguous and difficult to chronicle in popular narratives. Hence, the utilization of historical narratives of South Asians during the British Raj or as model minorities in the United States offers an easy way to identify national origins and eliminate the racial ambiguity of South Asians in American culture. What becomes problematic is that South Asians are continually framed in colonialist and Orientalist narratives that reinforce South Asians as alien and foreign to America.

Indian Accents analyses representations of South Asian American identity and racialization using theories of Orientalism and American racial performance. Focusing on South Asian Americans brings these two theories in dialogue with each other because South Asian American racial performances are linked to both traditions. Scholarship on American ethnic and racial performances, such as blackface, portrays the acculturation process of marginalized racial and ethnic others to American dominant culture. Theories of Orientalism, on the other hand, are associated with British colonialism and imperialism and establish boundaries between what a domestic or national practice is and what is considered exotic and foreign. Similar to the practice of Asian yellowface performance, South Asian American racial and ethnic performance relies on the appeal of the exotic to emphasize the difference between Eastern and Western cultures. Indian accents can also be seen as culturally exotic and foreign, but the historical presence of the British in India and the use of English by immigrant Indians place South Asian American racial performances as a hybrid of the East and the West. The emphasis on South Asian American racial performances of brown voice and brownface allows for an alternative narrative of Indian accents that disrupts cultural conversations about race and citizenship beyond the conventional binaries of black versus white *and* foreign versus domestic in American popular culture.

The first half of this book looks at the use of Indian accents, such as vocal accents and brownface, in popular culture and at racial impersonations of Indians and Indian Americans in mainstream film and television; the second part of the book examines how the work of Indian and Indian American actors pushes back against brownface and brown-voice performances.

South Asian American and Indian American Identities

While South Asians hail from diverse geographical locations (Afghanistan, Bangladesh, Bhutan, India, the Maldives, Nepal, Pakistan, and Sri Lanka), the majority of images in popular culture tends to focus on Indian immigrants. Often, characterizations associated with Indian immigrants are extended to all South Asian groups even though the nationalities and ethnicities have different historical, social, and cultural practices. How South Asians are named and name themselves stems from the legacy of British colonialism and U.S. legal classifications. Prior to Indian and Pakistani independence from the British in 1947, the subcontinent and its inhabitants were known as Indian (and sometimes named by the religious majority Hindu) in world and U.S. history. In contemporary times, South Asian American, like the term "Asian American," functions as a political identity that comprises several ethnic, religious, linguistic, and national identities. Despite the diversity within the group, the description "South Asian American" remains a useful category to discuss populations and individuals living in the United States who can chart their ancestry from the political geography of the Indian subcontinent. In the current geopolitical climate, the distinctions among Pakistan, Sri Lanka, and India, for example, have been broadcast by multiple groups and media outlets, but popular portrayals of South Asians in the United States still tend to lump all South Asians into an Indian identity via food, fashion, religion, language, and music. Thus, although the title of this book is *Indian Accents*, I also utilize the more general term "South Asian" to underscore how the "lumping" of multiple histories under one label occurs and can be both problematic and illuminating in U.S. discussions of race and ethnicity.

South Asian Americans are often labeled a "model minority," but, significantly, they are also seen by both dominant and minority groups as a "privileged minority" in relation to other racial and ethnic groups, including other Asian Americans.[20] It can be argued that the general (though not necessarily accurate) view of South Asian Americans is that of a privileged community because many read, write, and speak the English language (with a

British-influenced accent), come from a colonial-based and English-speaking educational system (for the middle and upper classes), and have a familiarity with Western culture because of South Asia's historical ties to Great Britain. Additionally, many South Asian immigrants often have or are represented as having advanced and postgraduate educational and professional degrees. Most vitally, more than half of all South Asians immigrants are professionals, such as physicians, engineers, and computer scientists, who have significant economic cachet.[21] Since the passage of the 1965 Hart-Cellar Immigration Act and the introduction of the H-1B Specialty Occupations visa in the 1990s, South Asian immigration to the United States has exploded at an exponential rate to make them the third-largest immigrant group, after Mexicans and Chinese.[22] South Asians, along with Filipinos, earn the highest median income of all nonwhite racial groups in the United States, and over 60 percent are in managerial and professional positions.[23] But alongside this majority are also South Asians in multiple occupations and classes, including grocers, cab drivers, motel owners, and gas-station owners. In current times, South Asian immigrants and South Asian–looking peoples are also victims of discrimination and hate crimes, but these stories are rarely discussed.[24] For the most part, like other Asian groups in the United States, South Asian Americans are often represented as undifferentiated from each other and are seen as a highly educated and successful minority.

In American Studies and Asian American Studies, scholars have argued that focusing on South Asian Americans allows for a rethinking of the "points of origin" national-identity model that considers how transnational movements and international consumer practices reframe what is perceived as American culture.[25] As Rajini Srikanth points out in *The World Next Door: South Asian American Literature and the Idea of America*, contemporary literary narratives of the South Asian diaspora not only employ and react to American stereotypes of South Asian Americans but also create narratives that challenge and modify American ideas of independence, citizenship, and culture.[26] This study lies at the intersection of American Studies, Asian American Studies, media studies, and South Asian American Studies, contributes to recent work on Asian American representations in popular culture, and chronicles how Asian Americans engage with different forms and genres of popular culture.[27] South Asian diaspora studies scholars, such as Jigna Desai, Gayatri Gopinath, Sandhya Shukla, and Madhavi Mallapragada, examine the representation of the South Asian diaspora in British, Indian, and American independent cinema and new media. Despite the rise of online sources and the prevalence of transnational independent cinema, Hollywood film and American television remain as the most dominant representations of American culture influencing both local and global expressions of race and ethnicity as well as national identity in the United States. This book adds to previous scholars' discussions by being the first study to focus on portrayals of South Asian Americans in American mainstream television and film.

Popular Culture, Orientalism, and Racial Performance

In the field of American studies, the area of popular culture has been important in depicting the relationship between Asia and America and Eastern and Western culture. Edward Said's influential theory of Orientalism argues that Western constructions of a monolithic Orient (East and Middle East) as "the exotic other" created a normative national and cultural identity for the West (Europe and the United States) that marked the United States, for example, as culturally, politically, and socially superior.[28] In Asian American Studies, Lisa Lowe points out that Asian American identity destabilizes the monolithic notion of the Orient (the East) because of the contradictions of their subjectivity and cultural expressions within the complex systems of capitalism, patriarchy, and race relations.[29] The ideals and contradictions of American identity are evident in mass culture, and popular culture is a powerful medium to express and portray the ideals of American national culture in domestic and international spheres. Many scholars have used popular culture, such as film, music, theater, and pulp fiction, to discuss American national identity, including Mary Beltrán, Susan Douglas, Philip DeLoria, Christina Klein, Robin Kelley, Robert Lee, George Lipsitz, Jeff Melnick, and Gina Marchetti. I share these scholars' investment in the power of popular culture to influence the construction of American identity. How national identity is parlayed through popular culture establishes expectations about what is normative and nonnormative. Cultural mannerisms and performance reinforce ideas about power relations between nations and cultures (East and West), acculturation, and belonging to a national culture and power hierarchies and elitism within national cultures.

Focusing solely on a narrative of East versus West is an approach that literary scholar David Palumbo-Liu warns against, because he argues that the separation between Asia and America essentializes racial difference as to what constitutes domestic and foreign.[30] Instead, he contends that historical relationship between Asian and American "implies both exclusion and inclusion, 'Asian/American' marks *both* the distinction installed between 'Asian' and 'American' and a dynamic, unsettled, *and* inclusive movement."[31] How-ever, in contrast to Palumbo-Liu's examples, South Asian Americans' racial position was constantly at odds with dominant racial categories of black and white (as well as Asian). South Asian racial identity disappeared and then reappeared in various guises to the extent that South Asian Americans today have difficulty identifying what race box they should check. South Asian Americans, thus, are both distinct and included in the categories of what is Asian and what is American and what is Asian/American and exemplify the unsettled and political nature of the term "Asian American." Although Palumbo-Liu does not examine South Asian Americans in his literary and historical study, his theorization of the Asian American position being both distinct and included is a characteristic that South Asian American narratives build on in unexpected ways. For example, Palumbo-Liu argues that model minority narratives support the narrative of the American Dream "where upward mobility is possible for anyone—but race does not disappear, *race is 'muted.'*"[32]

Returning to the example of Apu, I argue that race is not muted but has a very loud and specific sound. Palumbo-Liu and other scholars rely on the visual in which the only two positions are to be visible or invisible. By foreground-ing vocal accent, Apu can attempt to "mute" his race by changing the way he speaks so he can be seen as an assimilated American citizen. His change in accent, however, does not make his race disappear but draws attention to it and his uncertain relationship to citizenship. Apu's race is "unmuted" and thus exposes the inclusion and exclusion of his position through accent. To have an "American" accent establishes belonging to a national community, and to have an "Indian" accent or other ethnic accent also indicates different hierarchies of access to American citizenship and the American Dream.

In studies on domestic U.S. racial performance and minstrelsy, scholars have discussed how different racial and ethnic groups have been depicted in popular culture to establish and reinforce American images of citizenship and national identity. The development of popular stereotypes of racialized others in American culture can be traced back to the performance of the minstrel show after the Civil War. The shows featured male racial and ethnic caricatures, such as Jim Crow, Zip Coon, and John Chinaman. In Eric Lott's seminal work on nineteenth-century black minstrel shows, *Love and Theft: Blackface Minstrelsy and American Working Class*, he argues that blackface performance "mirrors rather than distances" the other.[33] The opportunity to try on "blackness," he argues, allows actors to test and blur the color line of black and white. Blackface performance is dependent on creating an African

American character with exaggerated racialized features, such as coal-black skin contrasted with red lips and white eyes. Indian accent as a brownface performance is both a mirror and a means of distancing that continually moves between these two poles of black and white because racially South Asians are at once part of and outside the black-white racial binary. If the only racial positions are black and white, South Asian performances are constrained by this definition, but the very presence of an alternative challenges the racial categories.

Ethnic performance can also comment on how racially unclassified or ambiguous groups are categorized in American culture. Michael Rogin, in *Blackface, White Noise: Jewish Immigrants in the Hollywood Melting Pot*, describes blackface performance, instead of class mobility, as "the instrument that transfers identities from immigrant Jew to American."[34] His interest in cross-ethnic affiliation opens up insights about the process of assimilation for new immigrants. Blackface allows for the ascent and assimilation of marginalized Jewish immigrants into white mainstream American culture and keeps the other racial group, blacks, "fixed in place" at the bottom rung of a black-white racial hierarchy.[35] The theory of brown voice combines accents and hierarchies together in American studies and, therefore, intervenes in the black-white paradigm that dominates both studies of whiteness and critical race theory. Brownface, however, does not necessarily reinforce the racial hierarchy but instead questions the black-white model and the necessity of assimilation to this racial narrative. Performing brownface, unlike blackface, does not make an immigrant American but instead allows for the ability to create a hybrid character that has some privileges but also retains cultural differences.

While blackface performance reinforces a binary definition of racial positions in America, yellowface exacerbates the difference between America and Asia. Josephine D. Lee, in *The Japan of Pure Invention: Gilbert & Sullivan's The Mikado*, comments that in blackface minstrelsy shows, Japanese characters and skits were used to add a touch of the exotic and the fantastic to the shows.[36] White performers and black performers played Chinese and Japanese (and Native American) characters as outsiders to American cultural ideals. Yellowface is the practice of mostly white performers, altering their skin tone with makeup and taping their eyebrows and eyelids to narrow the roundness of their eyes in order to resemble Chinese or Japanese features. Yellowface evokes both the foreign element of being outside the nation and can bring in the alien (dangerous threat) and the exotic (mystical, magical, and spiritual contrasts). Robert Lee, in *Orientals: Asian Americans in Popular*

Culture, notes that yellowface "exaggerates racial features that have been designated 'Oriental' such as 'slanted' eyes, overbite, and mustard yellow skin."[37] Lee uses the term "Oriental" to define the popular culture stereotype of Asians that exaggerates racial features in opposition to whiteness. Yellowface performances reinforce narratives of Orientalism that elevate American identity to a superior position over Asia and Asian immigrants. The persistent use of Orientalism to represent Asian immigrants as foreigners continues to position Asian Americans in opposition to whiteness and at the same time denies them a place in America, where the most recognizable racial hierarchies are black and white. Indian accents, such as the performance of brownface and brown voice, traverse the black-white racial hierarchy slightly differently because brown implies the status of "not quite black" and "not quite white" and suggests a hybrid identity that includes elements of racial privilege and difference rather than a distinct exotic other.

Vocal accents became an important part of Hollywood performances with the introduction of sound in the motion-picture industry in the late 1920s. With the transition of silent film to the "talkies" from 1928 to 1930, established film actors in American silent films faced an end to their careers if they could not speak without an accent. This was especially true with Latino/a actors in the industry. Beltrán points out in her study of Mexican American film star Delores Del Rio that studio executives and production heads had to figure out what an American accent should sound like in the movies.[38] Often, it became an idea of what an American should not sound like. Del Rio was allowed to make the transition and become a Hollywood icon in the role of the Mexican spitfire. However, while many British actors saw their careers flourish in the talking-film industry, former leading actors with Spanish accents "faced the end of their Hollywood careers or were relegated to roles that incorporated (and often exaggerated) their accent."[39] Latinos/as and Latin American identity in the popular consciousness became associated with an exotic look, a foreign language, an accent, and musical dance numbers.[40] The cultural racialization of South Asian Americans through vocal accent mirrors the early history of Latinos/as in the film industry and warrants a larger comparative study of these two groups. The racialization of Mexicans as white in immigration law in the early twentieth century, however, did not subject them to the same restrictive practices conferred upon Asian Americans and South Asians as aliens ineligible for citizenship. The images associated with yellowface and brownface connote an exotic, foreign, and distant group not welcome to live and work in the United States except as temporary sojourners.

Lee indicates that yellowface performance also includes exaggerations beyond the visual because "on the minstrel stage, Canton English and nonsense words were often deployed together in the construction of John Chinaman."[41] Nineteenth-century performances accentuated the fact that Chinese immigrants could not speak English without an accent. The sound of broken English or grammatically incorrect English sentences with words out of order transferred to other Asian immigrant groups, including the Japanese and Koreans. This, however, was not the case with South Asian immigrants and Filipinos, whose facility with English is not characterized by "nonsense words" and broken English. The performance of an accent in the acting world also recognizes accent as a cultural construct. In her article on how actors learn to perform different types of accents, Angela Pao analyzes how acting books and Oriental-accent instructional manuals combine phonetic tones with a specific cultural subject matter.[42] The acting manuals are different from learning a foreign language, because in performance, authenticity is not the goal. The studio executives do not want an authentic accent but rather an "oriental intonation" that would add the "Chinese flavor" to the dialogue.[43] In this case, the representation of the perceived sound of a foreign language is more important than the language itself. Like blackface and yellowface performances, brown-voice performance also manufactures a racialized identity constructed in opposition to whiteness that promotes a racial hierarchy with whiteness at the top of the hierarchy. Instead of exaggerated physical features, brown voice is built on a performance that is not as easily visually identified and, therefore, has not been examined closely.

Comedy and Racial Performance

With Apu's vocal accent as the springboard, this book examines the cultural impact of Indian accents as a racializing representation for South Asian Americans. The examples discussed in my chapters largely involve comedic portrayals of South Asian Americans. Part of the reason is that most of the roles for South Asian Americans in American television and Hollywood film tend to be comic roles. Historically, comedy, unlike drama, offers the opportunity to satirize American culture in a nonthreatening manner that pokes fun at and shifts the ground of the status quo.[44] Drama offers an opportunity to empathize with a particular group, but comedy can challenge cultural assumptions, particularly through parody and satire with a critique of social conventions. Parody focuses on taking something recognizable and changing it into something where the difference is emphasized more than the similarity. In the case of Apu's performance of an American accent, the parody is taking a familiar representation of an Indian immigrant who speaks with a foreign accent and making him unfamiliar by changing his accent. Comedy and the use of irony, parody, and satire are prone to controversy because what is funny to one group may not be funny to another. For example, irony works by challenging truth or authority so that a situation, or even a word, is something different (or opposite) than what we think is true. Apu speaking with a John Wayne accent challenges how we think about Apu's identity. What assumptions do we make or not make about his citizenship, and how do different characters in the show aid him in his attempt to become a citizen?

Historian Lee describes how the minstrel shows positioned the European ethnic characters such as Mose the Irish fireman and Siegel the German as assimilable by developing standards of comedy about what behavior could be laughed at and what behavior could be so outrageous as to elicit punishment.[45] He says, "By distinguishing between funny but acceptable behavior among various white characters and ridiculous but punishable behavior among colored characters, these minstrel shows enacted the bounds of acceptable working-class behavior and resistance. In this regard, minstrelsy can be understood as a ritual response to boundary crisis."[46] The anti-immigration and exclusion acts of the late nineteen century attempted to solidify geographical boundaries and create hurdles for Asians in the United States.[47] Federal and local laws related to Asian American labor such as the 1858 Page Law and 1882 Chinese Exclusion Act prevented many Chinese women from immigrating to the United States and prohibited Chinese immigrant laborers from entering the United States until 1943.[48] The Chinese were depicted as foreign low-income labor that threatened American jobs. In the nineteenth century, being Asian meant that immigrants were not allowed to become legal citizens because Asians were not considered white or black. The early twentieth century focused on the rise of rise of Japanese militarism in the Pacific. The popular press coined the term "Yellow Peril" to describe Asia's threat to the United States, and the series of wars in Asia (World War II, Korean War, and Vietnam War) created another stereotype of Asians as military threats.[49] Indians, because of their status as a British colony and later as a fledgling democracy, were not associated with the "Yellow Peril." Instead, Indians were portrayed as resisting the British or as spiritual figures.

The performance and use of ethnic and racial humor knowingly and sometimes unknowingly reveal political and racial hierarchies of the audience in ways that can create a national furor. Linda Hutcheon argues that irony creates hierarchies or discursive communities of who is "in" on the joke and who is "out" or on the margins or who is a patriot and who is the enemy.[50] Exploring the roots of why a character, situation, or performance is ironic can sometimes strip away the humor from a joke, but in the end, dissecting why something is humorous at one time and not at another also attends to the changing nature of American culture. The proliferation of South Asians in comedy roles is another example of how South Asians are racialized as accents. Comedy is dependent on exaggeration and embellishment. Comedy takes the threat out of difference and makes accents palatable and laughable and sometimes loveable.

This book follows how the performance of South Asian racial identity begins with the Indian vocal accents of Apu and progresses to how Indian accents highlight American discussions of racialization even when the Indian characters do not speak with accents. Chapter 1 discusses the history of South Asian American representation in American film and television and argues that narratives about South Asians continuously emphasize India's colonial history or depict Indians as exotic others or aliens. The chapter chronicles how Peter Sellers's brownface performance as Hrundi Bakshi in the film *The Party* (1968) originates from a British colonialist portrayal of Indians and helps generate the characteristics associated with representations of Indian immigrants that endure in popular culture today. Chapter 2 returns to a discussion of the character Apu, exploring how his appearance on the television show *The Simpsons* in the 1990s was a departure from previous Hollywood and television representations of South Asians in the United States. Whereas South Asians were previously depicted as brief visitors or exotic foreigners, Apu symbolizes a permanent Indian immigrant presence in the United States. Yet, his brown-voice performance racializes and differentiates him from other Americans. This chapter theorizes the use of brown voice and discusses how animated characters, in particular, become a significant subject to study vocal accents and voiceovers. Animated characters are unique because one of their most important defining features is their voice, and, thus, animation emphasizes the voice as a site of interest in thinking about racial performance. Chapter 3 discusses how the Indian American character is the accent or the suburban "sidekick" character to the dominant narratives of young, white masculinity that are prevalent in American culture. The representation and use of the historical figure Mohandas Gandhi in the MTV animated series *Clone High* revisits and challenges American representations of Asian Americans and South Asian Americans as model minorities. The use of the historical leader Gandhi as a teenage "geek" sidekick without recognition of how

Gandhi fits into South Asian history and influences South Asian American communities shows how American stereotypes dwarf any other representation of South Asians or South Asian Americans in the United States.

Returning to live action actors in film, chapter 4 explores how, in the comedic parodies *The Guru* (2002) and *The Love Guru* (2008), new-age spirituality is used as an Indian accent to reflect on the strange, foreign practices of Indians and at the same time to show the American desire for difference. This chapter discusses how the role of the Indian guru is predicated on stereotypical cultural performances for American consumption. The performance of brownface by Mike Myers as Guru Pitka in *The Love Guru* repeats stereotypes Peter Sellers created fifty years earlier. British Indian actor Jimi Mistry in *The Guru*, on the other hand, offers a response and a critique to racialized performances of brown voice and brownface when he plays an Indian actor attempting to do brownface performances to cater to the expectations of his American admirers.

While the first four chapters depict brown-voice and brownface performances as Indian accents that separate or exoticize South Asian Americans from other Americans, the last two chapters focus on Indian and Asian American actors offering critical commentaries on established Hollywood stereotypes. Mistry's role leads the way in rethinking how immigrant Indians are portrayed, and the Harold and Kumar films go one step further by removing the brownface performances and vocal accents to make Korean American Cho and Indian American actor Penn the center of the narrative. Chapter 5 focuses on the film comedy *Harold and Kumar Go to White Castle* (2004), an alternative to the immigrant journey often seen in Hollywood films where the old country is full of hardships, but the new country of America offers freedom and opportunity. Because the film is a stoner comedy, it is not readily recognizable as an Asian American story. However, within the genre of the stoner comedy, these films create a new narrative that normalizes Asian Americans and South Asian Americans as a central part of American culture and in the process redefines the boundaries of American regional, cultural, and national identities. The concluding chapter examines how the sequel film *Harold and Kumar Escape from Guantanamo Bay* (2008) establishes Harold and Kumar as patriotic, racialized American citizens who are able to question American federal policy towards outsiders and regional stereotypes in the south in a post–9/11 heightened-security era. In this film, Indian accents are one type of many of racial and cultural accents that appear in the United States. Harold and Kumar are the narrative insiders, and all the other characters in the film are depicted as outsiders or paranoid conspiracy theorists.

In the film, institutions associated with federal authority, such as airport security, law enforcement, and the government agents of the George W. Bush era, are portrayed as incompetent because they cannot distinguish between different national and cultural identities.

Historically, according to Cedric C. Clark, representations of minorities in the media follow a trajectory in which, first, minorities are invisible and, second, minorities are comic characters that entertain dominant culture and exaggerate racial difference from mainstream culture or criminals that need to be taken out of mainstream culture.[51] Finally, minorities are elevated to figures of authority in dramas that enforce the status quo. Although there have been variations to this paradigm, minority groups tend to follow this pattern of representation. The majority of South Asians and South Asian Americans appear in comedies, and, hence, as I argue, the racialized performances tend to exaggerate the difference and foreignness of South Asians in the United States. The appearance of Apu in 1990 represents a static and caricatured image of South Asians that is performed by white America. Apu is a racialized performance of what American media imagines South Asians look and act like. His portrayal represents the model minority stereotype associated with post-1965 South Asian immigration to the United States. But in the years since Apu's debut, South Asian American immigrants and their children speak with different accents and offer up complicated images of how America defines both South Asian American racial and American cultural identity in the aftermath of 9/11. However, the images on TV and film often dwell on and repeat the same racialized narrative to the extent that the stereotype overdetermines any other performance. As a result, not only do these stereotypes become a dominant image of how South Asian American identity is depicted to non–South Asians but also influences South Asian American performances in television and film. *Indian Accents* examines how the aural and cultural characteristics associated with racialized (and mostly white) performances of South Asian Americans in animated television shows and comedic films allows for a reevaluation of how racial categories are socially constructed. This book discusses the different permutations and evolutions of accent as a marker of foreignness, assimilation into dominant culture, representative of neo-Orientalism, and a site of negotiation.

1

South Asians and the Hollywood Party

Peter Sellers and Brownface Performances

Even though it seems as if South Asians are ever present in contemporary television and film, this was not the case in the twentieth century. Prior to 2000, the most recognizable South Asian characters on American network television was the animated character Apu on *The Simpsons* (1989–).[1] In the film industry, independent filmmakers, British and Canadian producers, and Indian and other South Asian media outlets created and showed multiple media images of the South Asian diaspora throughout the latter half of the twentieth century; however, Hollywood made very few films that featured the South Asian immigrant experience or South Asian Americans. This chapter gives a short history of the portrayals of South Asians in American film in the twentieth century and focuses on how the origins of brown-voice and brownface performance are re-creations of Orientalist roles that diminish the threat of Asian immigration through the portrayal of comic and harmless South Asian characters.

One of the most influential racial performances of a South Asian in the United States is Peter Sellers's Indian character Hrundi V. Bakshi in the film *The Party* (1968), directed by Blake Edwards. Sellers's humorous portrayal of an immigrant Indian relies on reinforcing the cultural differences between Indians and Americans in the 1960s. Actors and comedians, such as Hank Azaria, the voice of Apu, and Mike Myers, *Saturday Night Live* alumni and actor who plays an Indian guru, both credit Sellers's performance as inspirations for their development of cross-racial and cross-ethnic characters. Azaria admits that his vocal accent for Apu is loosely based on Peter Sellers's

Bakshi.[2] Myers, while he was growing up in England and Canada, was raised on British comedy and fondly recalls watching Peter Sellers on television with his father.[3] Hence, an influential model for contemporary brownface and brown-voice performances is grounded in earlier work established in British comedy. As a prolific British radio performer and screen comedian, Sellers had previously used vocal accents and cultural mannerisms to create Indian characters in British films such as *The Millionairess* (1960), directed by Anthony Asquith. Sellers's role in *The Party* is a departure from previous characters because he is playing an immigrant Indian actor working in the American film industry. He is not a colonial native or a British citizen; instead, his character is representative of the post-1965 wave of immigrants from Asia and South Asia to the United States. *The Party* and the role of Hrundi Bakshi mark the transition from prior British colonial-native narratives to American model-minority narratives and a transition from British understandings of South Asians to American interpretations of South Asians.

Although scholars of race and ethnicity in American film have devoted more studies to Asian Americans in film, most of them have neglected South Asians as a racialized group outside of British or Indian film history. Key texts about the portrayals of Asians and Asian Americans in film and television history include works by Peter Feng, Darrell Hamamoto, Robert G. Lee, Gina Marchetti, and Kent Ono, to name a few, but rarely have any of them have discussed in detail the history of South Asians in American film or television.[4] This chapter discusses the film *The Party* to show the historical change of portrayals of South Asians in American films from colonialist narratives to model-minority American immigrants and citizens. Later representations of brownface performance in animated shows magnify the role of the vocal Indian accent. The next chapter theorizes brown voice and the relationship to language and accent as a racializing aspect of South Asian identity. This chapter focuses on the history of brownface performance in American narratives that includes brown voice as one component of Indian racial impersonations. I argue that the characteristics of brown-voice and brownface performance are rooted in early film narratives that emphasize the history of British imperialism and colonialism in India that are later carried over and rewritten to encompass Indian immigrants in the United States.

From British Colonial to American Immigrant: Role-Playing in *The Party*

Blake Edward's *The Party* (1968) features Peter Sellers in dark-brown makeup (brownface), playing the bumbling Indian actor Hrundi Bakshi. Bakshi's character is expressed through physical humor that emphasizes the contrast (seen as comedic ineptness) between him and Hollywood . . . American culture. The film is a one-joke comedy sketch developed around the idea of what happens when a small-time Indian actor in the United States is inadvertently invited to an exclusive Hollywood studio head's party. The action of the film centers on Bakshi's fish-out-of-water status at the party that includes him trying to retrieve a missing shoe, finding a place to sit at the formal dining table, attempting to make small talk, falling in and out of the water pools, and frolicking around the premises with a baby elephant. The reaction to the film was mixed, with some critics lauding the pairing of Edwards with Sellers and others deriding the film as too long and too narrowly focused on one joke.

Sellers's characterization of Bakshi depicts him as an object to be commented on and responded to for comic effect rather than an individual with his own story. Bakshi, in effect, becomes an accent and a "cultural thing." The verbal misidentifications that confuse Bakshi's national identity as an Indian with Native Americans ("Hey, Chief") are secondary to his physical awkwardness at the party. His performance in *The Party* is based on physical and visual comedy but also includes an Indian vocal accent. Comedy, rather than drama, tends to be a more suitable genre to use exaggeration as a central plot device because the notion of equality is diminished when the exaggeration emphasizes a complete dissimilarity to what is perceived as normal and renders the situation humorous. Comedy tends to objectify difference.

While Sellers may don a brown face and perform an Indian accent that depicts the character as a comic simpleton, the film, in fact, shows the transformation of South Asians from supporting characters in colonial narratives to South Asian immigrants and foreigners in U.S. culture. Bakshi's character is introduced through his film role as a native in the British colonial army, his morning ritual of meditating and playing the sitar, and his interactions at the Hollywood party. Critic Mandel Herbstman points out that the main plot and action of the story revolve around the contrast between "the artless, uncomplicated actor from Asia" and "the nervous ambitious actors of Hollywood."[5] However, this description by the critic misses the fact that the portrayal of an Indian actor is far from uncomplicated.

We see this complexity from the beginning of the film. The first scene opens with an empty, barren, and rocky landscape. There are no credits, and the only sound is the approaching music of Scottish bagpipes and whistling British troops. The director does not need to set up a time or place because the first person to appear in the film is a brown-skinned man in a white turban, British military jacket, and loose Indian trousers (Sellers). The sound, the landscape, and the exotic native evoke the familiar tropes of the colonial narrative. The scene shows the villains are the native men in turbans, hiding in the hills with guns and waiting to ambush the unsuspecting British military company. Sellers is the loyal Indian bugler who warns the troops and as a result is shot by the rebels even as he blows his horn to save the British. The move from colonial drama to comedy occurs when Sellers turns his character's heroic death into an extended and exaggerated death act that goes on for several minutes with his last breaths punctuated by the toot of his horn until the director's "CUT" finally stops the scene. The film changes from a colonial adventure set in 1878 where Sellers has been cast as an expendable native to a narrative about the actor, Hrundi Bakshi.

Hrundi Bakshi
(played by Peter
Sellers) as a colonial
native in *The Party*
(MGM, 1968)

The reference to colonial dramas in the film highlights the previous historical representation of South Asians in Hollywood film. Unlike other Asian American groups, South Asian Americans (until recently) do not have a history inflected with war or colonialism in relation to the United States but instead are linked to the United States economically and politically by the ties of capitalism and a British-based democracy; India is represented as an Asian country with seemingly Western (if not American) values. Thus, early Hollywood portrayals emphasized Indians in the context of British history. As film scholar Marchetti points out, Hollywood films were not catering to Asian Americans at the box office so their interest was to use "Asians, Asian Americans, and Pacific Islanders as signifiers of racial otherness to avoid the far more immediate racial tensions between blacks and whites or the ambivalent mixture of guilt and hatred towards Native Americans and Hispanics."[6] Although she does not discuss South Asian portrayals, the idea that South Asians in British Raj narratives offered a safe and escapist fantasy of racial otherness explains the limited subject matter for South Asians. Depictions of South Asians often emphasize the differences between Indian culture and Western culture and, hence, support Orientalist narratives of the East. Although Americans derived pleasure and paid at the box office for the stories of Gunga Din, Mowgli, and the Arabian Nights, these narratives intentionally drew strong lines between English identity and Indian identity that discouraged the crossing of cultural, national, and racial boundaries.

In early film history, most Hollywood images of South Asians were confined to British (and sometimes American) tales of adventure or spiritual discovery set in colonial India.[7] In her study of the representation of China and India in Hollywood film from 1896–1955, Dorothy B. Jones argues that before Indian Independence, Hollywood focused on three thematic threads that characterized narratives of India and Indians: impoverished and wily villagers, mystical wise men, and either treacherous or noble natives rising up against the British.[8] The repetition of these stereotypes emphasizes what Homi Bhabha has called a "productive ambivalence" in colonist discourse: the idea that racial otherness is both "an object of desire and derision."[9] Colonial narratives addressed the desire for the other as the crossing of racial boundaries through the interactions of the native and the colonizer. The act of cross-dressing or performing as the native other was the topic of popular narratives ranging from the exploits of Lawrence of Arabia to Rudyard Kipling's *Kim*. In American studies, Eric Lott characterizes nineteenth-century blackface performance by whites as "theft" in playing the other but also as "love" that allows white men to participate in taboo relationships between blacks and whites.[10] The act of desiring the other is intimately linked to racial impersonation, but Bhabha's term of "derision" evokes the comedic turn that these roles evolve into in American culture. In extending Bhabha's argument to Indian accents, I posit that the origins of brown-voice and brownface performances stem from the interplay between the idea of playing the desirable role of the other and a role that needs constant repeating through ridicule and contempt to ward off the temptation of the other.

The first theme in colonial narratives emphasized India as a mystical place with religious cults. Many of the distinctions among different religions in India, including Hinduism, Islam, Sikhism, and Christianity, are lost or lumped into the idea of power-hungry, blood-sacrificing religious cults who threaten the rule and order of the British. The first motion picture that simultaneously visualizes and describes Indians is Thomas Edison's film entitled *Hindoo Fakir* (1902). Jones chronicles a series of films that feature Indian mysticism as a recurring theme, such as the *Soul of Buddha* (Fox, 1918), *The Green Goddess* (Distinctive Productions, 1923; Fox, 1929), *Mystic India* (Twentieth Century Fox, 1944), and *Mysterious Ceylon* (Warner Bros., 1949).[11] In *The Young Rajah* (Paramount, 1922) Rudolph Valentino plays a man (adopted as a child) who believes he is white. He discovers he is a long-lost Indian prince when he experiences mystical flashbacks that identify him and prove to others that he is heir to the Indian royal family whose members have been blessed by the gods with special powers. Buddhism was featured in films about China and the Far East, so there was some differentiation between Asian religions, but they were linked to specific nationalities where Buddhists lived in China and Hindus lived in India.

The second thematic thread depicts India as a foreign geographical landscape that emphasizes the differences between the poor and the wealthy. The mud-hut villages and starving natives are contrasted with the opulent palaces and forts. In films such as the *Rains of Ranchipur* (1955) and *The Rains Came* (1939), the drought-stricken fields lie next to vast, lush jungles readily available for elephant and tiger hunts and illicit romance. The desire to cross racial and class boundaries usually results in the death of characters who do so, and the repetition of this fate in subsequent narratives emphasizes that certain lines should not be crossed.

The third and most prolific theme in Hollywood films depicts the primitive hordes and rebels in the northern frontier of India (also known as the Trunk Road, which goes from India through Pakistan to Afghanistan) defying and rising up against the heroic forces of the British Indian Army.[12] The films repeat stock characters, such as the orphaned waif, the loyal native, the religious fanatic or fakir, and the snake charmer.[13] In *The Party*, Bakshi's role as native who dies for his British companions references the title character from one of the most famous films in this genre, *Gunga Din* (1939). In the film, Gunga Din (played in brownface by actor Sam Jaffe) is the native water boy who is mortally wounded but manages to warn his British soldier friends of an impending attack by sounding a bugle. However, Bakshi's exaggerated death scene not only brings humor to what was traditionally depicted as a melodramatic moment but also heralds the end of a certain type of role for Indians. The role of an Indian is no longer to save the British but rather to discard old narratives that are not relevant to the 1960s. The film establishes its "modernness" by seeing British narratives as part of the past and celebrating America as the center of entrepreneurship and capitalism. In one instance, for example, the director has to reshoot a scene because he notices Bakshi is wearing a wristwatch. The narrative is separating out the role that Bakshi plays in the film from his role as an actor in the modern era. To punctuate the point that the film is offering an alternative narrative from previous colonial stories, Bakshi literally sets off the explosives (accidently) that blow up the British fort and bring about the demise of the film. But while this narrative may be over, what is Bakshi's role in Hollywood?

The opening of the film showcases that although the old narratives may be repeated, this film presents an alternative narrative where there is inter-action between the former native/new immigrant and mainstream popula-tions across previously strict boundaries. In the action of the film, it is only when Bakshi is fired and dismissed from the set that the opening film credits begin to roll. What follows are images of Hrundi Bakshi playing the sitar and meditating in his garden with his pet monkey, Apu, set to a psychedelic soundtrack infused with Indian sitar music. Bakshi is transformed from a co-lonial subject of the British to an Indian cultural object (in the United States) that is associated with Indian spirituality and Indian music. He receives an invitation to the studio head's party when his name is mistakenly pulled from the fired pile and put into the invitation pile. Even though Bakshi is at the party by mistake, his presence is not questioned by the guests because the "things" or Indian racial difference he offers complement American identity but do not threaten American interests.

Metaphorically, *The Party* focuses on what happens when South Asians get to the United States. The different ways the character is featured anticipate the complex issues associated with depicting South Asians in film and tele-vision. On one level, in the plot, the actor Bakshi is acting in a Hollywood

The Party
(MGM, 1968)

historical epic during the British Raj. But on another level, the actor is at a party in 1968 California during the height of the black-, yellow-, and red-power movements and the escalation of the Vietnam War. The film poster, however, foregrounds the absurd elements and images in the film, including Bakshi standing in a pool of water and young people marching behind an elephant. The Indian actor is being played by a white actor in brown makeup, so even while the intent may be to shake up stereotypical roles, the film is utilizing a white man to portray the new immigrant. While the film moves easily from narratives of British imperialism to hippie culture in the 1960s, it neglects any reference to British decolonization and the emergence of the United States as a dominant world power. The film replaces British stereotypes with a revised American Orientalist model that depicts Indians (as played by non-Indians) as a model minority who do not challenge racial hierarchies. Indian participation in economic or social movements of the times is minimized and reduced to comic mannerisms.

Decolonization and the Arrival of the Indian Immigrant

India, after independence from the British in 1947, was the largest English-speaking democracy in Asia. When Hollywood made films about Asia in the post–World War II period, most of them focused on China, Korea, and India.[14] Cultural historian Christina Klein argues that even though post-1945 American interests in Asia and the Pacific increased substantially and Americans from the military, diplomatic corps, educational ranks, business and industry, missionary workers, and tourists entered Asia, the "expansion of U.S. power did not occur in a smooth or uncontested fashion. It coincided—and existed in tension with—the revolutionary process of decolonization."[15] This meant that new depictions of the former colonies had to take into account the change in government and politics in the area. For example, film treatments of China and Japan had to reverse who were the heroes and who were the villains. Film treatments also showed the Americans as the ultimate heroes of the war and the hope for the future. During World War II, the United States was allies with China and at war with Japan, but after World War II, Communist China became the enemy of the United States, and Japan became a staunch U.S. ally. Previous films that were sympathetic to the Chinese, such as *The Good Earth* (1937), were replaced by compassionate treatments of Japanese-U.S. interracial romances, such as *Sayonara* (1957) and *The Teahouse of the August Moon* (1956).[16] With South Asia, the political shift was complicated because the newly independent countries of India and Pakistan were also engaged with decoupling from the British and establishing their own sense of national identity.

One of the few films that discussed decolonization in South Asia was Paramount Studio's film *Elephant Walk* (1954), starring Elizabeth Taylor. Film scholars James Chapman and Nicholas J. Cull identify the film as an example of how British imperialism is criticized in the time of decolonization in the country of Ceylon, now Sri Lanka. The story features a native servant who wants to preserve the old ways, while the rest of the natives are depicted as impoverished, child-like, third-world inhabitants who need the assistance of the whites. However, there are no representations of the native civil servants and government officials of the newly independent country. What the authors hint at but never fully explore is how the film focuses on what the process of decolonization means for the British and the Americans but not for the native population. In the case of *Elephant Walk*, for example, Luigi Luraschi, Paramount's head of domestic and foreign censorship, was corresponding with the U.S. Central Intelligence Agency (CIA) on the representations of the natives. Luigi noticed the only portrayals of natives in a newly independent Sri Lanka were servants and in order to show an alternative wrote to the CIA, "Have made sure Dr. Pereira (good character) will be cast with an actor impersonating full-blooded Ceylonese. Very dignified doctor who takes care of our sick male lead. . . . Educated Ceylonese will handle themselves on an equal level with when dealing with Europeans."[17] The idea, according to studio heads, is that the educated brown people can be represented as equals to the well-meaning Europeans (and Americans), but they can only be played successfully by a white actor (Abner Bieberman) doing a racialized brownface performance.

As Klein points out, popular-culture narratives about Asia and America focus on what Asians mean for American identity. Brownface performance by white actors operates with the same idea. The brownface performance is how Americans want natives to act and has to do more with the dominant group and how the minority group fits into the dominant narrative. However, brownface performance requires an exaggeration of racial difference that includes different skin color, cultural mannerisms, and vocal accents. The irony is that in order to portray natives interacting with Westerners on equal terms, the studio requires that the difference between South Asians and Westerners be more pronounced.

In general, during this period, Hollywood produced few films that focused on South Asia and instead made films associated with China, Japan, and Korea during the 1950s and early 1960s. While Hollywood was reducing its portrayal of India onscreen, the Indian film industry was in the midst of the golden age of Hindi film (1940–60), but those films rarely played in American theaters. Internationally acclaimed films, such as Satyajit Ray's *Panther Panchali* (1955), garnered a favorable critical reception in art-house theaters but was not widely distributed in the American domestic cinema market. The civil-rights era and the 1965 Hart-Cellar Immigration Act brought about a change in depictions of Asians and South Asians in the 1960s from former colonial citizens to new immigrants to America. The primary action following the opening credits of *The Party* depicts how South Asians become part of the model-minority narrative of the late twentieth century.

Indian Immigrants and Citizens in the United States: Crashing the American Party after 1965

In the 1960s and 1970s, most Hollywood depictions of South Asians were focused on the hippie and mystical aspect of the culture and led to the characterizations of brownface performance that are the precursors of contemporary portrayals. The new wave of South Asian students and professionals to the United States (primarily from India and Pakistan) were immigrating as a result of the Hart-Cellar Act but were largely ignored in American media culture. When South Asians did appear, they were associated with three major themes. First, although the population was increasing, South Asians in the media were associated more often with cultural artifacts and practices than with individuals or a people. Second, South Asians were depicted as sources of comic amusement, and third, most of the narratives were displaced into alternative times (the future or the past) or into different genres, such as animation, to avoid discussing the realities of the present for immigrants.

In the 1960s, India entered American popular culture through the counterculture movement. Historians Jeffrey Melnick and Rachel Rubin argue that the musician Ravi Shankar was a catalyst for the movement, which "was finding a new way to welcome brown people into the center of life in the United States," but the price was that the immigrants had to give up "some measure of control over their cultural stuff," such as cultural arts, fashion, and music.[18] South Asian culture became disassociated from people and, instead, was rooted in cultural artifacts that were mass produced for an American audience who could play at being exotic without necessarily meeting with Indian people. Brownface performance, in this case, encourages Indians to be thought of as a collection of cultural mannerisms and objects that can be used for comic effect. Sellers's role as Bakshi is one of the only contemporary depictions of South Asians in the 1960s, and it originates in a British performance of brownface where the Indian accent that Sellers uses continues to proliferate and influence others.

Ironically, it is the British actor Sellers and the British director Edwards who put an Indian in America, and, yet, the America shown onscreen in The Party is one that is distanced from its own cultural history. For example, in the film, the international cultures that appear in the film are primarily European. The female guests are foreigners from Italy, Britain, and Russia. The guest of honor is a young French actress named Michele Monet. The rest of the guests are older, white, American men and slightly younger, white women. There is no reference to the civil-rights movement or the Vietnam

War protests or third-world movements that are taking place in 1968. The youth and counterculture movements make a brief appearance at the end of the film in the form of clean-cut college students who have been at a "protest," but any sort of political message has been eliminated from the film, including any other people of color. Bakshi is distinctive as the only brown person in the room. Of course, since Bakshi is being played by Peter Sellers in brownface performance, there are actually no people of color in the film. Both political and racial challenges have been eliminated in the film, and, instead, the film is reduced to the comic antics of a racial impersonation of an Indian foreigner.

Actor and comedian Sellers is most widely known for his portrayal of the clumsy and heavily accented French Inspector Clouseau in the popular *Pink Panther* film series.[19] But what is not as well known is that Sellers, in *The Party*, is also famous for originating one of the first brown-voice performances of an Indian immigrant in the United States. In *The Party*, Sellers speaks with an Indian accent, and his acting relies on the physical exaggeration of his racial difference through both visual and aural mannerisms and thus can be identified as brownface performance that includes an Indian accent.[20] When he speaks, he is always smiling, even when the situation is a serious moment. The words come out rapidly in a high-pitched tone, but the phrasing is lyrical. His sentences are littered with extraneous cultural exclamations ("Ooh, goodness gracious") and half sentences that are deferential ("Indeed, sir" or "No indeed, sir"). When he puts together a sentence, it is short and enunciated, but the words are sometimes out of order, such as "Especially I thought your song was very beautiful," and "That is what my name is called." All these verbal habits create the basis of how he and others eventually perform an Indian accent up to the 1990s and 2000s, such as the case of Hank Azaria's brown-voice performance of Apu and Mike Myers's brownface performance as Guru Pitka in *The Love Guru*.

One of the first portrayals of Sellers's brownface performance appeared in *The Millionairess*, also starring Sophia Loren. A film adaption of a Bernard Shaw play, the romantic comedy is set in London and features Loren as a spoiled heiress determined, after several wrong choices, to marry the Indian émigré physician, Dr. Ahmed el Kabir. In playing the role, Sellers wore a Nehru-style suit and triangular hat and spoke with a fabricated Indian accent. In addition, Sellers and Loren recorded the song "Goodness Gracious Me" as their characters of the Indian doctor and the Italian heiress in the film.[21] While Loren is using her own Italian-inflected English, Sellers performs the song in a nervous, high-pitched English inflected with his performance of an

Indian accent. To further accentuate the difference of his speech patterns and his exoticism, the lyrics of the song emphasize his cultural background by naming places in Indian geography. He sings, "From New Delhi to Darjeeling, I have done my share of healing," and also references the Punjab. Two years later, Sellers reprised his role as an Indian physician, but this time, he is a supporting player to some of the great Americans comedians of the time. He appears, wearing brown makeup and a Nehru-style jacket and speaking with a manufactured Indian accent, in Bing Crosby and Bob Hope's final installation in the Road series films, *Road to Hong Kong* (1962). His depiction of brownface performance is dependent upon the visual, cultural, and auditory characteristics of what is Indian. This includes saying the word "curry," using a Hindi (rather than an English) alphabet eye chart, and acting as a snake charmer playing a flute to entice a cobra from his basket. His performance comprises a collection of Indian things that are exaggerated for comic effect. This includes being obsequious to Americans and Europeans yet also being wily enough to try and cheat them.

As Hrundi Bakshi, Sellers's performance as an Indian in the United States deviates from earlier portrayals because his character is more reactive rather than proactive. While a guest, he does not speak to anyone about what is happening at the party. It is difficult for him to engage with anyone in the room, and so he is always outside the conversations. He misses the punch lines of jokes and laughs at the wrong things, leading one guest, a congressman, to ask, "Who's the foreigner?" The response is no one knows who he is. Later, Hrundi meets another actor who plays a cowboy named Wyoming Bill. Hrundi is a big fan of his work, and they do an impromptu line quotation where the cowboy calls him an "Injun" (after hearing he's from India) and says, "He's a cute little feller." In these examples, he is first a foreigner and then mistaken for a Native American, which points to the ambiguous racial position that Indians occupy because Indian national identity (unlike other Asian national identities) also shares a historical link to American Indian and Native American first encounters with Europeans. As Christopher Columbus misidentified whom he was meeting and where he was going, so does the film rely on a similar set of misunderstandings.

The Party is well known in Hollywood circles and is continually shown in film festivals and Peter Sellers retrospectives. Brownface performances (that include Indian accents) of South Asians are continually repeated, and American performers learn to emulate Peter Sellers, whose performance is celebrated as "a masterpiece of mimicry."[22] As a result many comics, such as Hank Azaria, view Sellers's performance as the standard upon which to base their own acting, especially with regards to his Indian accent. And, yet, although Indian things were fashion commodities of the 1960s and 1970s and present on television and film, other than *The Party*, South Asians were mostly absent from both the small and silver screens until the revival of colonial narratives in the 1980s.

The Return of the Colonial Narrative

Even though Hrundi Bakshi blew up the sets of the colonial narratives in *The Party*, these stories continued to thrive, especially during the neoconservative movement in the 1980s, which saw the decline in American industrial and manufacturing dominance and the increased competition with Japanese and other Asian economies in global markets. The reemergence of colonial narratives fortified the notion of Indians as still subordinate to Western culture and needing aid from the Americans. These narratives recall Bhabha's notion of "productive ambivalence" because they relegate Indians to the colonial past, where they are not a threat to American identity in the 1980s.

The themes Jones outlines in her study of films before 1955 reappear in popular films, such as *Indiana Jones and the Temple of Doom* (1984) and the James Bond film *Octopussy* (1983). An updated version of pre–World War II serial adventures for the 1980s, Steven Spielberg's second Indiana Jones film, *Indiana Jones and the Temple of Doom,* was primarily set in 1930s India. The plot features adventurer and archeologist Dr. Jones as an American hero who rescues a Hindu idol and saves the native villagers (and his friends) from the blood cult of Kali. Even reviewers made note of the portrayal of Indians eating monkey brains in the film as a bit farfetched and tasteless for late-twentieth-century sensibilities.[23] The film emphasizes the exotic and foreign nature of Indians and India.

Octopussy, however, is set in the modern Indian nation of the 1980s and includes a small role for then-celebrity Indian tennis player Vijay Amritraj. He plays the Indian intelligence liaison to MI-6, but his character is killed by one of the villains while Bond is having a romantic interlude with a Bond girl. In other words, Indians are expendable to the central plot and romance of the story. Despite the contemporary setting of India, the film manages to show Bond in the midst of a tiger hunt in the jungle, where he is pursued by a power-hungry South Asian prince, threatened by a henchman with a turban, and has a liaison with one of many white Bond girls dressed in Indian clothing. In this film, India is the exotic background and playground for exiles and white Westerners rather than a thriving, modern democratic nation.

The two prominent South Asian roles in the film are the villains, Prince Kamal Khan, an exiled Afghan prince, and his menacing Indian Sikh bodyguard and servant. Prince Kamal Khan as Bond's chief rival is well dressed, wealthy, and fluent in English. He can easily mingle and fit into the upper echelons of Western culture. French actor Louis Jourdan performs his racial impersonation by dressing up in Indian clothes and wearing brown makeup, but he does not affect an Indian accent to play Khan. Instead, he speaks English in his normal voice that has a European accent. As in earlier films, it is the British and the Europeans who dominate the narrative, and India becomes the backdrop for a story about British and American interests. The Bond girls are both white women (American and British) who happen to be living in exile in India, and Indian actors are given small roles. Veteran Indian actor Kabir Bedi plays the role of Gobinda, the turbaned servant who obeys his master without question and rarely speaks in the film. The film repeats the themes

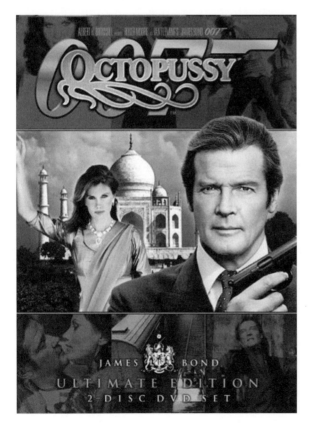

James Bond film
Octopussy (MGM, 1983)

of the imperial adventure films of the 1920s and 1930s rather than showing a changed or modern India. As a result, the image of India is viewed through the lens of the British Empire and characterized as a colony of Britain even forty years after Indian Independence. Indian and other South Asian immigrants in post–World War II films are characterized by their colonial history rather than being seen as a part of the American landscape.

The most famous portrayal of a South Asian story in Hollywood film is the critically acclaimed biopic *Gandhi* (1982) that garnered eight Academy Awards including best picture. The historical film was made in conjunction with the Indian government. British director Richard Attenborough introduced an Indian hero to America, and this film is discussed in further detail in the third chapter of this book. The film centers on the history of the Indian Independence movement and covers Mohandas Gandhi's life from the 1920s until his death in 1948. Although the depiction of Gandhi's story was new for Hollywood, the time period is still that of the British Raj. Subsequent films and television series, such as *The Jewel in the Crown* (1984) and *The Far Pavilions* (1984) continued to focus on the British Raj but did not reflect contemporary life in India or for South Asian Americans in the United States.

Science Fiction and the New Colonial Frontier

In addition to the adventures of Indiana Jones and James Bond, the 1980s introduced South Asians in Hollywood science-fiction films as experts in science, engineering, and medicine. Brownface performance in science fiction operates through both the colonial narrative and the model-minority lens. Historically, Asians as aliens have been a constant presence in American science-fiction narratives and include memorable villains and mad scientists, such as Ming the Merciless and Fu Manchu. In these roles, Asians are cast as the threatening foreigner who seeks to disrupt the status quo. Science-fiction narratives associated with conquering a new frontier or establishing new colonies, such as the *Star Trek* franchise, draw on histories of colonialism and empire, so alien creatures are often metaphorically used as stand-ins for a native population or for the menacing threat to the established order.

In the 1980s, Lee characterizes the model minority as having two sides: "The myth presents Asian Americans as silent and disciplined; this is the secret to their success. At the same time this silence and discipline is used in constructing the Asian American as the new yellow peril."[24] Lee points to Ridley Scott's film *Blade Runner* (1982) as a dystopic vision of a corporate global culture that is controlled by Asian (specifically Japanese) capital and labor and represents an economic yellow peril. Although Indians do not appear in the film or Lee's discussion, this characterization applies to brownface performances of Indians in science fiction. But instead of being an economic threat, brownface performances of Indians act as intellectual threats to the establishment and often as emotionally controlled individuals who have difficulty with personal relationships. In these roles, they are scientists who are cast as villains or as secondary characters who use their intellect to save humanity. These characters are often seen as much smarter than the average human being but who also have the ability to contribute to the existing society. Stephen Hong Sohn points out that characters with technical expertise are often Asian or Asian American characters, but the premise of these narratives is that the reliance on too much technology is inhuman or alien. While Asians are depicted as outsiders, those who temper technology with morality tend to be white humans.[25] Science fiction, as a genre, is an outlet to introduce East Asians and South Asians as part of a future both as leaders and villains but usually in relation to a specific doctrine. Those who preserve the West or who are allied with Western ideals of individualism, democracy, and freedom are representative of a hopeful future and cast as the heroes.[26]

Most scholars tend to focus on the history of East Asian representations, but South Asians, like East Asians, are often cast as the technical experts or scientists. Into the 1980s, the South Asian roles were still being played by non-Indian actors in brownface performance. For example, the comedies *Short Circuit* (1986) and *Short Circuit 2* (1988) starred white actor Fisher Stevens performing in brownface as robotics scientist Ben Jabituya (Jahveri in the second film). He is an example of a reclusive technical genius who has difficulty making human friends and creates an artificial intelligence in order to feel connected to the world around him. He is representative of a model minority that is successful in America yet also at the same time is distinguished by his cultural difference. His character is a precursor for the Indian geek or nerd character that appears, for example, in the film *Van Wilder* (2002) or on the television series *The Big Bang Theory* (2007–).

The first film in the Star Trek franchise, *Star Trek: The Motion Picture* (1979), cast Indian actress Persis Khambatta, a former Miss India (1965), as Lieutenant Ilia, a bald Deltan (humanoid alien) Star Fleet science officer of the next generation, but she was one of the few exceptions. One of the most memorable villains in the Star Trek universe is Khan Noonien Singh (a character of South Asian origin played by Mexican American actor Ricardo Montalban), a genetically engineered superhuman Sikh from Earth's past who ruled Asia. Khan was first introduced in the original series' episode "Space Seed" (1967) and later was Captain Kirk's nemesis in *Star Trek II: The Wrath of Khan* (1982). He is played as a smart, resourceful, and charismatic leader who in later years blames Kirk for the death of Khan's wife and the abandonment of his people. In this case, the character of Khan is elevated from native henchman who follows orders to the charismatic villain who challenges authority and the status quo. Because he threatens the Western ideals of the federation, he has to be killed.

Recent studies of Asian Americans and science fiction discuss how representations are related to revised versions of Orientalism such as "techno-orientalism," which is used in the study of cyberpunk, new media, and internet studies. "Techno-orientalism" is a term used to discuss the ways East Asian peoples and places have become linked with technology to produce a collective fantasy of East Asia as the future in narrative and culture.[27] In *Yellow Future*, Jane Park introduces the idea of "oriental style" in East Asian Hollywood narratives that goes beyond techno-orientalism and includes the manner of how Asians and the East offer conditional visibility and invisibility of certain bodies, objects, and images in future narratives. In furthering her observations, I argue that oriental style is a kind of accent that draws attention

Ricardo Montalban as Khan in 1967 *Star Trek* original series' episode "The Space Seed" (series aired on NBC 1966–69)

to what is different but continues to support the mainstream narrative. For South Asians, the majority of Hollywood narratives of the future continue to cast them as technological experts or villainous outsiders. In the latest installment of *Star Trek* (2009), brownface performances have been replaced with South Asian and South Asian Americans actors who are cast as supporting actors in the Star Fleet universe. The opening scenes of the film feature a South Asian captain (Faran Tahir) who valiantly faces the enemy (and dies in the first five minutes) in order to buy some time so the rest of the crew can escape. This is a variation of the colonial narrative and the character of Gunga Din, who sacrifices his life to save his compatriots. Although he is a captain of a starship, he is not the main story in the series yet. In contemporary science-fiction films, South Asian Americans continue to appear as scientists, government officials, and secondary characters.

Before Apu's appearance on *The Simpsons* in 1990, there were small parts on television and in film, but unlike other Asian Americans groups, such as Chinese, Japanese, Korean, or Filipino/a or Vietnamese, who were associated with early American history, spiritualism, and American military action and movements, South Asians (as a population rather than consumer items) were not as visible in popular American mainstream media.

The fall of the Berlin Wall and the end of the Cold War ushered in a new era of economic and immigrant labor flows, particularly in the communications and technology industries in the 1990s. The dramatic increase in H1-B visas given to South Asian immigrants created a professional middle-class immigrant community with money to spend and ties to South Asia. Many of the immigrants were settling in Silicon Valley, Los Angeles, Houston, and other centers in the country. Non-Indian actors playing stereotypical roles in colonial stories or acting as model minorities in some distant future were no longer the only images of South Asians in mass media. Independent filmmakers created shorts, documentaries, and feature-length films that presented diverse images of Indians in the United States played by Indian actors. South Asians made financially successful films in Britain, Canada, and the United States that featured South Asian immigrants in the United States as the main characters in dramas, including *Mississippi Masala* (1991), directed by Mira Nair, with Denzel Washington.

By the end of the 1990s, Hollywood was not only taking notice of South Asian Americans, but, as Jigna Desai notes in her study of Indian film, the Hindi commercial film industry located in Mumbai, and known as Bollywood, was beginning to send films abroad with box-office success.[28] More important, Hollywood was beginning to invest in the lucrative Bollywood film industry. The influx of wealthy South Asian Americans, the large audiences in India and other South Asian countries, and the box-office receipts of Bollywood compelled Hollywood to take notice of the South Asian American population for financial reasons, if nothing else. Films that featured Indians at the center of the narrative, such as the critically acclaimed *Monsoon Wedding* (2001) and *The Namesake* (2006), both directed by Nair, as well as the 2009 Academy Award–winning *Slumdog Millionaire* (2008), directed by Danny Boyle and Loveleen Tandan, were some of the first films in the English language to be widely recognized by an American audience. Many of these films (as the ones in the 1990s) are dramas that focus on immigration journeys, generational conflict, and the reality of life as a cultural and numerical minority.[29] And, yet, these films are the exception rather than the rule, as most narratives continue to repeat the comic characters or the native characters from the past rather than continue creating new roles and new histories for South Asian Americans.

Conclusion

The Hollywood history of South Asian representations were associated with the past (the British Empire) or the far future in the genre of science fiction, but contemporary portrayals of South Asians on American television and in film were few and far between. Recurring parts for South Asians started to appear on a regular basis during the 1990s and 2000s as their roles in world business and entrepreneurial areas became more prominent. Although the introduction of Apu was a turning point in 1990, his character must be put in context. As an animated figure that is voiced by a white man, his portrayal, as argued in the next chapter, is yet another way to avoid dealing with the physical presence of South Asian Americans.

This chapter has presented how brownface performances or racial impersonations of South Asians by non-Indians is tied to an earlier history of British colonial narratives that begins to shift with the introduction of Peter Sellers's comedic portrayal of Bakshi. Historically, the portrayals of South Asians emerge from colonial natives that emphasize South Asians as exotic natives who have the ability to assimilate to Western ways but are subordinate to or subordinated by dominant culture. The film *The Party* announces the presence of Indian immigrants in the United States after the 1965 Hart-Cellar Immigration Act, and both literally and figuratively frees Indians from a colonial legacy and instead places them within the civil-rights and race narratives of the United States. But although the geography and context for South Asians changed, Sellers's brownface performance continued to emphasize the foreign accent and cultural mannerisms he developed earlier and influenced brownface performances seen in contemporary times, such as in the film *The Love Guru* and with the character Apu in *The Simpsons*. Sellers's performance is part of the historical trajectory of depictions of South Asians that do not disappear after a specific time or progress in a linear fashion. Instead, brownface and brown-voice performances continue to reappear in American media narratives with minor variations and comment on cultural practices and ideas about immigration, American materialism, and racial difference.

2

Apu's Brown Voice

The Simpsons and Indian American Accents

I cannot deny my roots and I cannot keep
up this charade. I only did it because I love
this land, where I have the freedom to say,
and to think, and to charge whatever I want!
Apu, "Much Apu about Nothing," May 5, 1996

The Simpsons' ninth-season episode "Much Apu about Nothing"
reflects the conflict between the promise of the American Dream for immigrants and the pressures of cultural assimilation that lead immigrants to
deny their cultural identity and focus on how the vocal nature of brown voice
operates as an Indian accent. Apu vents his frustration, after masquerading
in both dress and accent, as someone who is culturally and stereotypically
American—an identity that does not reflect his experience. Apu expresses a
love for the freedom of speech and free enterprise in the United States, but his
"charade" to appear as American reveals to him that the values he loves about
the United States do not apply to someone like him (an immigrant without
legal papers). In the episode, Apu is compelled to purchase false citizenship
papers in order to avoid being deported as an undocumented immigrant. He
then dresses up in what he thinks is the persona of an American citizen—a
man who wears a cowboy hat and baseball shirt and talks with a John Wayne
accent. This is the only occasion in the series when Apu does not speak in
his signature accent. As mentioned in the introduction, it is his lack of an
Indian accent that draws attention to how Apu is racialized in the show.

This chapter begins with a discussion about the representation and performance of South Asian American voices and accents in American culture
in the 1990s. The term "brown voice" identifies a specific racializing trait

among South Asian Americans in Hollywood productions, which simultaneously connotes both foreignness and familiarity because the accent is identified with an English-speaking identity and hence offers some cultural privileges of assimilating into American culture. Apu is identified as Indian in the series, so when he is referenced here, his accent is Indian, but his accent stands in for a more general South Asian accent. Despite the inclusion of Apu in a social satire of American culture, his signature voice, I argue, is an example of a racialized performance of South Asians in the United States that reinforces rather than challenges stereotypes of South Asian Americans and, more generally, Asian Americans in American media.

Ultimately, the practice of brown voice is a form of cultural inflection: a variation on cultural citizenship that reinforces a static, racialized position for South Asian Americans regardless of their status or occupation in the United States.[1] South Asian American groups are represented as one undifferentiated group who are saddled with one accent and one voice. This image frames South Asian Americans as an acceptable and privileged ethnic group (in comparison to other minority and immigrant groups) that in current times also has considerable political and economic consequences in terms of business deals, state security, or celebrity status. This static and fixed position, signaled by a singular and stable "voice," develops through the particular historical representation of difference in mass media in the United States and combined with prior and current relations of the Indian diaspora with both British and U.S. culture. This static position is illustrated by what may arguably be the most recognizable and definitive Indian accent to American audiences established by Hollywood in the 1990s: that of Apu Nahasapeemapetilon on the long-running animated series *The Simpsons*.

In the first scene described, Apu's cultural appropriation of American icons is extreme and, thereby, emphasizes how different he is with respect to the other citizens of Springfield. Apu's flawed attempt to impersonate an American with a celebrity accent attaches him to an American cultural history and, hence, (in his mind) an American cultural citizenship. But to the audience (including me), this is a humorous scene because we know Apu is not culturally American. Our expectation of Apu when we see him onscreen is for him to speak English with what we have been culturally primed to hear as an "Indian accent." This satire of ethnic assimilation illustrates how racial and ethnic identities operate beyond the visual and are influenced by the reception of accented speech. It also illustrates the notion of "the charade" of taking up another's cultural behavior by performing a cultural accent. I am less interested in the phenomenon of cultural masquerade than in the

Apu from
The Simpsons
(Twentieth Century
Fox Television, 1989–)

meaning generated by this practice in relation to Indian Americans in the United States. The character of Apu offers an ideal case study to portray how Indian Americans are situated and understood in the popular American imagination. Unlike Peter Sellers's Hrundi Bakshi, who is distinguished by his break with colonial narratives and his outsider status in 1960s Hollywood, Apu is a part of the Asian American (rather than the British) immigrant narrative in the United States. As a character, he represents many of the key themes from the 1990s to current times associated with Indian Americans in popular depictions, such as the model-minority image, subdued or hypomasculinity, and an informant on Indian culture and religion. Apu, a fictional construction, helps us to revise theories of racial performance and, therefore, examine American racial hierarchies and the formations of Asian American communities in popular culture.

This analysis links Asian American notions of accent to the prevailing theories of minstrelsy and racial and ethnic performance not only on the small and silver screens but also in the largely understudied realm of animated cartoons.[2] By focusing on the concept of voice, we can move the discussion of racial subjectivity beyond the visual aspects of racial recognition and expose alternative cultural factors that build on the idea of Peter Sellers's performance as a voice impersonator and influence racial perceptions of immigrants. Sociolinguists, such as Rosina Lippi-Green, have chronicled how language and accent stereotyping influence social-identity formation and how these stereotypes are reinforced in educational institutions and media outlets. Feminist theorists, such as Kaja Silverman, have explored the power dynamics of masculine and feminine voices but have not explored national and ethnic accents in relation to the articulation of power.[3] I am interested in studying the value of vocal accents in relationship to the concept of cultural citizenship. By focusing on cultural definitions of what an Indian accent means and how it is used in performance, this chapter explores how television sanctions a limited vision of Indian American and South Asian American presence in the United States as a foreign immigrants rather than cultural Americans. The emphasis on the aural sound allows for a reevaluation of how racial categories are socially constructed through representations of Asian Americans and South Asian Americans.

In a well-known study of undergraduate students' comprehension of lecture material at the University of Michigan, students listened to a lecture recorded by the same speaking voice (a native speaker of English from Ohio). Half of the students were shown a slide of a white woman, and the other half were shown a slide of an Asian woman. Students who saw the photo of the Asian woman recorded lower comprehension scores and were more likely to register the presence of a foreign accent in their responses to the lecture.[4] In this case, the physical image of the supposed teacher heavily influenced the understanding of the material by students even when there was no accent. This study illustrates that accent reception is subjective. It also matches representations of Asians in the popular media, which usually portray one type of "Asian" accent even though the difference between a Beijing accent and a Hong Kong accent is as distinct as that of Chicago and Boston accents. In popular culture, Asians are shown as speaking "broken English," which is a cause of frustration and anger or ridicule to those listening to them. Indian-accented English, on the other hand, is not depicted in this way and offers an alternative way to understand representations of race and ethnicity in American popular culture.[5] Lippi-Green asserts, "Accent serves as the first point of gatekeeping. . . . [A]ccent becomes a litmus test for exclusion, an excuse to turn away, to refuse to recognize the other."[6] Accent discrimination is not a novel experience in the United States, but it is rarely expressed in discussion of racial hierarchies or racial performance except to indicate difference or foreignness.[7]

Practicing Brown Voice

The representation of an Indian American voice and in particular an Indian-accented English voice gestures toward a special status for Indian Americans, a status that mirrors the historically amorphous and ambiguous position that Indian Americans occupy in American racial hierarchies. The performance of this accent, which I term "brown voice," is the act of speaking in an accented English associated with Indian American nationals and immigrants. While any person can perform an accent (as comic relief, to accentuate a point, for example), the cultural meaning changes depending upon the actor. The manner of speech is just as important as what is being said. For example, a South Asian speaking brown voice sounds very different from a white actor acting out an accent and playing an Indian American.

To be clear, brown voice is a performance in both senses of the word, not only does someone speak but someone also has to receive and recognize the implications or at least the intent of the accent that marks someone as Indian American. The "affect" of vocal accents and how they are socially constructed are topics that sociolinguists, such as Lippi-Green, have explored in productive ways.[8] Understanding another person's speech is often dependent on the listener's good will. Prejudiced listeners cannot hear what a person has to say because accent, as a mirror of social identity and a litmus test for exclusion, is more important.[9] While an Indian American may be speaking English in the way in which s/he is educated and not be aware of speaking brown voice, American dominant culture will hear the English as accented. Brown voice is just as much about how we "hear" and understand Indian accents as who is doing the talking.

The performance of brown voice comes out as an inflected version of English. In terms of linguistic form, these are not words out of order, such as "Milk, where can get I?" instead of "Where can I get milk?" Inflected English, I argue, is an accessible dose of foreignness rather than an irritating form of speaking. Inflected English bears a similarity to American English.[10] The implementation of brown voice is how Apu speaks in *The Simpsons*, a rote and consistent accent that is foreign but understandable.

Unlike other forms of Asian English often seen as broken English, Indian-accented English has a unique phonetic signature in which meaning is indicated by which syllables are stressed in certain words.[11] John Honey, in

Does Accent Matter: The Pygmalion Factor, describes reactions to accents as "distractions" rather than unintelligibility—the distraction from what one is saying to how one is saying it creates a notable effect when it comes to Indian English: "[T]he greatest source of unintelligibility in the Indian English accent is its pattern of word stress—that is deciding which syllable in a word gets the emphasis" (106). Unlike Australians, New Zealanders, or South Africans, Indians tend to stress different syllables (one researcher estimates one in five of all the words used in Indian English is stressed differently). Significantly, these words are "made up of mostly 'content' words which carry most of the meaning of the sentence rather than 'connecting' words which are often less crucial" (107). Some examples include words such as deVElop versus DEvelop and NECessary versus neCESSary and prePARE versus PREPare and casSETTE versus CASSette.

Word stress is a promising approach to the study of cultural communication because it does not ridicule the intelligence or aptitude of the speaker but rather comments on the process by which intelligibility is registered by prioritizing meaning. It asks not, "Why can't you speak my language?" but *"Why are you speaking it that way?"* so that the basic structure is correct, but the interpretation of what is emphasized in communication is variable. With brown voice, the cultural perception of the accent is associated not only with a model-minority Asian immigrant group but specifically with a privileged minority, such as Indians who are understood to speak a more culturally receptive accented English. In other words, since the language has already been learned and mastered, the most difficult barrier in achieving cultural assimilation to overcome is the reception and communication of the meaning of one's speech.

Brown voice, then, can be understood as the cultural performative practice of manipulating meaning and creating a cultural difference. Although perceived and received as a "foreign accent" in American culture, Indian English is, in fact, a native form of speaking in India, where the two national languages are English and Hindi. Many middle-class Indians are educated in English-speaking schools (also known as English medium schools), where all subjects are taught in English. However, there are a multitude of accent variations. So although it would be more appropriate to think of Indian English as an inflected version of English that more closely resembles British English, American culture perceives Indian Americans as talking with an accent of a nonnative speaker.

In Asian American studies, cultural citizenship for Asians is often linked to the ability to speak and be fluent in English. In Hawaii, for example, the interplay between pidgin and Standard English is directly related to the historical legacy of immigrant labor, American colonization, and citizenship.[12] The ability to speak Standard English is associated with class and upward mobility through better schools and better jobs. As in the case of brown voice, local speech does not destabilize the legacy of colonialism but rather highlights the effects of that history. In Hawaii, the class system emphasizes the primacy of speech over racial and ethnic position. In other words, the way one speaks determines the way one is treated and the community to which one belongs even before one is visually recognized. The development of an educated class in the context of an American empire is about access to the privileges of whiteness, which is associated with enunciated English.

In contemporary America, Indian American culture and cultural products (bindis, henna, mendhi, clothing, and fabrics) are available as fashionable consumer commodities. To imitate an Indian accent (in theater, film, or just for fun in both ethnic and white communities) is not considered a sign of bad education or breeding but, in fact, the opposite—Indian accents imply one type of an Asian model minority, and in multicultural politics, this is the type of minority the United States wants to promote because its members fit the image of entrepreneurs, computer engineers, and successful immigrants, in general. The constant performance of brown voice, therefore, establishes one sound and one image for Indian Americans in the cultural imagination and, hence, freezes the perception of the group in a static definition. Thus, although Indian Americans occupy the privileged position of being recognized as successful foreigners, this position does not allow the perception of Indian Americans to expand and, thereby, prevents Indian Americans (immigrant or second- or third-generation Indian Americans) like other Asian American groups from establishing any kind of presence other than as outsiders and foreigners in American communities. If the image of Indian Americans and South Asians is continually that of immigrant foreigners, then how can Indian Americans ever be seen as movers and shakers, let alone stakeholders and cultural citizens, in American life?

Brown voice is also instructive in thinking about how race is located beyond the realm of the visual. Voice and vocal inflection also are integral markers of cultural subjectivity. Perceiving race beyond the visual aspect of the body helps us to identify and question racial constructions of identity that remain buried under the title of Asian American or in a binary black-white paradigm. By placing voice at the center of our analysis, we can reevaluate social constructions of racial hierarchies both within and between racial groups that are related to visual images.

The Sounds of Difference
in Radio and Animation

Racialized performances of voice first occurred on a national level on the radio and set the standards for later forms of mass media, such as television. For obvious reasons, voice was crucial to the articulation of difference in radio. As Michele Hilmes points out in her study in the field of radio, *Radio Voices: American Broadcasting 1922–1952*, not only is the history of radio the precursor to narrative forms in television but it is also directly linked to the formation of American national identity. "As the English language spread into every corner of the nation, 'homogenization of the American' would follow."[13] The growth of radio stations and public practices of listening to the radio emerged during the national debates over naturalization and immigration laws in the 1920s. Hilmes maintains that the linguistic unity fostered by national American radio influenced the perception and judgment of voices that deviated from what was considered the national norm. During the same time, the national radio of Great Britain (BBC) was actively creating a national voice that spoke with a manufactured upper-class Oxford accent, even though most of the population spoke with an entirely different phonetic deviation.[14] Other forms of English might be present on the radio, but the voice of the BBC reflected an intentional performance of a fabricated national accent. To the British, accent had already become more important than appearance as a class indicator as seen, for example, in George Bernard Shaw's stage drama *Pygmalion*. In the United States, however, racial and ethnic characteristics were broadcast to all audiences through the use of radio drama.

In the early days of radio serial programs, writers borrowed from the vaudeville traditions of racial dialect and consciously re-created these accents to construct and indicate race in a nonvisual medium. The common narrative device through which difference and humor (and, in particular, "blackness") was expressed was the theme of "cultural incompetence."[15] Hilmes describes: "One signification of cultural incompetence involves language use and 'funny accents,' a device milked by 'Dutch' acts, Irish acts, Jewish caricatures, and the state Italian since the dawn of vaudeville. Other 'ethnic' traits involved the common situation of the immigrant: 'humorous' native customs that clashed with American norms," including plays on language pronunciation and cultural misunderstanding.[16] Ethnic humor was based on the disparity between immigrant and racial cultural expressions in speech and the American national accent that was established by radio. Apu's brown voice is the contemporary (and not much changed) legacy of ethnic vaudeville humor. Hilmes argues that although radio had the technology and opportunity to create a "race-less" society, instead it solidified the racial hierarchies of the 1920s and 1930s through the continued production of accents, and in the case of black drama (the popular show *Amos 'n' Andy*, for example), the continued practice of blackface minstrelsy in which whites voiced black characters.[17] The theory of brown voice combines accents and hierarchies together in Asian American studies and, therefore, intervenes in the black-white paradigm that dominates both studies of whiteness and critical race theory. Instead, brown voice redirects attention to how the expression of national language exposes social rankings of identity among racial groups in the United States.

In an animated series, the fact that the bodies are physically drawn and, therefore, not real brings the voice (as in radio) to the forefront. Most animation, unlike radio and film, is predicated on the notion of fantasy and make-believe.[18] Early animated shorts of Felix the Cat and Mickey Mouse emphasize the simultaneously humorous and fictional nature of the medium. Although the process of animation from conception to production is grounded in the visual, when coupled with the dynamics of voice animation, we can examine how racial representations are not just visual but also reinforced in the voice. In the case of animation, the analysis of race transitions from the physical to the vocal performance. That the impact and importance of voice actors has long been recognized by the television industry is indicated by the fact that the cast of *The Simpsons* has won multiple Emmy Awards for best voice-overs for a series.[19] The award not only implies knowledge (on the part of the industry and the audience) of who plays the voices but also recognizes the proficiency and importance of voice in the creation of a character.

Speaking with brown voice is more than a ventriloquist performance because with ventriloquism the manipulation of the puppet or the dummy is a visual as well as aural joke that the audience understands and has accepted. This does not happen in animation because we usually cannot see the living body (as opposed to the fabricated animated representation) from which the voice emerges, except in shows where vocal identification has become the gimmick. In *The Simpsons*, for example, celebrities often do heavily hyped guest voice-overs that overshadow the character illustrations. As an animated series, *The Simpsons* rearranges reality and allows the audience an even-greater distance from the characters than do live-action situation comedies. Characteristics that emphasize this freedom from reality include a controlled environment, such as the unchanging town of Springfield, a frozen time in which characters do not age, and the two-dimensional, visual nature of ani-mation. Because of the audience's suspension of disbelief, animated series can often tackle issues and situations that would register as unbelievable or inappropriate on live-action sit-coms.[20] Events ranging from alien takeovers to political satires to social commentaries are now common fare for shows such as *The Simpsons, King of the Hill, Family Guy,* and *South Park.*

Unlike blackface, the manufactured voice also allows racial and ethnic accents to proliferate, because unlike physical acts of discrimination, vocal mimicry is meant to be humorous and is not seen as insulting or demeaning. Peter Sellers's portrayal of Indian Hrundi Bakshi in *The Party* (1968) would not go unchallenged in contemporary times because of the very visual im-pact of racist stereotyping in the film.[21] Mike Myers's rendition of brownface in *The Love Guru* (2008) was explained away in the narrative as part of his childhood experience—his character was a white American who grew up in India so technically he was not playing an Indian. The practice of brown voice avoids most challenges based on racial stereotyping because it is not physical.[22] Animation foregrounds the sound and resonance of voice but not the person whose voice it is. The voice is disembodied from the speaker and attached to something else (animals, fictional people, ogres, trees).

With the advent of *The Simpsons,* however, guest voices and celebrity voices became the vogue. In *The Simpsons,* the producers and creators want us to recognize these voices and often pair up the celebrity with an animated body that looks like the individual. Animated feature films have latched on to this practice and promoted such films on the basis of whose voice is starring as a particular character.[23] But the actors depicting the main characters in *The Simpsons* do not want to be recognized for a single voice but instead pride themselves on the number of different voices they can do. While celebrity voices are linked to the singularity of the actor's physical image, animated characters provide an opportunity to perform voices for characters of any race, gender, age, or accent. It is this anonymity that allows Hank Azaria to voice the character of Apu, because although most of America (and the world) know about the character Apu, they cannot identify Azaria as the man who voices him. If a celebrity like Paul McCartney or Tom Cruise per-formed brown voice, the reaction among the public and Asian American groups would be very different and liable to generate the furor that fueled the protests against the musical *Miss Saigon* in New York City when actor Jonathan Pryce performed as the multiracial character of the Engineer in the musical. In 1992, Asian American groups protested the New York production casting of Pryce, a white British man, in the role of the Eurasian engineer in the production. Although he had played the part in the London version, Asian American groups were appalled by his yellowface makeup. But the main objection was that no Asian Americans were allowed to audition for the part. After the initial run on Broadway, subsequent shows all cast Asian or Asian American actors in the role of the Engineer.

To perform an accent is to be technically superior at one's craft (Meryl Streep and Nicole Kidman, among others, are considered masters of the accent). However, the performance of brown voice should foster a recognition and acknowledgment that there are particular racial histories and hierarchies that allow certain accents to be read as funny and others to be vilified. Eric Garrison from *The Simpsons Archive* writes, "Apu started out in concept as a simple convenience clerk. According to show writer Mike Reiss, though, when Hank Azaria (the voice of Apu) started to voice act the script, Azaria couldn't help but give Apu an Indian accent. 'We couldn't help it,' says Reiss. 'Once Apu was given an Indian accent, Apu Nahaseemapetilan [*sic*] was born.'"[24] The idea that a convenience clerk and Indian character/accent were inevitable ("We couldn't help it") is a telling sign of how the creators and actors perceive Indians in American culture. What comes first, the accent or the character? In this case, the accent defined Apu and created not only a "humorous speaker" but also a culturally popular and significant Indian American representation on American television.

The Emergence of the Fox Network and the Simpsons

When the Fox Broadcasting Company debuted in 1986, it was not legally considered a network at all because at the time it was not offering on its stations and affiliates the minimum fifteen hours of programming per week that the Federal Communications Commission (FCC) required. Owner Rupert Murdoch and Fox Inc. CEO Barry Diller, along with Jaime Kellner, president of the Fox Broadcasting Network, were the central players in the creation of the fourth network. Their innovations in launching what we now know simply as FOX changed the landscape of network television in the 1990s in terms of industry practices and television programming. For example, in the beginning, Fox began with a modest five hours of original programming on Saturday and Sunday nights. The commitment to building a new audience and counterprogramming gave Fox the reputation of being progressive and open to new programming ideas, as opposed to the traditional fare offered by the big three networks (ABC, CBS, and NBC). Kristal Brent

Zook in her book *Color by Fox: The Revolution in Black Television* argues the network specifically targeted urban and young audiences in their programming to the extent that they actively "counterprogrammed" against the big three, and "[b]y 1993, the fourth network was airing the single largest crop of black-produced shows in television history."[25] In an interview with Zook, Keenan Ivory Wayans (creator of the comedy-sketch show *In Living Color* (1990–94), which featured black comedians, writers, and directors) stated, "They wanted to be the rebel network."[26] In particular, the network wanted to reach out to an urban and multicultural demographic that the other networks were not serving.

Fox debuted in Sunday prime time in March 1987 with *Married with Children* (1987–97), which began garnering Emmy Awards after its first season and received a nomination for best comedy series at the Golden Globe Awards in 1990. The comedy (created by Michael Moye and Ron Leavitt, a black and white writing team, respectively) was known for its over-the-top stories that were not always considered family friendly. It aired in the Sunday 8 P.M. time slot and was followed by the parent show of *The Simpsons*, a variety and sketch comedy show *The Tracey Ullman Show* (1987–90), hosted by the British comedian and singer Tracey Ullman. In December 1989, the two-minute shorts from *The Tracey Ullman Show* expanded into a thirty-minute Christmas episode and premiered with thirteen new episodes as part of the Fox Sunday lineup in January 1990 and became the first Fox series to break into the top thirty of the Nielsen ratings. The network became a contender with one show and, at the time, only four nights of prime-time programming. Sunday evening became a prime-time powerhouse for Fox built on the high Nielsen ratings for *Married with Children*, *The Simpsons*, and *The X-Files*, plus teen programming, such as *21 Jump Street* and *Beverly Hills 90210*. The big gamble came in the 1990–91 season when Fox elected to kick off its new Thursday night programming by pitting its most popular show, *The Simpsons*, against NBC's *The Cosby Show* (1984–92). In the fall of 1990, *The Simpsons* was near equal to the ratings winner of *Cosby* in its time slot and "was actually beating Cosby among such key demographics as teenagers and men 18–49."[27]

Daniel Kimmel points out in his book *The Fourth Network: How Fox Broke the Rules and Invented Television* (2004) that this move gave Fox the legitimacy to negotiate a deal with Tele-Communications Inc. (TCI) cable and resulted in delivery of their signal from 90 percent to 100 percent of the country. *The Simpsons* became a consistent Thursday-night ratings winner for Fox's target demographic of teens and men. When Fox acquired National Football League game televising rights in 1993, the network moved *The Simpsons* back to Sunday to retain that demographic in its nightly programming, and the program has remained there as the lynchpin of the Fox Sunday night lineup, and today is one of Fox's most consistent and largest viewership nights.

As with *Married with Children*, Fox programming came to producer James L. Brooks to negotiate the expansion of the short into a series. According to an interview with Harry Shearer, Brooks negotiated a noninterference clause with the network.[28] Matt Groening and the writers were free to air any content, including satirizing the network that supported them. And although the reputation of the network has shifted from its "rebel roots" to become the home of the conservative Fox News, the television programming appeals to a wide urban-and-youth demographic through its programming and the continued affiliation with the NFL. Thus, in its twenty-plus seasons, *The Simpsons* is one of the most popular and pervasive American culture icons of the time, and the show runs parallel to the historical time period in which a new wave of Indian immigrants came to the United States as part of the 1990s technology boom.

The Voice of Apu: White Face, Brown Voice

The Simpsons is broadcast (both new episodes and repeats) in syndication to more than sixty countries around the world including Japan, India, and the United Kingdom.[29] Apu Nahasapeemapetilon, the proprietor of the Springfield Kwik-E-Mart, represents not only the most recognizable Indian American character on television but he (an animated character) was also one of the *only* Indian American characters on television in the 1990s. The series chronicles the escapades of the middle-class family the Simpsons. Homer Simpson is the lovable patriarch who works at the local nuclear power plant. He is married to Marge, the blue-haired, second-wave feminist-turned-housewife. They have three children, Bart (fourth grade), Lisa (second grade), and Maggie (the crawling infant who does not speak for most of the series). They live in the small American city of Springfield with a wide host of characters that have become central to the narrative of American popular culture.

For over twenty-five years, Apu has appeared in a variety of episodes. His first extended appearances took place during the first season of the series on the fledgling Fox Television network in 1990. Throughout the series, we learn that Apu is a Hindu (in "Homer the Heretic") and a vegetarian ("Lisa the Vegetarian"). He emigrated from India to the United States to pursue his doctorate in computer science at Springfield Heights Institute of Technology (also known by its initials). While he was a computer-science PhD student, he began working in the Kwik-E-Mart and eight years later eventually bought and ran the store ("Much Apu about Nothing"). Later, he gets married ("The Two Mrs. Nahasapeemapetilons"), romances his wife ("I'm with Cupid"), and has eight children ("Eight Misbehaving"). He acts (both literally and figuratively) as a vehicle to introduce current views and debates about minorities in the United States.

As a result of the fame and singularity of his character, Apu emerges as a highly politicized representation of a Hindu from India who fulfills and also complicates the "model minority" stereotype of success through tolerance and hard work. For example, in the show, Apu is depicted as one of the central members of the Springfield USA community, where he is portrayed despite his accent as just another member of the community. Apu is a volunteer fireman, Lisa's hockey coach, a participant in Homer's barbershop quartet and bowling team, an aspiring screenwriter, and at one time, Homer's boss. For all practical purposes, he is merely a citizen of Springfield until creator Matt Groening chooses to frame an episode specifically around his character. In these cases, his foreignness and "Indianness" are highlighted in relation to issues of immigration, citizenship, arranged marriage and its consequences, and spirituality.[30]

In "Much Apu about Nothing," Apu is concerned about his citizenship status because he entered the United States on a student visa and ended up staying in Springfield without applying to be a citizen. His character becomes representative of all immigrants (legal and undocumented) as he makes every attempt to "pass" as a citizen. In another episode, "Lisa the Vegetarian," Apu says, "I learned long ago, Lisa, to tolerate others, rather than forcing my beliefs on them. You know, you can influence people without badgering them always."[31] By preaching the doctrine of tolerance and articulating the politics of strategic influence, Apu Nahasapeemapetilon becomes a spokesperson for working within the system and within the community in order to facilitate changes in attitudes. In essence, his contract as a character is to not rock the boat and to use alternate ways of bringing his issues to the table; it denotes a philosophy often associated with the image of the model-minority Asian American community. It's a rare moment in the series when we hear Apu confess (without irony) to Lisa (often considered the most enlightened child of the Simpson family) how he copes with his position of difference in the fictional small town of Springfield, USA.

In 2003, Nancy Basile, a correspondent for the Web site animatedtv.com, listed Apu as one of her top-ten Simpsons characters, after the Simpson family members and Mr. Burns: "Apu seems to always have a quip ready at the counter of his Kwik E Mart. He cleverly gauges [sic] Springfield citizens with his prices. His patient explanations of Hinduism to Homer tickle me silly. He's got a killer singing voice, as proven in 'Streetcar Named Marge.'"[32] Her affection for the character showcases his versatility and, more important, his patience in teaching Homer. Part of Apu's appeal, in reading her description, is his role as a cultural spokesperson. However, in the Indian American community, debates run between whether Apu's popularity and presence in the show symbolize a sign of Indians making it in the United States or whether the success of Apu only reinforces Indian immigrant stereotypes and limits all future Indian characters to Apu-like roles.[33] In the film *The Guru* (2003), the main character and his friends (all Indian immigrants) in the film all bemoan the fact that the only famous Indian in America, Apu, is a cartoon.[34]

The character of Apu that Groening and his writing team developed went from being a greedy storekeeper obsessed with crime to a cultural and spiritual spokesperson for India to a naturalized citizen and family man.[35] Azaria, the son of Greek immigrants, has been the voice of over a hundred different characters on *The Simpsons*, including Moe Szyslak (the owner of Moe's Tavern) and Police Chief Wiggum, but his most famous character is Apu Nahasapeemapetilon. For over twenty years, he has been the voice and character of Apu and, hence, the de facto voice of all Indian Americans on television.[36] Because of the popularity and longevity of his character, Azaria has been instrumental (whether he claims this position or not) in standardizing for television culture what Indian immigrants are and what they sound like because there are no other types of characters. As Joe Rhodes reports in *TV Guide*, "It was Groening who suggested that Apu be Indian, though 'we were worried he might be considered an offensive stereotype,' writer Al Jean says. 'But then we did the first read-through, and Hank said, 'Hello, Mr. Homer' with his accent, and it got such a huge laugh, we knew it had to stay.' The writers made Apu a Pakistani of great dignity and industry."[37] So the writers did think about the consequences of brown voice, but the impression of a good joke trumped any concerns they might have had with the stereotype.[38] In the case of Apu, Groening's decisions have been a mixed bag of results. When Apu is featured in an episode, it is his cultural behavior that is the focus of the show and dictates his comedic actions that are often at the expense of Indian religion and culture.

In an interview in the weekly *India Abroad* (highly subscribed to by Indian Americans), while Azaria admitted he did not have any training for his Indian accent, he said he learned his accent "from listening. In Los Angeles, going to 7-11s, hearing Indian and Pakistani clerks."[39] Interestingly, as Al Jean's quotation shows, even the writers have difficulty in identifying Apu's roots

Actor Hank Azaria

and like Azaria cannot distinguish the difference between India (a democracy that has a largely Hindu population) and Pakistan (a military-based government with a primarily Muslim population), nor are they aware of the tensions that currently and historically have defined these two nations. This lack of understanding on the part of the writers signals how Indian Americans are lumped into one group regardless of significant linguistic, religious, political, and cultural histories. And it is this representation that is perpetuated and influences many other characterizations of Indian Americans and, hence, the popular conception of Indian Americans, in general.

To be clear, the figure of Apu can be read through dual, though not necessarily competing, points of view. The first is through a close examination of the character of Apu. Groening, in one sense, is able to present a diverse and liberal exchange of ideas about various issues involving government, big business, social issues, art, and politics. Indeed, it might be argued that Groening presents a progressive vision where Apu is an integral part of the Springfield community, and his ethnicity and cultural background do not determine his activities in Springfield. Apu is a member of the volunteer fire-men brigade, part of a town glee club, and participant in the bowling league. Groening describes Apu, "I think he really loves his job and the power that it gives him to frustrate other people."[40] Apu is also shown as a founding member of the community where his Indianness does not define all his roles in the community.[41]

Apu bears a closer scrutiny through an analysis of his voice. As has been shown, Apu's voice holds great power and influence over how Indian Ameri-can cultural identity is seen in the United States. In a speech delivered to the American Society of Newspaper Editors in 1991, Groening pointed out that the subtext of his show is, "The people in power don't always have your best interests in mind."[42] Media portrayals of Indian Americans on television shows, such as the character of Babu on *Seinfield* (1989–98) and *The Simpsons*, have ignored or de-emphasized racial categorizations of Indian Americans and, instead, in comedic formats, focused on how cultural categorizations of religion and marriage emphasize the foreign nature of Indian Americans.[43] To have a brown voice is to be heard and read as foreign but also to register a status that reflects a highly specialized educational and class status that is seldom associated with other Asian American immigrant groups (in terms of their relationship to accent) and is fairly specific to individuals from the Indian subcontinent.

How Do Indians Speak English?
Mimicry and the Model Minority

In 1835, Lord Thomas Babington Macaulay, the governor general of India, instituted an educational policy in India that he believed would transform natives into perfect British citizens. His "Minute on Education" proclaimed that Indian natives educated in English and taught an English curriculum would produce "a class who may be interpreters between us and the millions whom we govern; a class of persons, Indians in blood and color, but English in taste, in opinions, in morals, and in intellect."[44] The English could thus reproduce themselves in the Empire through the education of a select number of natives. The resulting "class of interpreters" would serve, according to the British point of view, as a bridge between the British in India and the masses of India—Indian intellectuals created without any sexual overtones or hints of miscegenation between the English and the natives. The creation would be the hybrid of the best in Indian and British culture.[45] This educated class could also represent India in the Western world.

The creation of a new class of English Indians was another way for the British Empire to construct a tangible other and, simultaneously, reinforce British identity. However, in his 1984 essay, "Of Mimicry and Man: The Ambivalence of Colonial Discourse," Homi K. Bhabha points out the subversive potential of creating an imitation Englishman who may speak English but who may not necessarily agree with the philosophy of the imperialism. British colonial mimicry is about the native adopting the habit and mannerisms of colonizer, or in this case the Indian becoming the perfect British citizen. But as Bhabha argues, mimicry also exposes the flaws in the British imperial project because the Indian can never truly be a British citizen. If s/he were, then the Empire could not maintain the hierarchies on which it was built. Mimicry, he explains, employs both "resemblance and menace."[46] The resemblance aspect of mimicry is comforting because of its familiarity. Its menace, on the other hand, exposes the contradictions of trying to reproduce the native in the colonial's image, because that very image is unstable and susceptible to misinterpretation. The recognition that the colonial project may be flawed undermines the entire act of mimicry and the solid, comforting image of British superiority. Thus, full transformation is prevented, and the native is only a potential project that is always trying but never succeeding.

Brown voice is particularly useful in reevaluating postcolonial theories of native-colonizer relations by rethinking Bhabha's theory of mimicry. Brown voice is mimicry in reverse but not its opposite. The two concepts are connected because brown voice, like mimicry, depends upon the notion of an authentic native figure by which to gauge one's identity. However, while mimicry exposes the cracks in the imperial effort to reform natives into proper subjects of the British Empire, brown voice operates in a slightly different manner because brown voice is also related to the comedic genre of parody. Like mimicry, parody depends on the idea of an original or authentic subject, and the action behind parody is to aim for more than an imitation. However, the intent of parody is to highlight the performative aspect of imitation. Instead of exposing the performer to ridicule because a true transformation (mimicry) cannot take place, brown voice gives the performer control over how he or she is going to be received. Brown voice is about the performance rather than the actual result and, hence, culturally constructed. The performative nature of brown voice is what also allows for a humorous (or not) response. Brown voice elides difference into one manageable aspect of difference. The idea of reducing complex differences into a single, manageable form is evocative of how American liberal multiculturalism also homogenizes ethnic and racial differences under the label of diversity or describes America as a "melting pot." As such, the sanctioning of brown-voice performance is an endorsement of conservative social policy with regards to race, because it is humorous (and so not taken seriously).

Like mimicry, brown voice exposes the flaws of being cast as a privileged or model minority. When I saw the accent emerging from Hank Azaria's mouth on an episode of *The Actor's Studio* on the Bravo network, I found the experience jarring because the physical image did not match the voice. Instead, Azaria's verbal and facial expressions and his attempts at parody were not humorous to me. The utilization of brown voice in this case highlighted how someone else, namely a white actor, was staging Indian cultural fluency and the glass ceiling of what Indians could achieve in terms of cultural citizenship.

The implementation of brown voice also seeks to divorce accent from race and thereby remove any hint of racial overtones from voice. In other words, the performance of brown voice participates in the simplification of racial identities. As a result, the accented voice becomes a consumer product that can be traded without regards to cultural, ethnic, and racial history. For example, in *The Simpsons'* seventeenth season (2006) episode "Kiss Kiss, Bang Bangalore," Homer's company is downsized, and he is forced to move to India. While he is there, he meets Apu's cousin, who speaks and looks exactly like Apu. There is no differentiation between Apu and the one other Indian person whom Homer meets. Simultaneously, the practice of brown voice ensures that although the Indians are striving for cultural citizenship, the nature of the accent will always be read as foreign, and the racial hierarchies of the United States will remain intact.

Conclusion

In terms of American immigration and assimilation politics, a corresponding argument can be made that accented English in any form makes us reflect on who and what can represent a true American or occupy the space of a "cultural citizen." The concept of brown voice brings with it the full force of colonial legacy. Over 150 years of interaction with British English have influenced how Indians and Indian Americans respond to and utilize English in daily life.[47] However, since Indian Independence (in spite of the flurry of British Raj dramas of the 1980s), the notion of brown voice also reflects the idea of educational expertise, particularly in the areas of medicine and computer and software technology. One only need scan the headlines to see how India and Pakistan frequent the news or the business and economics sections or the technology sections to see the influence of Indians, Indian Americans, and South Asian immigrants in global and national economies.

Ultimately, the theory of brown voice causes us to rethink how we see and hear racial identity beyond the visual and how we process the cultural meaning of accents. In the case of Indian Americans, the accent has been rendered a part of American culture by the character of Apu, who has made it familiar, loved, and also funny. But the performance of brown voice also connotes class privilege, a particular type of poshness associated with education that we hear from Salman Rushdie or in Merchant Ivory films or Dr. Sanjay Gupta or Deepak Chopra on American television. To break out of brown voice through accent variation, for example, is to defy expectations of the audience and to allow other accents to emerge out of brown bodies. It redesigns experiences of racial and national identity.

3

Animating Gandhi

Historical Figures, Asian American Masculinity, and Model-Minority Accents in *Clone High*

MTV US apologizes if we have offended the people
of India and the memory of Mahatma Gandhi.

January 31, 2003

During the last week of January 2003, the Indian Press attacked MTV USA programming choices and Maxim magazine's publishing decisions by protesting the "attempt to humiliate the father of the nation," Mohandas Gandhi.[1] Indian politicians condemned MTV's promotion of the teenage character Gandhi on the television broadcast animated series *Clone High*; Om Prakash Chautala, chief minister of Hayarana, and other politicians announced they would conduct a political hunger strike to protest the images in Maxim magazine, claiming it was "gross insult to the icon of non-violence" and condemned the television show, an "insult heaped" on Gandhi by MTV USA.[2] According to various reports, over 150 politicians and activists staged a one-day hunger strike at Gandhi's memorial in New Delhi to protest a character on a show that they hadn't seen (nor were likely to because the show was not going to air in India) but only heard of through the popular grapevine of the internet and the non-resident Indian (NRI) population.[3] A few days later, the U.S. division of MTV apologized to the people and nation of India about any misunderstandings concerning the depiction of Gandhi on the series *Clone High*.[4]

Why was there a controversy? After all, Apu from the television series *The Simpsons* had been on American television for thirteen years at the time, and although there are still discussions about his portrayal and the ramifications for South Asians and Asian Americans, his character is not a source of national

The cast of *Clone High*: Mr. Butlertron, John F. Kennedy, Cleopatra, Abe Lincoln, Joan of Arc, Gandhi, and Principal Scudworth (lying down)

or international protest. *Clone High*, like *The Simpsons*, was an animated series that parodied everyday life; it ran for thirteen episodes from November 2002 to March 2003 before MTV cancelled it. Although the series is not as well-known as *The Simpsons*, the controversy it generated is symptomatic of how racial performance becomes the dominant narrative of how Indian and Indian Americans are represented in American culture.[5] The protest directed at the show centered on the issues of cultural appropriation and American ignorance (read as lack of respect) of Indian history. This ignorance results in the erasure of Indian Americans characters' awareness of their own history in order to assimilate to American narratives. This chapter marks an addition to representations of Indians in America as new immigrants (1960s) and convenience-store owners (1980s and 1990s), such as Apu, and focuses on the roles of Indian American teens and young adults who have a more complex relationship to cultural and national citizenship. *Clone High* represents the next generation of Indian Americans—the suburban teenager and American-born Indian (*desi*), who bear no visible vocal accent but are still racially performed in a variation of brownface roles. The characteristics of an assimilated brownface performance are present in the roles of the model-minority immigrant and the second-generation Indian American. This chapter discusses the racializing aspect of Indian accents and brown-voice performance in relation to the depiction of the model-minority sidekick and American masculinity.

In further developing the discussion of the national community of America, it is important to discuss the gendered and racialized representations of Indian American men in the media. Although the characters Gandhi and Apu have individual names and storylines, they often become representatives of Asian American men, in general. While growing up, Indian American actor Kal Penn (one of the stars of the film *Harold and Kumar Go to White Castle* [2004]) remembers the effects of the character Apu on his everyday life: "A lot of Indian kids took a lot of heat." So in his films, he tries to directly address and then counter the idea that every Indian American looks, acts, and speaks like Apu.[6] With the exception of his role in the film *Van Wilder* (2002), Penn is featured in roles where he does not have an Indian accent. Scholar Richard Fung describes the stereotypes of Asian American men in popular culture: "Asian men (at least since the 1920s) have been consigned to one of two categories: the egghead/wimp, or—in what may be analogous to the lotus blossom–dragon lady dichotomy [for Asian American women]—the kung fu master/ninja samurai. He is sometimes dangerous, sometimes friendly, but almost always characterized by a desexualized Zen ascetic."[7] Apu and the character Gandhi are in the first category of eggheads and wimps, although in the case of Gandhi, his masculinity is linked to being seen as a typical American teenager who struggles with fitting into the dominant group.

Because Apu is a fictional figure, his character is not scrutinized in the same way as a depiction of Gandhi. Indeed, the lack of cultural and historical memory allows for a certain measure of ignorance with regards to Apu, but with a respected figure such as Gandhi, the controversy allows us to examine how the media frames cultural and racial groups in the United States and the consequences of those depictions in a global environment where India is one of the major players in the world economy. The controversy is about the image of the "father of the nation" versus the satire of the iconic image, which has grown larger than life. Now, while American heroes, such as George Washington and Abraham Lincoln, are also venerated historical figures who are routinely satirized, the benefit of time and distance has allowed variations (rather than one single image) to be seen about these individuals; Gandhi has not had the same exposure. The character Gandhi on the animated television series *Clone High* offers an opportunity to discuss the portrayal of South Asian masculinity and American citizenship in the new millennium.

National Apologies and World Interests

Less than one week after the premiere of *Clone High* in January 2003 in Canada and the United States, MTV issued the above statement in response to protests about the portrayal of Gandhi in the Indian and British press. The immediate response may also reflect MTV's considerable business interests in Asia and India with an audience of over two billion.[8] An excerpt of the statement reads as follows:

> MTV wants to make it clear that 'Clone High' *was created and intended for an American audience.* We recognize and respect that various cultures may view this programming differently, and we regret any offense taken by the content in the show. The animated show parodies several historical figures from around the world, including the United States, *where this form of comedy is common.*[9]

While MTV's apology seems contrite, the defense of the show and the need to explain the idea of parody to India are condescending and indicative of how consumption of the exotic or racialized other without knowledge of social and cultural history can be problematic. The tone of the apology implies that American audiences (unlike Indian audiences) would not be offended because parody of historical figures is common.[10] This separation of American audiences from an Indian audience points to the fact that humor, especially parody, is culturally and nationally specific. It validates the idea the Americans are a monolithic group who all look and think the same and does not take into account that Indians live in the United States and other parts of the world. But this distancing also makes it clear that this is an Indian problem, not an American one, and puts the onus of blame on the Indian reaction rather than considering that the show might have overlooked something in relation to its historical portrayals. The language of the release assumes that Indians do not understand parody—a form of satirical drama used in India before the United States was a recognized country! What MTV and the producers of the series did not understand is that it was not the "what" or the form of series that was objectionable, it was the "who," the revered figure of Gandhi, that was problematic. While MTV did not pull the show immediately from its lineup, *Clone High* was not renewed after the airing of the thirteen episodes in Canada, although it became available on the internet and now is a DVD set.

In discussing the show, co-creator Phil Lord describes *Clone High* as a "social commentary" and claims, "Gandhi is based on people we knew in school, the kind of kid from those very intense, high-achieving families. No kid would feel more pressure to be a high achiever than the clone of Gandhi."[11] In other words, the creators utilized Gandhi to stand in for a "model minority," a stereotype often attributed to Asian Americans. Historically, Gandhi has been described as many things, but model minority is not usually one of them. Clearly, he was picked because he was the only famous Indian person that the creators could think of to fit into their vision of a high school spoof, and they wanted someone to physically stand in for the stereotype of the high school geek.[12] And yet, though Gandhi is physically drawn as "brown" in the show, he does not perform "brown voice." All the characters, including Gandhi, speak with recognizably American accents or what Americans might identify as no accent at all. The single character that possesses an accent (and a slight stutter) is the character JFK (John F. Kennedy), who speaks with his signature Boston accent. The storyline that features Gandhi's attempt to learn and perform JFK's regional American accent provides an illuminating commentary on American immigrant assimilation after 1965 and on modern depictions of American ethnic masculinity. It is not my intent to comment

The character Gandhi in the television show *Clone High* (Touchstone Television and MTV, 2002–3)

on whether these portrayals are wrong or right but instead to examine how they reflect and challenge social and political discussions surrounding the formation of American identity and the representation of Indian Americans.

In the previous chapter, Apu's accent is defined as a manufactured sound that reinforces the representation of Indian Americans as welcome, though not entirely assimilated foreigners and immigrants. It could be argued that the character Apu is the adult manifestation of an Indian American male figure that is prevented from achieving narrative white assimilation because of his accent and storylines. Gandhi, in *Clone High*, is a second-generation American teenager who is a biological clone of the historical figure. In the twenty-first century, Indian Americans are not only convenience-store owners but now are American teenagers who live in the suburbs and go to high school. The show, however, reduces Gandhi, an influential figure, to the stereotype of a model minority without any historical context or background. *Clone High* encourages the idea that all Indians occupy one single niche in American culture—the smart, racially nonwhite, out-of-place, emasculated geek who is always the sidekick and never the leader. The lack of explanation in using this image in the show diminishes the historical significance of a figure such as Gandhi and the reality of Indians in United States and international consciousness.

As the political backlash against the program shows, the attempt to make Gandhi into an assimilated model-minority sidekick conflicts with the historical legacy of Gandhi as the pioneer of modern, mass civil disobedience and a hero of India. Gandhi challenged the established colonial British presence and also tackled internal prejudices within the Indian community, such as religious, caste, and sex discrimination. So although the creators wanted to include minorities in the spoof of a high school drama, instead, I find, they end up emphasizing essential stereotypes about Indian Americans and Asian American men who are always subordinate to the dominant, white, male characters.

The controversy generated by Gandhi the animated character challenges how Indian Americans redefine twenty-first-century notions of American nationality and masculinity. The 1960s developments contrast with the depictions of Asian American men and masculinity in a post–9/11 world that features television programs such as *Clone High*. New youth cultures influence programming and broadcast choices, as do transnational business markets in the global world of the twenty-first century. Programming on MTV promotes certain images of America but also has to be sensitive to world economies because MTV Networks Corporation (which has a \$7 billion per year operating budget) also has an international corporate identity as a global network.[13] Youth comedies such as *Clone High* are central to MTV's target demographic of young men seventeen to twenty-five. The television show *Clone High* utilizes the comedic genre of satire to appeal to a young male demographic and reinforces the status quo of heteronormative masculine ideals at the expense of the racialized figure of Gandhi. The analysis of one of the most memorable episodes of *Clone High* shows the transformation of the character Gandhi into "a shorter, browner Kennedy," which represents a sophomoric (or one might say stereotypical teenager) approach to dealing with gender relations where Indian Americans are cast as racial outsiders in American national identity politics.

The Politics of MTV Programming in the Twenty-First Century

Since MTV first aired in 1982, the channel has positioned itself as the site for counterculture and youth movements in American music and culture. However, the cable channel's initial refusal to show black music videos because the channel catered to a white middle-class demographic represents the uneasy relationship MTV has had with programming related to race. Their change in policy only occurred when record companies, at the behest of black artists, threatened to deny MTV access to all their artists. For example, in 1982, CBS Records represented both Michael Jackson and Billy Joel on its label. Faced with the threat of economic losses it could not recover from, the fledging cable channel reversed its position and soon benefited as the meteoric rise of stars such as Jackson, Lionel Ritchie, and Prince became intertwined with the music videos on MTV.[14]

In the late 1980s and early 1990s, MTV began to counterprogram to neutralize charges of racism and discrimination. Andrew Goodwin writes how the creation of black programming, such as *Yo! MTV Raps*, the airing of controversial music videos by Public Enemy, and the Free James Brown event (when the singer was in jail on drug possession), was an effort to promote liberal politics and racial representation.[15] The 1990s featured the introduction of reality shows, such as *The Real World*, and animated series with adolescent male humor, such as *Beavis and Butthead*. Scholar Jon Kraszewski argues that MTV subsequently "redefined its brand from explicitly liberal to subtly conservative channel to capture the mood of the George W. Bush presidency and a post–9/11 America."[16] Kraszewski specifically points out how in reality shows, such as *The Real World*, liberal black-white racial dialogues were replaced by more conservative portrayals of difference that are often embodied in the multiracial characters who "register racial difference but who do not talk explicitly about racism in America." The network executives made a concerted shift by hiring in 2003 a new director of social programming, Ian V. Rowe, who formerly worked in the Bush administration.[17] At the same time that MTV America was developing a more conservative approach to programming, MTV International had become a global empire that had expanded across the world. Large consumer markets in Asia and, in particular, in India led to the launch of MTV Networks Asia in 1995 and expanded to include twenty-four-hour programming on MTV India, MTV Mandarin (China, Hong Kong, and Mainland China), and MTV Asia (focusing on Southeast Asia).[18] MTV India is one of the most popular channels on Indian television today, and as in the United States, the station caters to a vibrant and consumer-savvy urban youth culture.[19]

Although MTV has never disclosed why the series *Clone High* was cancelled, it can be surmised that economic interests in Asia might have affected their programming decision, even though the show was not scheduled to be broadcast in India. In terms of North American programming, *Clone High* was introduced when MTV's domestic agenda featured shows in which race is "handled" or managed by the individual rather than explored as a societal and systemic part of culture.[20] The controversy around the character of Gandhi is the center of these two counterpoised social and cultural moments. Gandhi as the brown character stands in for racialized minorities in the United States. But in the case of this model minority, the historical legacy of a world-renowned figure and the country where he comes from (in which MTV has vested commercial interests) did trump American satire and programming interests.

Media Representations and the Model-Minority Man

Anxieties about new immigrants to the United States have historically appeared in film and television. Depictions of Asian American men in American popular culture have consistently cast aspersions on Asian American masculinity and sexuality.[21] Common characteristics associated with Asian American men on television include the passive or effeminate but intelligent nerd and the foreign student who cannot speak American English. These roles are typically supporting characters that serve to provide a negative contrast to the white-male narratives. The martial arts expert, associated with Bruce Lee films in the 1960s and 1970s, represents a more physical masculinity that is usually showcased in fight scenes or violent behavior. The roles Asian American men routinely play are the evil threat to the established law or the servant and sidekick to the interests of the status-quo majority.[22] In the case of South Asians, political cartoons and articles historically focused on Gandhi's resistance to the British Empire and later looked at the Indian Americans as spiritual figures.

Gandhi's image as a lone man in a robe or piece of cloth combines the ascetic image with a small, wizened body. These stereotypes of the spiritual guru were continually reproduced in American media and continue to flourish in contemporary times (see chapter 4). The image of Gandhi is popularly represented worldwide and is associated with Gandhi's political protest against the British and with the Indian Independence movement.

Gandhi on the Salt March statue in front of the Indian embassy, Washington, D.C.

In the photograph of the Gandhi statue, the statue is in front of the Indian embassy in Washington, D.C. The other stereotypes that *Clone High* address through the character of Gandhi is the representations of Asians and Asian Americans as a model-minority stereotype or the variation of the model minority in which the Indian American is the highly intelligent and reliable minority sidekick that does not challenge the status quo and assimilates into the existing culture. The idea of the model minority is a comparative model used by the dominant racial group to distinguish Asian American immigrant behavior and Indian American immigrant behavior from other racial minorities, such as African Americans and Latinos/as. The depiction of Gandhi in *Clone High* persists in perpetuating existing stereotypes of ethnic masculinity and the model minority.

The term "model minority" first appeared in 1966, almost immediately after the passage of the 1965 Hart-Cellar Immigration Act, which eliminated quotas from U.S. immigration policies and opened up immigration to people from the Asia and the Indian subcontinent. India, Taiwan, Korea, and, in particular, the Philippines had a surplus of medical and engineering personnel. Many middle- and upper-class professionals ended up coming to and residing permanently in the United States. This small but new highly educated professional class combined with existing Asian American populations in the United States attained more economically prominent positions. In the media, the *New York Times Magazine* celebrated the efforts of Japanese Americans to assimilate into everyday American life, and later that year, *U.S. News and World Report* printed a story that praised the hardworking Chinese and the successful economic enterprises in Chinatown.[23] Both articles emphasized that Japanese Americans and Chinese immigrants were productive members of the American economy and had overcome racial prejudice and discriminatory practices. However, the constant reinforcement of Asian Americans in the media as a model minority can limit and even cover up the diversity of experiences of Asians in the United States.

The mid-1960s marked a tumultuous change in American racial politics. The success of Asian Americans was pitted against the claims of the black-power movement that America was an unequal and racist society. In an article in *U.S. News and World Report*, Keith Osajima claims, "At a time when it is being proposed that hundreds of billions be spent to uplift Negroes and other minorities, the nation's 300,000 Chinese Americans are moving ahead on their own, with no help from anyone else." Asian Americans were touted as the embodiment of the American Dream and proof that America was an egalitarian society where dreams could come true. Osajima argues, "Asian achievement confirmed that the United States was indeed the land of opportunity. It defined success in narrow, materialistic terms."[24] Minority success is tied to family values, good education, and the willingness to fit into mainstream society, rather than challenge the tenets of dominant culture. This success is reflected in the rise of the Indian American professional class and the movement of Indians to the affluent suburbs. Portrayals in television and film can also reinforce the idea that Indian Americans, including second-generation Americans, are seen as cultural outsiders in the United States. Apu of *The Simpson* is representative of the complex mix of the multiple and often contradictory positions of ethnic and racial immigrants with regards to American political and social culture. Whereas in the 1980s and 1990s depictions of Indian Americans were confined to professional adults, the new millennium features young characters that emphasize the new generations of immigrants to the United States during the rise of the informational technology boom but also the children of the post-1965 immigrant generations. At the beginning of the twenty-first century, in contrast to the adult Apu, the next generation of Indian Americans—immigrant students and second-generation teenagers—began to appear as model-minority characters and sidekicks in American media.

South Asian Sidekicks and Model-Minority Students

On American television, South Asian American youths are present as sidekicks to white Americans in situation comedies, but these roles tend to emphasize the stereotypical qualities of the model minority that are similar to Apu but in younger characters. For example, the CBS comedy *The Big Bang Theory* (2007–) features particle astrophysicist Rajesh Koothrappali (Kunal Nayyar) as an Indian scientist—a kind of young Apu—who speaks with an Indian accent, has difficulty speaking to women, and is part of the egghead/wimp stereotype. The series *Aliens in America* (2007–8) focused on a Muslim high school exchange student from Pakistan named Raja Mushsharraf (Adhir Kalyan) who lived with a white family (the Tolchucks) in Wisconsin. The show is a coming of age in high school comedy. Even though the character of Raja Mushsharraf was one of the first Muslims to be portrayed in a situation comedy and the intention of the creators was to offer an alternative view of Muslims as Arabs or terrorists, the show still framed him in the role of a model minority in high school.[25] Like many of *The Simpsons* plot lines that focus on the cultural habits of Apu to mark his difference from a normalized view of American culture, *Aliens in America* also homes in on Raja's religious beliefs as accents that show how different he is compared to the people (Americans) around him. Raja is polite to women, studious, faithful to his religious practices, reliable, does not lie, and does not sell alcohol to underage boys (Justin's friends). He becomes a catalyst for the family, but his character is rarely shown (except when he starts smoking) to deviate from acting as a moral center for others in the show.[26] Since he is an exchange student, the show implies that he will be returning to Pakistan, and his presence is a temporary one that is outside of American culture.

In *National Lampoon's Van Wilder* (2002), Kal Penn (before his fame in the Harold and Kumar comedies) also plays a foreign-exchange student named Taj Mahal Badalandabad from Banglapore, India. The character is not named after a person (like Gandhi) but after one of the most famous sites in India, the Taj Mahal. This type of role reduces him to a cultural thing or accent. Like Apu's last name, Nahasapeemapetilon, Taj's last name of Badalandabad is a made up and unpronounceable name that has no meaning and makes fun of Indian names. Their last names do not reflect their individuality but instead their symbolic status as stereotypes of South Asian Americans, who are often interchangeable.

In the film, Taj is hired as a personnel assistant to Van Wilder (Ryan Reynolds), a wealthy, white student who has been in college for seven years. The humor associated with Taj resides in how he is compared to the American Van Wilder. Taj is funny because of his verbal slips of tongue, his Indian accent, and his overall clothing choices.[27] Penn, an Indian American actor who does not have an Indian accent, plays the role of Taj by performing an Indian accent. The character wears preppy but slightly out-of-style American clothes and is obsessed with losing his virginity. In essence, Van becomes Taj's guru and teaches Taj everything he needs to know about excelling in the college social scene, including wooing women. At the end of the film (when Van Wilder graduates), Taj reverts to wearing an Indian tunic (rather than preppy American clothes) and falling in love with an Indian woman who is a transfer student from Banglapore. His character is a combination of Gandhi from *Clone High* and the unmarried Apu from *The Simpsons*. The implication is that he has saved the protagonist of the film, Van Wilder, by helping him graduate, and Taj will also soon graduate and go home. The film represents a conventional narrative of a foreign student who arrives in the United States and adopts American cultural mannerisms of fraternity-boy behavior and ends up as the faithful sidekick to the hero of the story. Although Gandhi in

Clone High is not a foreign student, the role Gandhi plays in the series mirrors the character in the film.

In the sequel *National Lampoon's Van Wilder 2: The Rise of Taj* (2006), Taj is the star of the film. However, the sequel takes Taj out of the United States and places him in the fictional Camford (Cambridge/Oxford) University, where class difference rather than racial difference fuels the plot of the film. This reflects a modern twist on the colonial narrative where Indians go to Britain and fend off English prejudices against the groups that were former territories or colonies, such as the Irish, the Scottish, the working class, the Americans, and the Indians. The character retains his Indian accent, but the British refer to him as an American. In both films, the accent is integral to defining Taj's character, and what creates laughs are his "Taj-isms," which are spoken with an Indian accent, but his position has shifted from model minority to the brash can-do stereotype of an American.[28] The film now introduces him as an Indian American immigrant whose parents live in Milwaukee, rather than as a foreign student. The second film demonstrates the inability of Hollywood, generally, to deal with the complexity of a South Asian character as the central character in an American setting so they reorient the plot to a British setting where class rather than race can drive the narrative of the film.

The show *Clone High*, on the other hand, portrays Gandhi as an American in an American setting. His nationality is never questioned, even though he is clearly drawn as racially different (dark brown) from the other characters. Indian Americans are not foreign-exchange students or relegated to the ethnic spaces of convenience stores, gas stations, and motels but now are teenagers who are being educated in American high schools. Cultural anthropologist Shalini Shankar notes in her study of desi teens in Silicon Valley that success for teenagers goes beyond material expectations. In addition to their affinity for Indian languages and culture, South Asian teens are dependent on peer interactions and connections, including social circles and dating practices, to measure their success.[29] The show normalizes Gandhi as a middle-class suburban teenager and does not acknowledge the cultural affinity Shankar describes as vital to a desi teen identity. His outsider status is related to his social status among his peers in high school and specifically models of American masculinity. The show is working with three models of masculinity and satirizes characteristics of the sensitive man (or emo), the hypermasculine jock, and the cerebral geek. In her work on 1990s South Asian youth culture in New York City, Sunaina Maira discusses the concept of cultural nostalgia as integral to South Asian identity formation and, in particular, highlights (as does Shankar) how South Asian youth are engaged in figuring out the relationships and hierarchies of American consumer images of Indian culture and their own experiences.[30] The show, however, neglects giving Gandhi cultural knowledge or a background that addresses his genetic heritage, and so he becomes a teenager whose only concern is what is happening with his peer group in high school. He is enacting an assimilated brownface performance that erases racial difference to the realm of the physical because he is drawn as tan. Gandhi becomes one Indian name among many, and the historical legacy of Gandhi disappears and is replaced with an American teenage drama.

The Legacy and Representation of Gandhi

To most people, Gandhi is an iconic quasi-religious figure who helped to free a nation from the shackles of British colonialism. Indeed, the honorific "Mahatma" means "great soul," which is a religious title. Mohandas Gandhi is also considered one of the most influential persons of the twentieth century and pioneered the practice of nonviolent protest and mass civil disobedience (known as *Satyagraha*) first in South Africa (1893–1914) and then in India (1915–45). Civil-rights movements in the United States and throughout the world continue to be influenced by his examples and teachings. Both Martin Luther King Jr. and Nelson Mandela read and utilized Gandhi's methods. Monuments to Gandhi, as a world-renowned figure, range from his statue at the Martin Luther King Jr. Museum in Atlanta and in front of the Indian embassy in Washington, D.C., to his appearance on Indian currency, and celebrate Gandhi's life and work.

In recent times, the first encounter that many Americans had with Gandhi was through the 1982 Academy Award–winning film *Gandhi*, directed by Richard Attenborough.[31] The film garnered eight Oscars including best film, best actor (Ben Kingsley as Gandhi), best director, and best screenplay. Much of the press coverage centered on the remarkable resemblance between Gandhi and Kingsley (who is half Indian) and on Attenborough's twenty-year-long desire to make a film about Gandhi.[32] Two independent British companies, Goldcrest Films International and International Film Investors, and India National Film Development, which the government of India and Prime Minister Indira Gandhi supported, financed the film; Columbia Pictures distributed it.[33] Interestingly, Attenborough made a comment that he passed on a Hollywood version of a film on Gandhi because he felt it would not portray Gandhi in a "true" manner.[34] Most of the film was shot in India, and although identified as a British film, Indian influences and Indian actors were a central part of the film.

In the United States, reviewers described the film in glowing terms as one of the most important films ever made. Critic Jack Kroll said, "As it is, he [Kingsley] mounts a powerful challenge to his audience by presenting Gandhi as the most profound and effective of revolutionaries, creating out of a fierce personal discipline a chain reaction that led to tremendous historical consequences. At a time of deep political unrest, economic dislocation and nuclear anxiety, seeing *Gandhi* is an experience that will change many minds and hearts."[35] The language and the presentation of Gandhi accentuate his role as a revolutionary and someone who is a change-maker, not someone who is meek, an outsider, or even a model minority. In the film, his approach to revolution is portrayed as calm, planned out in advance, and compassionate. Even though Satyagraha does not condone violence, it is a strategic practice

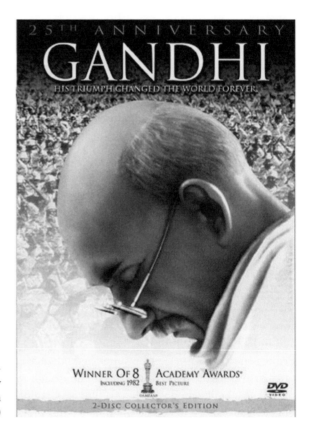

Gandhi, twenty-fifth-anniversary DVD edition (Columbia, 1982)

of civil disobedience that flies in the face of the image of a compliant model minority who excels in American culture but does not make waves or challenge the system.

Ultimately, the film was an international success that collected multiple awards from around the world and that Indians also embraced.[36] Vincent Canby of the *New York Times* notes, "Of more overall importance is the possibility that the film will bring Gandhi to the attention of a lot of people around the world for the first time, not as a saint but as a self-searching, sometimes fallible human being with a sense of humor as well as of history."[37] In this case, Gandhi was not just associated with a religious aspect to his identity but also the fact that he was involved with setting policy and directing a campaign of independence. Since 1982, very few films (and none of them American) have chronicled the life of or even featured Gandhi.[38] Part of the reason may be the controversial nature of his historical legacy that touches upon Hindu-Muslim relations.[39] The other might be is that he is a revered figure, and any attempt to give a new or critical opinion of him will always be met with skepticism or resistance just as with other great figures. Since Gandhi's assassination in 1948, there have been few Indians that are easily recognizable to Americans. Gandhi is India's most famous figure in the world, and, yet, Gandhi's role in world history remains relatively unknown to Americans except for his association with phrases such as "nonviolence" or visual cues, such as his half-naked body and bald head. In my informal poll of students and colleagues, most associated Gandhi with "peace" or pacifism, as well as nonviolence. Some also read nonviolence as passive. But Gandhi was also a strategist, a smart legal mind, and a wily diplomat. The migration of his legacy in the United States from civil protester to passive pacifist (one who will not act or fight) is an indicator that the popular image of Asian men inflects how Gandhi is perceived and how the creators of *Clone High* could be influenced by this perception.

The film *Gandhi* is a historical drama for which the director and producers went out of their way to gain public and media support for their project. As Attenborough indicates, he was interested in representations that respect the "true" legacy of Gandhi. *Clone High*, on the other hand, does not make any such claim. Many of their characters are famous historical figures, such as Joan of Arc, Abraham Lincoln, and John F. Kennedy. The key critique of the representation of Gandhi on *Clone High* is that unlike Lincoln or JFK, most Americans would see the satire before they ever learned the history. How can a writer satirize someone when that person's history is not culturally mainstream, and how might that take over any image the audience might have? Also, what other images do South Asians have in terms of great historical figures that are seen in popular culture? Vijay Prasad discusses the role of South Asians in U.S. race relations in *The Karma of Brown Folk* by addressing the question, "How does it feel to be [seen as] a solution?"[40] In the case of Gandhi, he's being used as a model minority to stand in for all minority populations.

Gandhi's Debut and Makeover: Making an American Man

Premiering in January 2003 on MTV, the animated satire *Clone High* featured high school students who are all clones of famous historical figures. The premise of the show revolves around a group of shadowy figures in the 1980s that retrieved DNA samples of famous and infamous world historical figures (most of whom had been killed violently) to create clones for some nefarious purpose. The series, which starts sixteen years into the project, depicts the clones as having deep angst about living up to their historical predecessors' images. Cinnamon J. Scudworth, the Clone Program administrator, is the manipulative principal of the high school. He and his mechanical butler/ vice principal (Mr. Butlertron) monitor the progress of the clones, primarily Lincoln, Cleopatra, Joan of Arc, Kennedy, and Gandhi.

The series satirizes American racial and gendered norms and also every conceivable plot device associated with high school dramas. Each episode parodies the issue-sensitive dramas that appeared on American television in the 1990s (the "very special episodes") that often dealt with narratives about drug abuse, AIDS, alternative lifestyles, racism and ostracism, and conse-quences of the prom. Most of the series is centered on school narratives, such as class elections, the prom, school athletics, and fund-raisers. Adults and parents (all foster parents of the clones) have cameo appearances. A blind, black jazz musician named Toots raises Joan of Arc, and JFK's parents are a gay couple. Gandhi's parents are Jewish, and Abe's parents are ringers for the American Gothic couple. The writers have created a sexually and racially diverse society that is exaggerated and over the top so that their depictions also critique narratives of diversity and cultural stereotypes even as they are showing them.

Gandhi is portrayed as a short, bald, party kind of guy who wants to be in the popular crowd and be a ladies man. He wears an earring in his left ear and wants to be the life of the party. He sees himself as an undiscovered rap-music artist and calls himself the "G-Man." He is best friends with Lincoln, the tall, awkward kid with a conscience. And yet, Gandhi is a maverick as he interacts with various minor characters in the school, including Genghis Khan and Marie Curie. As the fifth wheel among the four other characters, he is not part of the heterosexual pairings that put JFK and Abe in competition for Cleopatra (the popular and narcissistic teenage girl) and Joan of Arc (the feminist activist and girl sidekick). And yet, he exhibits all the longings and lust of a sixteen-year-old high school teenager. If Abe is seen as soulful and representative of the sensitive kid (and coveted by Joan), and JFK is the jock who wants to sleep with every girl in school, where does Gandhi fit in as a masculine trope?

In the second-to-last episode, "Makeover, Makeover, Makeover," everyone is scrambling to change her/himself into someone who will be asked to the high school prom. Reminiscent of the teen films such as *Clueless* (1995) and other makeover films that feature how one's physical look reveals or hides the inner person, the "Makeover" episode chronicles literal makeovers on three of the cast members, one of whom is Gandhi. In their work on television reality shows, authors Laurie Ouellette and James Hay argue that makeover TV "conveys the idea that the quickest route to success is 'strategic' self-fashioning, a practice that includes remaking one's body, personality, and image in calculated ways to bring about personal advantage in a competitive marketplace."[41] In the world of high school, getting one's preferred date for the prom is the competitive market that Gandhi has to venture into. When we first see him in the episode, he bursts into the girl's locker room and asks all the girls if they will go to prom with him. His tone and manner are filled with bravado, and his attitude is one that only sees women as object—someone to dangle on his arm. Everyone turns him down. He has to physically and psychologically "rebrand" himself as a normative, white, hypersexualized male in order to successfully get a date, and so he strategically turns to the representative of this seemingly preferred model of masculinity—JFK. As the episode progresses, Gandhi is turned into an objectified person as a result of his makeover by JFK. Gandhi revels in his position until he realizes that the makeover was a bet and a superficial means of becoming popular. This chapter's interest is how the narrative transforms Gandhi the geek to GFK the stud or to "a shorter browner Kennedy."

JFK's desire to change Gandhi is not only an American version of George Bernard Shaw's drama *Pygmalion* that chronicles how to change one's speech and class and dress. It is also an attempt to clone himself. Homi Bhabha in "Of Mimicry and Man" points out the fallacy of turning the native into the colonizer, because it usually exposes something wrong or deficient in the identity or enterprise of the colonizer. The inability of the native/minority to be "not quite" white is both the appeal of assimilation and also the ambivalence (Bhabha's term) that encompasses the act of mimicry. The difference, despite the effort to change, is always apparent. Accent, like mimicry, is dependent on the contrast between the minority figure and the dominant narrative, but in the American context, changing the speech and the clothing is part of the assimilation narrative and also an individual endeavor. Gandhi functions as an accent because his character is malleable—he can "fit" in with the popular crowd. JFK's attempt to "school" or educate Gandhi out of "Gandhi-speak" into JFK Boston-inspired dialect is his desire to recreate more versions of himself and thus inflate his own importance as the most popular boy in school. In this case, the positions and terms are cleverly switched around, and yet the goal is still the same—"Be like Me and you will achieve a particular kind of respect and identity" and embody the icon of American masculinity.

What the creators of the show fail to capitalize on is the irony that the biological clone of the first Irish Catholic and, hence, the first ethnic President of the United States is Gandhi's teacher. As Matthew Frye Jacobson points out in *Roots Too*, Kennedy heralded the romantic narrative of the ancestral European immigrant who through fortitude and gumption makes her/his way to the United States and becomes a success.[42] The series does not overtly address JFK's religious identity as the first Catholic president or his ethnicity as Irish, except in the form of the Boston regional accent. The vocal accent, however, is not a marker of JFK's ethnicity. Instead, in a reverse move, JFK's articulation of a Boston regional accent identifies him as undeniably American. When Apu attempts to speak with a John Wayne accent in *The Simpsons* episode "Much Apu about Nothing," it is a caricature of a caricature and an attempt at sounding American. With JFK, his accent is exaggerated, and, yet, his Americanness is not questioned.

Historically, Kennedy's accent also represents an upper-class, educated background as well as a regional accent. In the context of the series, the accent is miming the way Kennedy talked, even though his speech, as a clone, would not have an accent because he was raised with the other clones and not in Boston. He is the only clone to possess a regional vocal accent that differentiates him from the other students. But it also identifies who he is to the audience. There is never any doubt about who JFK is in the mind of American audiences because he is such an iconic figure in American history. Even though JFK is portrayed as a schizophrenic hypermasculine jock, he can be compared to a multitude of other images (both historical and manufactured) in American culture. In the case of Gandhi, the extent of his role as one of the leaders of the Indian Independence movement and creator of modern nonviolent civil disobedience is not as well known or understood in American popular culture. His numerous imprisonments for his protests against the British and his economic boycotts against the British are only two parts of a historical legacy that defies casting him as a model-minority sidekick. But in the series, he is reduced to a multi-ethnic and perhaps multi-racial depiction of Asian Americans and model minorities.

When JFK first addresses Gandhi in the episode, he does not call him by name but unleashes a verbal cascade of racial epithets that represent the ambiguity of Gandhi's racial position, citizenship, and masculinity. In the scene, JFK calls him a "Half-Pint," "Junior Mint," "Pip Squeak," "Tiny Tim," "Yardstick," "Snack Pack," "Wee Fella," and "Brown Leprechaun." JFK first tries to label Gandhi with every insolent epithet there is, but none of them really stick, and he has difficulty getting Gandhi's attention. Gandhi responds, "Are you talking to me?" As in any teen drama when the popular kid talks to the disenfranchised outsider, Gandhi is surprised that JFK is addressing him, but another way to interpret this interaction is that the labels do not apply. There is no connection between what JFK is saying and who Gandhi is, so Gandhi cannot hear him. In the episode, since names and labels cannot describe Gandhi, JFK attempts to change the way Gandhi speaks to make him over into someone JFK can recognize. JFK makes a bet with himself that he can make Gandhi into a mini-JFK. When offering Gandhi the opportunity to study with him, JFK tells Gandhi he needs a "round high ass" in order to get a date or a "Betty" that would be acceptable to JFK. Gandhi responds with a high-pitched cackle and falls into slang—"You let the dogs out, J-slides." Gandhi speaks in slang that resembles typical teenager banter, but his verbiage also resonates as "talking street," or racially black. He tries to speak "black" to assert his masculinity, but, instead, it comes out as a comical mishmash. JFK immediately quashes this type of racialized performance and identifies Gandhi's speech as the first part of him to fix: "Let's start with that. . . . Your 'Gandhi-speak' is all wet." "Gandhi-speak" resembles an amalgamation of racially black speaking styles. To get rid of his Gandhi-speak, or stop Gandhi from speaking "black," JFK teaches Gandhi to speak "white." There is no brown-voice accent depicted as an option. Speech is framed as racially black or white. Of course, JFK's version of speaking "white" involves teaching Gandhi to speak with a regional Boston accent.

Gandhi initially has no viable or audible accent in the episode or the rest of the series (just word choice and phrases). His intonation is not racialized until Kennedy makes it so by teaching him (in a scene right out of *Pygmalion* or *My Fair Lady*) how to talk by making Gandhi repeat the phrase, "For supper, I want a party platter" (instead of the phrase associated with *My Fair Lady*, "The rain in Spain stays mainly in the plain"). The speech-therapy lesson allows JFK to exaggerate his own pronunciation for extreme comic effect. Gandhi's success at mastering JFK's accent physically alters his body. Instead of a change in skin color or the development of a well-muscled torso, Gandhi suddenly produces a nicely rounded backside that represents potent masculinity and sexual prowess. In his study of Asian American masculinity and sexuality, David Eng asserts that most minority and mainstream depictions of Asian American masculinity are interested in creating normative representations of sexuality.[43] Asian American men are "racially castrated," in Eng's terms, though it is both racial and sexual emasculation in comparison to mainstream white heteronormativity. Both mainstream and Asian American narratives focus on the process-of-assimilation stories and the tension between the Asian American man being the outsider and wanting to be accepted as part of mainstream culture. In order to assimilate to a normative masculinity and also a racially normative position, JFK must show Gandhi how to get back (or for JFK to give him back) his ass, not in the attempt to woo Gandhi himself but instead to remake Gandhi for female consumption. Gandhi's masculine appeal resides in his white, racial, and gendered voice and the physical characteristic of his body that mimics but is not quite the same as JFK's body. Gandhi becomes representative of the "model minority" male figure that can be assimilated.

Initially, despite Gandhi's best efforts, he is unable to emulate JFK's intonation. Only after JFK threatens him with emasculation and tells him that he will never be able to "dry hump," or approximate sex with a girl, is Gandhi able to deliver the line with the JFK pronunciation. Here, JFK is threatening to deny Gandhi the dream or idea of ever fitting into the mainstream unless Gandhi changes in the way JFK prescribes, and so there is no alternative presented to Gandhi or, in general, for Asian American or South Asian American men. The route to acceptance is on the terms of JFK's, white, normative hypermasculinity. The cartoon depicts the process of Gandhi developing a high, round bottom and breaking through the language barrier with the long, drawn-out syllables of a JFK accent. Although the homoerotic nature of Gandhi's transformation could be argued, a more compelling reading casts Gandhi as JFK's recreation of himself. As JFK talks, Gandhi repeats, and a clone of JFK is the result. JFK is not only asking Gandhi to change his speech patterns but also his habits of consumption to become JFK. The rest of the physical transformation includes learning how to walk (balancing books on his square wig, rather than his original, round, bald head), sporting a red-and-white-striped polo, and wearing dark sunglasses instead of his round eyeglasses.

Gandhi debuts his new look at school and is announced with his new name GFK. He is the miniature representation of JFK, a brown Mini-Me, a virile, young stud whom all the females in school ogle and describe: "He's like a shorter, browner Kennedy!" The young women all fawn over him as he speaks with the words and intonation of JFK, "Don't damage the merchandise, ladies, and by merchandise I mean MY JUNK." It's not only the accent that is the same as JFK but also the mannerisms and words. JFK appreciates Gandhi's new look and compliments him like a proud parent, "You look like an angel." Later, when he sees how Catherine the Great wants Gandhi to take her to prom, and she starts to kiss and maul him, JFK says, "They grow up so fast." The paternalistic attitude reflects his pride in his creation but also the assimilation of Gandhi into JFK's culture. Clearly, the show is mocking JFK's actions as much as Gandhi's makeover, but at the same time, JFK is the dominant model for virility and masculine appeal to the females.

The verbal mimicry, as Bhabha points out, does expose how masculinity and virility can only be superficial and emphasizes under the veneer of the makeover, the native still remains independent and will act independently. In the episode before his transformation into GFK, Gandhi first asks Marie Curie (an anomaly and giant mutant of a girl) to the prom. As GFK, he ignores her in favor of the svelte and sexually licentious Catherine the Great. This plot device satirizes the modern makeover in narrative teen films, such as *10 Things I Hate about You* (1999) or *She's All That* (1999), but takes on a different connotation with Gandhi in the role. Historically, Gandhi is a man who was educated in England and followed the tenets of British culture but ultimately rejected them in favor of a return and resurgence of his own rights to cultural individualism.

Gandhi's rejection of his persona of GFK at the end of the episode is the expression of his faith in his own individuality: "I am no longer GFK [in JFK speak], my name is Gandhi [with no accent]." His assertion of his identity is delivered quietly but forcefully and does not have any of the previous mannerisms. This act supports the mainstream narratives that say although racialized minorities can be successful model minorities, there is something inherently different that prevents them from changing completely. Others might read this as a liberal narrative of the triumph of the individual differences over dominant culture and peer pressure to change. In teen dramas, the assertion and validation of individual differences are key staples of the narrative. The makeover genre builds on this idea by focusing on how individuals in a "neo-liberal economy" can work on the self as "a pre-requisite for personal and professional success."[44] The pressure is on the individual to change, but the emphasis is that change is a state of evolving and developing from within rather than being imposed from without, but it still involves consumer spending and physical alterations. The makeover genre also gives the individual the perception of agency in her/his own transformation where professional success is less secure. This theme is not only a staple in teen makeover dramas (the right to be different) but also mirrors in some ways the real history of Gandhi (who abandoned Western suits in favor of his Indian homespun *dhoti*). However, in the effort to create comedy, this moment is undermined when Gandhi's virility and sexuality are stripped from him. In order to revert to his original self, Gandhi takes the dark wig off his bald head, puts back on his round eyeglasses, and takes seven (!) socks out of his jock strap. In this instant, he is seen as physically impotent (or castrated), and Catherine immediately dumps him as her date. As he casts off the garments and trappings of JFK, he also is less appealing to women, and even the giant genetic mutant Marie Curie turns him down. He has to shed an appropriated masculinity but is unable to create an image for himself that is not the butt of a joke. The show once again relegates his masculine appeal to nonexistent and leads us to question whether his assertion of independence was a triumph or the maintenance of the status quo.

JFK creates his own clone and the image and success that come with being "JFK." This is significant in two ways. First, assimilation for racialized others is possible and even reaps rewards for masculinity—Gandhi "gets" Catherine the Great. He becomes the great white man who gets the girl. But, second and more significant, it is because he becomes the image of John F. Kennedy, which is associated with youth, vigor, and American nationalism. If one is a Kennedy clone, then not only is one a cultural American (think of Bill Clinton's photo with John F. Kennedy) but one is also attached to a legacy of greatness and a historical path of change in American history. The phrase "He's like a shorter, browner Kennedy" implies that the standard for success and Americanization is to be a Kennedy.[45] The conventions of the teen genre emphasize that a person should be her/himself, but the teen genre does not work for Gandhi. The only way he is able to "succeed" within the contexts of the genre is by being GFK, but at the end, he has failed to get a date for the prom and is alone.

Conclusion

The controversy that the Indian press and government generated about Gandhi's representation in the show is associated with the loss of cultural memory, where Gandhi is used for his celebrity name recognition but with no understanding of the man himself. No prominent black figures are regulars in the series, such as Rosa Parks or Martin Luther King Jr. King appears briefly in one episode with Moses about conflict mediation, but the co-creators did not seem to want to risk including him as a regular member of the cast. Satirizing a prominent and legendary African American would create a controversy in the United States, so, instead, by focusing on individual who is seen as a model minority and won't make waves, the network, the producers, and writers thought there would be no problems because this program was a comedy.

The use of Gandhi as a comic figure in *Clone High* vacillates between depicting him as a model minority and as normalized teenage boy. Brown voice is not used as a distinguishable racializing characteristic to identity him as Indian American, but, at the same time, he is racialized figure because of his name. Without that characteristic, he becomes a deracialized, suburban teenage outsider. In *Clone High*, accent is not necessarily only a racializing mechanism but also functions as a nationalizing aspect of identity. The most commonly parodied regional American accent in popular culture is the long, drawn-out tones of a southern accent. However, that accent is not necessarily associated with any one historical figure. The accent of the real John F. Kennedy has been heard and repeated all over the world, and so when someone performs that accent, it is associated with a former American president. As a form of comedy, we understand what is being parodied because we understand the original context. It is not Americans, or the Irish, or the Catholics who are being made fun of, it is JFK, and as an audience, we know the difference. The character of JFK is humorous precisely because he represents two recognizable exaggerations of American culture. The first is President John F. Kennedy, and the second is the high school jock who dates the popular girls. As contemporary times show, the ability and desire to emulate Kennedy and be compared to Kennedy carry great political and national resonance. The problem is that there is no other reference point for Gandhi. He is a leader who inspires others just as Kennedy and Lincoln do, and, yet, he is put in the position of being the outsider and the fifth wheel and the racialized other devoid of masculinity. He is a good sidekick, but he can never be the center of the narrative or a lead character.

When Gandhi speaks with JFK's accent (exaggerated for comic effect), he attempts to latch on to the legacy and representation of Kennedy, who was portrayed as successful, handsome, and smart. Gandhi looks like a wannabe without any distinct character of his own. Parody relies on the imitation of a commonly known idea or event, but without that knowledge, parody is unrecognizable and taken to be a genuine portrayal. The figure of Gandhi in American culture could have been an opportunity to showcase some of Gandhi's ideas about civil disobedience in high school, but, instead, in the series, Gandhi is a stand in for a deracialized or completely assimilated model minority.[46]

4

Indian Gurus in the American Marketplace

Consumer Spirituality in *The Love Guru* and *The Guru*

Move your feet to the beat of your heart.
Swami Ramu, *The Guru*

I speak of Intimacy, or Into-Me-I-See.
Guru Pitka, *The Love Guru*

One cultural value historically associated in American mass media with South Asians is the practice of Eastern spiritualism. Early Hollywood films depicted India as a land full of mystical powers and religious cults. American cultural representations of Indian spirituality in the 1960s and 1970s were associated with the new-age movement and hippie culture; Indian culture became part of the American consumer-goods market. The new-age movement is a modern, late-twentieth-century movement associated with Western and Eastern spiritual philosophies that is inclusive of all religions and cultures and borrows from the ideas of self-help and self-transformation as well as the arena of metaphysics. Religion and media scholar Jane Naomi Iwamura argues that Hinduism and other Asian religions gained more widespread exposure in the popular media in the middle to late twentieth century "not only as they were practiced in Asia but also as they were transplanted, transformed, and taken up by Anglo practitioners in the United States." But she also argues that the tolerance for different Asian religious practices was limited by previous racialized stereotypes of the Oriental monk as foreign in manner, dress, race, spiritual commitment, and "his peculiar gendered character."[1] To extend her argument to South Asians, an Indian accent with regards to Asian spirituality emphasizes the compelling yet foreign nature of Indian gurus. In addition, in the twenty-first century, Indian spirituality is aligned with tourist and consumer models of cultural appropriation that offer economic as well as spiritual rewards.

The representation of Indian spirituality is an example of how Indian Americans are racialized as exotic cultural objects. This chapter theorizes how new-age spirituality operates as an Indian accent in the era of neoliberalism. The transnational idea of becoming American for migrants and immigrants allows for multiple allegiances of language, culture, and religion that are not necessarily fluid and that are sometimes conflicted. And yet, despite the promise of a transnational and, hence, border-crossing national identity, in American film, the notion of an American identity is still tied to American images of Indians as foreigners and immigrants, and Indian spiritual practices as a salvation to the materialistic life in America. The genre of comedy works well as a starting point to deliver social and cultural critiques that comment on the modern-day consumption of spirituality and racial representations of Indians in the United States. The films examined in this chapter, *The Guru* (2002), directed by Daisy von Scherler Mayer, and *The Love Guru* (2008), directed by Marco Schnabel, are comedies that parody the consumption of American new-age spiritualism. Both films expose the material aspects of Indian spirituality in American society in the 1990s and 2000s, but *The Love Guru* fails to challenge the capitalistic co-optation of spirituality. *The Guru*, however, works more effectively as a parody of new-age spirituality and critiques consumer culture by continually emphasizing how spirituality is packaged and marketed for a mass audience. This chapter also marks the transformation of an Indian accent from brownface and brown-voice performances to roles in which Indian actors are the main Indian characters in the film. In *The Love Guru*, Mike Myers performs Guru Pitka as a hybrid of brownface performance and Orientalist stereotypes that reaffirm Indians and India as foreign in comparison to American culture. In contrast, Indian actor Jimi Mistry's performance as Swami Ramu Gupta in *The Guru* reveals the complexities of an Indian immigrant experience and interrogates brownface performances and stereotypes of an Indian guru.

The two epigraphs represent the spiritual philosophies that are marketed by each guru to the general public in the Hollywood films *The Guru* and *The Love Guru*. The first epigraph, "Move your feet to the beat of your heart," links the physical movement of dance to internal workings of the heart and emphasizes the relationship between physical actions and emotional strength and desire. Swami Ramu presents his philosophy in the language of dance that links the physical expression of dance to spirituality. This quote also reveals Ramu's former occupation as a dance teacher and his desire to be an actor (who dances) in the United States. The second epigraph, "I speak of Intimacy, or Into-Me-I-See," is a verbal pun that expresses Guru Pitka's philosophy to connect to the inner self through an advertising slogan rather than an active relationship. He follows this phrase with an explicit reference to the TM (trademark patent) that emphasizes that his words of wisdom are a profitable commercial enterprise. However, TM is also an abbreviation for the Transcendental Movement associated with the Maharishi Mahesh Yogi in the 1960s and so links Pitka's philosophy to an authentic religious practice. His catchphrase represents the dual roles associated with the guru figure: a spiritual guide who offers self-transformation and a moneymaking entrepreneur. Although both films attempt to parody the late-twentieth-century and early-twenty-first-century preoccupation with new-age spirituality, the difference is that *The Guru* questions the branding of spirituality as a marketing strategy for Indian American success in the United States, whereas *The Love Guru* ends up reaffirming the mass consumption of Indian goods sold to the public for material gain and superficial spiritual transformation.

Spirituality, Parody, and Guru Figures in American Culture

One of the most contemporary faces associated with new-age Indian spirituality in the United States is Deepak Chopra. As the author of over thirty best-selling books on spirituality, enlightenment, and the path to happiness, Chopra is the face of new-age spirituality that teaches that there is a metaphysical relationship between human beings and the world around them. The journey toward self-awareness and awareness of others is a vital part of world peace and personal contentment.[2] Originally trained as a physician specializing in internal medicine and endocrinology, Chopra left his private practice to pursue his interest in the healing relationship between the mind and the body. Chopra's foray into spiritual matters came in the 1980s and 1990s when his books on spirituality became top sellers in the United States. He is a highly educated, immigrant physician who speaks English and also dispenses Eastern philosophy to the larger American public.[3] Not only is he a model minority but also he is also symbolic of the American Dream of monetary success for immigrants, and his name has become a recognizable brand for new-age spirituality.

Chopra's success has also generated controversy about his brand-name recognition as a representative of Indian culture and spirituality. Historian Vijay Prasad argues that Chopra is a "complete stereotype willed on India by U.S. Orientalism, for he delivers just what is expected of a seer from the East. . . . He offers a way to be a better consumer and person within the system."[4] In other words, the image of Chopra and his brand of enlightenment sell a specific U.S. image of India and the East—a palatable dose of the "other" to be bought and sold.[5] The idea of the exotic figure of the guru as a teacher and CEO of spirituality is one that is celebrated in *The Love Guru* (in which Chopra makes a guest appearance).

Chopra also is linked to a lineage of famous South Asian gurus in the West. The term "guru" implies someone who possesses knowledge and wisdom. More important, a guru is a teacher who has knowledge and skills to impart to others (disciples).[6] Unlike the representation in American media of the Asian mobile monk who is isolated from his community, the guru is characterized as an individual who draws people to him by virtue of his knowledge to establish a community of followers.[7] The teachings of a guru in the modern age of capitalism can be measured by book sales, seminar sales, and income generated by personal appearances and product endorsements. The new-age movement has its roots in 1960s subculture (associated with hippie culture, Ravi Shankar, the emergence of Maharishi Mahesh Yogi and Transcendentalist Meditation, and Hare Krishna groups) but in contemporary times is the amalgamation of naturalism, Eastern metaphysical philosophy, self-help regimens, and spirituality.[8] Iwamura argues that Chopra is the modern incarnation of the Maharishi Mahesh Yogi. Chopra's entry into new-age spiritualism occurred by picking up a book and studying the teachings of transcendental meditation and Maharishi Mahesh Yogi. However, as Iwamura points out, unlike the long hair and saffron robes of the Maharishi Mahesh, Chopra presents the image of the assimilated immigrant who is clean-cut and wears Western clothes. Chopra is a representative of the post-1965 immigrant generation; he can draw on popular media images of the guru to promote his message and his style of Indian spirituality.

Traditional concepts of spirituality tend to emphasize ideas of unity and awareness of a reality larger than one person or the loss of an individual sense of time, place, and space in favor of a larger initiative. This chapter's interpretation centers on the idea of spirituality as the search, in the context of American films, for one's identity and future path in life. Definitions of the philosophy of spirituality tend to favor the collective good over personal material conditions. This way of thinking is at odds with what is arguably one of the most sacred American values—the rights of the individual. As such, the images of U.S. popular consumer spirituality do not emphasize a religious collective or community. Instead, popular consumer spirituality celebrates the idea of the individual and also the expression of individual enlightenment through material consumption. "Pop spirituality," then, is acceptable to conservatives and liberals alike because the practice of experiencing another culture is divorced from the tenets of the everyday practice of a non-Christian religion. Instead, spirituality is associated with the inner spirit or self and the ascension of an independent spirit—a very American notion of citizenship. When Christine Aguilera started wearing a jeweled *bindi* (a dot), the symbol associated with Hindu and Indian marriages became a popular fashion accessory in American culture. Madonna's album *Ray of Light* (1998), released by Maverick Records, Warner Bros., and her Drowned World Tour in 2001 featured South Asian spiritual chants in her songs and Indian fashions onstage. Bindis, religious portraits, and henna tattoos became merchandise for commercial consumption. Pop spirituality is not only tied to inner enlightenment but also nationalistic expressions of identity. Kimberly Lau argues that "the cultural ordering of spirituality in the business world exploits the transformative power" of spirituality so that it becomes instrumental to the market rather than engaged toward a wider social and ethical framework to promote change. The practice of popular spirituality supports capitalism rather than challenges the relationship between materiality and inner self-knowledge. The term "spirituality" has now become "the brand label for the search for meaning, values, transcendence, hope, and connectedness in advanced capitalist societies."[9] Indian spiritual practices and philosophies have become "cultural things" to be traded and displayed as a means to show personal transformation.

The historical representation of South Asians in Hollywood has revolved around the exotic depictions of South Asians and featured stories about Americans going to India and other places in order to flee personal problems or achieve a personal and perhaps spiritual transformation.[10] In Wes Anderson's *The Darjeeling Limited* (2007), three estranged brothers travel in North India, and through spiritual rituals and interaction with native Indians, the brothers resolve their difficulties with each other. The film *Eat, Pray, Love* (2010), based on the best-selling novel, features India as the site of spiritual knowing, where eating signifies Italy, praying represents India, and love happens in Brazil. However, the advantage of living in a transnational world is that the transformative powers of Indian spiritual enlightenment are now available in the United States, the United Kingdom, and all over the world in ethnic neighborhoods, boutiques, grocery stores, and marketplaces. Films such as *What a Girl Wants* (2003), directed by Dennie Gordon, and *Freaky Friday* (2003), directed by Mark Waters, portray ethnic markets and restaurants as examples of how teenage girls consume and are transformed by Asian and South Asian consumer goods. For example, in the first film, the protagonist is able to express her individuality by wearing ethnic clothes, and in the second, a mother and teenager daughter learn to understand each other when they "eat" and read a magical fortune cookie in a restaurant in Chinatown.

We must ask how this American citizenship manifests itself in relation to local and global practices and, especially in a consumer culture. Cultural anthropologist Sunaina Maira asserts, "We need to be more attuned to the new forms that citizenship takes in an era in which relations of social belongings are steeped in consumption."[11] Maira puts forth the idea of a new Orientalism and cosmopolitanism that is consumed through the mediums of trance dances and rave culture in the United States. She discusses how this new Orientalism is characterized by the invisibility of location. In other words, the notion that one can experience the world and, particularly, Asian culture without leaving the United States is the key to the new Orientalism—in which everything of importance that represents Asia will already be in the United States and be available to purchase. Indian pop spirituality represents another Indian accent that can be consumed and performed just like a vocal accent can be performed. With new Orientalist consumption, the product is disposable and conveniently available to everyone in venues all over the world.

The performance of an Indian accent in film can be more complex than purchasing cultural icons because in addition to superficial consumption or mimicry of a cultural practice, a racialized performance also requires the ability to create and act as a character with a backstory. The actor is connected to the character, such as Peter Sellers as Hrundi Bakshi or Mike Myers as Guru Pitka. As a result, the performance caters to the strengths of a particular actor; for example, Hank Azaria is excellent with vocal accents, and Mike Myers is a physical comedian. Their performances are readily available through mass media, but their product is meant to be an individual expression of their craft rather than something that is disposable. Both draw their inspiration for their comedic performances not from their direct experiences with Indian accents or Indian culture but instead from the brownface performances of the popular and successful Sellers. While Sellers's performance in *The Party* helped redefine the representation of Indians in the United States in the 1960s, there has not been a lot of progression in these roles through the early twenty-first century. The narrative of *The Party* is a departure from the mystical and British colonial narratives of the past, but the new performances of brownface have returned to the pre-1965 era where accent represents a racialized and spiritual exoticism.

Geography or location is also important to the depiction of spirituality. Asian culture or an Asian locale can be used to define significant moments of self-knowledge for movie characters. Spirituality becomes a commodity that can be bought and sold rather than an institution that has a long and influential history. Spirituality is religion-lite because it does not dwell on difference or conflict but instead focuses on the 1960s hippie version of love taught by a wise guru figure. *The Guru* and *The Love Guru* concentrate on the individual representation of spirituality in one figure and the followers who accumulate to buy that wisdom. *The Love Guru* is an example of the superficial and material transformation that new-age consumerism promotes but in the guise of Indian culture. Even though the film is a live-action movie, the characters act the same as the two-dimensional, animated figures in *The Simpsons* and *Clone High*. The film attempts to parody elements of Indian spiritual practices and capitalize on the success of comedies such as Sacha Baron Cohen's *Borat* (2006), directed by Larry Charles. Guru Pitka is a caricature of a white man raised in India trying to dispense Indian philosophy in America. While Chopra is evoked as the model to which Guru Pitka aspires, Indian spirituality is exaggerated as the practice of strange and funny rituals, but its commodification is not critiqued. The saffron robes and the unruly facial hair of Myers, combined with the images of flower power in the film poster, characterize the film as an exaggeration and a comedy. Guru Pitka ends up being an imperfect and unfunny imitation of Indian spiritualism because he is read as strange. There is no outlet for empathy or identification with his character because he is too foreign. He fails to be funny.

The Guru, on the other hand, engages with the fad of new-age spiritualism, but it employs the personal transformative power of spirituality to tell an immigrant story. The independent film features a talented cast that includes Mistry, Heather Graham, Marisa Tomei, Michael McKean, and Christine Baranski. Mistry, a British-born Indian actor, plays the lead role, Ramu, and the film includes other British Indian or Indian Americans in the cast, such as comic Ajay Naidu and Emil Marwa. Scenes feature a debate among the Indian immigrant characters about their desire for material success versus their personal and cultural integrity. In a progressive move, the film discusses the limitations of the American Dream for an aspiring middle-class Indian actor. Indians in America can dream of success but only

The Love Guru
(Paramount, 2008)

in specific industries (i.e., a waiter in an Indian restaurant) and roles that involve acting and speaking in certain ways. Ramu wants to make it as an actor in New York City, and his character is sympathetic because he wants be successful and emulate the actor John Travolta in *Grease* (1978). The film poster for *The Guru* does not emphasize the strange so much as the commercial appeal of dancing and singing as a part of the American Dream. As an Indian actor who wants to become famous in the United States, Ramu faces different challenges than other actors. The film shows how he utilizes U.S. stereotypes of India to become a popular phenomenon.

In animated comedies when the jokes are outrageous (and potentially offensive), such as Homer impersonating or invoking the Hindu deity, Ganesha, in *The Simpsons*, any type of offense can be dismissed because Homer is a cartoon character that is not associated with a real person. In addition, any

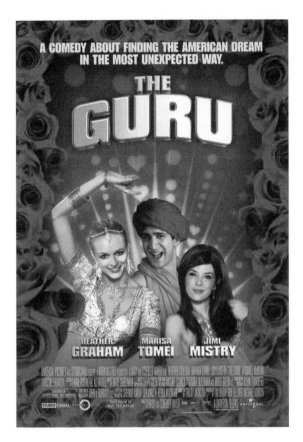

The Guru
(Universal, 2002)

physical portrayals or excessively violent images are rendered childlike and nonthreatening because they are being expressed through the medium of animation. Live-action comedies depend upon the physical performances of individual actors, and the success or failure of a film can be attributed to the acting ability of an individual. Some of the most common displays of live comedy in mass media include the use of irony, parody, and satire to critique society. *The Love Guru* and *The Guru* rely on parody, a genre that takes a familiar idea or topic and changes or exaggerates the idea to offer a new way of understanding of that idea. For example, Myers's Austin Powers films are a parody of the James Bond/superspy franchise. *The Love Guru* could replicate the success of the Austin Powers films though the creation of a guru figure, Guru Pitka, who could operate in the same way. Both guru films break down the idea of an all-knowing guru who dispenses the wisdom of Eastern philosophy and, instead, present men who are fallible and pro-mote a personal spiritual philosophy based on exotic rituals and consumer demand. Both films try to offer a comic social critique that has the potential to challenge American ideals about consumer spirituality. *The Love Guru's* parody seems to fail and be unfunny because it relies on an exaggeration of spiritual practices that overwhelms any type of social commentary. *The Guru*, however, offers the potential of a critique of consumer spiritualism.

Consumer Spirituality, Neoliberalism, and *The Love Guru*

During the 1893 World Parliament of Religions in Chicago, Swami Vive-kananda, a spiritual philosopher from Bengal who toured the United States from 1893 to 1895, introduced Hinduism to American culture. Vivekananda argued that the West might have technological and material superiority, but the West lacked spirituality. This, for him, made India the superior culture. His views supported a binary discussion of East and West and situated the Orient and the East as the romantic site of ancient tradition. As Prasad points out, Vivekananda also recognized the business aspect of Orientalism when he spoke to an audience in Minnesota: "You make commerce your business; we make religion our business."[12] He emphasized the split between the ma-terial and the spiritual but also linked the practice of Eastern spirituality to a business and capitalist enterprise that could be sold in the United States.

One hundred years after Swami Vivekananda, the popularity of new-age spirituality is a lucrative business that relies on media exposure and consumer appeal. One of the first popular Indian spiritual leaders featured in the media was Maharishi Mahesh Yogi, who embodied Indian spirituality with celebrity clients, such as George Harrison from the Beatles and actress Mia Farrow. The representation of Mahesh in 1960s print images and articles, Iwamura argues, vacillates between two competing images: the celebrity guru/con man who was a master of marketing the Transcendental Movement versus the spiritual teacher who embodies the teachings of India. The former is a threat to the status quo because of his ability to dupe unsuspecting youth and innocents, whereas the latter authentically represents ancient traditions of India. Iwamura comments, "Mahesh, an Oriental Monk, is no longer at the representational beck and call of a Western audience; they are not the ones who visually and spiritually 'take in' his image at will, but rather are the ones who are meant to be 'taken in.'"[13] In the world of consumerism and mass-media marketing, the person who controls the image and the message is vital to the popularity of a product. By making his movement a lucrative economic enterprise, Maharishi Mahesh Yogi paved the way for other gurus, such as Deepak Chopra, to hold some leverage over how he might be portrayed in the media to continue attracting more people to his products.

A more notorious example of the melding of spiritual practices with commercial interests is the story of Bhagwan Shree Rajneesh (later known as Osho), who from 1981–85 attracted a large following that had its headquarters near Antelope, Oregon. Rajneesh was a controversial figure that was known in the United States for his sixty-four-thousand-acre ranch and his collection of ninety-three Rolls Royce automobiles. Although now an example of quirky Eastern religious cults, Rajneesh developed a successful business model that also had ties to community businesses, local elections, and an international foundation. His combination of spiritual practices and business acumen led him to create a lucrative spiritual corporation, the Rajneesh Foundation, and legally rename the town around him Rajneeshpuram in Oregon. Eventually, Rajneesh was arrested on suspicion of fraud and alleged bioterrorism and deported from the United States back to India in 1985. Religion scholar Hugh Urban points out, "His [Rajneesh] ideal was not that of an ascetic renunciate who retreats into some otherworldly bliss, but rather what he called the Superman who unites material and spiritual, capitalist and religious impulses."[14] The fees for his seminars, retreats, and philosophies attracted all classes of people, though he was known for having wealthy clients. Prasad reports that the seminars earned up to $45 million and attracted business executives from companies such as BMW.[15] It is the practice of new-age consumption that both films attempt to parody, as *The Love Guru* and *The Guru* emphasize the business nature of selling Indian spirituality in the corporate and global trade culture of the twenty-first century.

In the era of neoliberalism, the context for understanding new-age discourse is the tension between the "good life" of corporate globalization and the "good society" of community-driven action. Lau comments that "marketing the spiritual allows companies and their consumers to pay lip service to the 'exotic,' rich, and historically significant religions" and also distance themselves from any deep engagement with religion.[16] This type of consumption encourages a superficial engagement with other cultures and ideas rather than an in-depth or critical interaction. Lisa Duggan defines the discourse of neoliberalism in the 1990s as characterizing multicultural politics as a "stripped-down, non-redistributive form of 'equality' designed for global consumption."[17] Individuals could show their political consciousness by buying products or wearing clothing from other cultures.

For example, corporations in the late 1980s and 1990s used slogans, such as the "United Colors of Benetton," to sell their fashion lines. The company featured ads with multiracial people from all over the world, creating a brand that promoted world unity through the purchase of luxury fashion goods. Consumption and capitalism become the driving forces of multicultural identity as global culture becomes a marketplace to buy and sell trade goods.[18] In contemporary times, global products are part of everyday market culture. Thus, the notion of consumer spirituality fits into the practices of global economics. Additionally, in the zeal to consume Indian spirituality and then enact that consumption, the performance of spirituality becomes a costume or "cultural thing." Multicultural issues and global knowledge are represented as a superficial collection of objects rather than cultural histories with a complex background. *The Love Guru* is full of the cultural trappings of Indian spirituality and tends to end up on the side of the "good life" of corporate globalization rather than revealing any tension between cultural appropriations and spiritual practices.

The Love Guru is a failed parody of the popularity of new-age spiritualism.[19] At the center of the film is Guru Pitka, a white orphan in India, who was tutored alongside Chopra by a cross-eyed whimsical guru (played by Ben Kingsley) in the art of spiritual guidance. The story has several beginnings including a preface, introduction, and then the opening credits. The scenes are strung together as a series of vignettes, but the story is framed around the Guru's self-promotion as a spiritual teacher who makes money by sharing his path to happiness in the self-help and new-age spirituality business. Pitka promotes a philosophy that says when a person finds her/his personal inner truth, s/he will also be able to have an emotionally and sexually fulfilling relationship and achieve any goal. His marketing slogans stress intimacy as the path to enlightenment, or as he says, "I speak of Intimacy, or Into-Me-I-See." The word "intimacy" is broken down into its phonetic components to create a definition of a word that does not require an in-depth consideration of the philosophy. Instead, it is the surface meaning that is important. Combined with his mantra is his deliberate attention to his ownership of this philosophy. After every slogan, he also adds "TM" to emphasize how his philosophy is a product to be sold. In this film, there is no division between the business of spirituality and the search for personal fulfillment. American studies scholars Jeffrey Melnick and Rachel Rubin argue that from the 1960s through the twenty-first century, "The consumption of Eastern goods was itself a spiritual practice—or at least a part of spiritual seeking."[20] The film, instead of critiquing the consumption of spirituality, exaggerates all the ways this consumption operates in Guru Pitka's business enterprise and participates in stereotyping and reifying Indian accents.

In the film, Guru Pitka is determined to dethrone Deepak Chopra as the number 1 "neo-Eastern self-help spiritualist." At the behest of National Hockey Team owner of the Toronto Maple Leaves, Jane Bullard (Jessica Alba), Pitka agrees to come to Los Angeles to counsel Canadian ice-hockey player Darren Roanoke (known as the "Tiger Woods of hockey"). The team management believes if Pitka can help Roanoke reunite with his estranged wife, the team can win the Stanley Cup championship trophy. Although Pitka tutors others in the philosophy of love, he has been unable to tap his own inner truth and, hence, his own sexuality. Pitka has been wearing a metal chastity belt since his youth, and he will only be released when he finds his own inner truth or true love. He falls in love with Jane, and at the end of the film, they return to India to celebrate his release from his chastity belt in a Bollywood-inspired dance scene (complete with Indian costumes) in an Indian village.

Initially, Pitka's interest is helping others is fueled by his ambition to be famous. His character teeters between that of a con artist and a sex-starved romantic. First-time director Marco Schnabel said the character of Pitka is a role that Mike has been trying out and refining in live comedy acts. Pitka, he says, represents "an entirely made-up faith—from Indian faith but not really."[21] Yet, the "made-up faith" draws upon the most prevalent stereotypes of gurus and new-age spirituality.

Although Myers does not do a literal brownface performance of playing an Indian character—he admits Guru Pitka was born in America and raised in India—he uses all the cultural trappings associated with South Asians, including speaking with an Indian accent. Pitka wears saffron robes, has long hair, and sports full facial hair, including a bushy beard, which for the movie, "the complete guru get-up required up to four hours a day in the makeup chair while various facial prosthetics, fake beards, and wigs were applied." Myers's look is deliberately modeled on the image of a rock-and-roll style Maharishi Yogi, such as Maharishi Mahesh.[22] However, as a white child raised in India, he represents a narrative that discusses how adopting Indian spirituality allows him to cross racial boundaries. But this potential to explore this intercultural crossing is not realized. If he were the sidekick rather than the main character, Pitka could be a humorous accent to the dominant narrative of someone searching for inner transformation. Instead, he becomes a character who is made up of cultural things that look and sound Indian, but his character does not exhibit any onscreen depth. Although the character he plays is a white man, Myers uses elements of brownface and brown-voice performance to represent Indian spirituality. His character is an example of a bad translation or perhaps a failed hybrid that shows how Indian spirituality is objectified through cultural capitalism. There are other examples of bad translations in the film, and they fall into different categories, such as verbal gaffes, imitations of Bollywood film scenes (because that's the popular representation of India), and the material consumption of India (with costumes and trademark branding). The verbal double entendres, for example, are sexual puns or names, such as Guru Tugginmypudha, that are setups for a laugh. In this film, Indian accents are the things that sound or look Indian to portray a foreign or different cultural norm and emphasize the silliness of Indian cultural ideas.

The film portrays Pitka's world as one that is filled with decadent opulence and Hollywood celebrities. Although the film opens and closes in India, the primary action occurs in Pitka's residence in Los Angeles and features a variety of celebrity cameos, including Chopra, Kanye West, Val Kilmer, and Jessica Simpson. The film stars Alba and Justin Timberlake in larger roles and includes comics, such as Stephen Colbert and John Oliver. The credits introduce Pitka through a series of images that reference and juxtapose older images of Indian celebrity "guru" figures, such as Ravi Shankar, Maharishi Mahesh Yogi, and Rajneesh with American celebrities. The Indian actors in the film are Pitka's sidekick, Rajneesh (Manu Narayan), and Chopra, in a cameo appearance as himself, who reinforce the images of Indians as guru figures.[23] Academy Award–winning actor Kingsley also appears in the film as cross-eyed Guru Tugginmypudha as the teacher of young Maurice (Guru) Pitka and Chopra. Like Maharishi Mahesh and Bhagwan Shree Rajneesh, Pitka is introduced as a "celebrity guru" whose clients and friends include the Beatles, Tom Cruise, Brittany Spears, Paris Hilton, and Lindsay Lohan.

Mike Myers and Graham Gordy are coauthors of the screenplay, and an Indian sense of spirituality is the baseline that Myers builds upon in his narrative. After the death of his father in 1991, Myers went on a personal quest to ease his own grief and visited different ashrams and gurus: "I started to realize that the whole idea of enlightenment is really, at heart, to just lighten up . . . and I love the idea of bringing irony and humor to the human search for happiness and love."[24] His idea was to write about the comic nature of spirituality, and the film is the culmination of many years of working on the character of Guru Pitka.[25] Myers revealed that he has been "fascinated with Eastern philosophy," but it is difficult to determine how the fascination is different from the material trappings of spiritualism he offers in the film.[26]

For example, in his mansion, Guru Pitka offers a greeting to his guests by clasping his hands together, slightly bowing, and reciting the name "Mariska Hargitay" (a television actress on *Law & Order: SVU*). There is no context for this greeting except when Hargitay appears in a cameo and is the recipient of this phrase, which is probably intended to draw a laugh. The made-up Hindi-like greeting "Mariska Hargitay" is a verbal word play on "Namaste," a common Indian verbal greeting that is meant to convey respect and hospitality. The phrase is often accompanied with the gesture of the two palms of the hand placed together over the chest and an inclination of the head and/or body. The film is full of moments such as this where an attempt at parody turns into a one-note gag that is uncritical and seems to poke fun at Indian customs and Indian words.

The film attempts to satirize the history of Indian spirituality in the United States in the first ten minutes. The film opens with a soundtrack that features the sitar in a psychedelic funk beat, and the first geographic feature is a snow-capped mountain that bears a striking resemblance to the Paramount logo (the studio that funded the film). The camera then pans down from the dominant image of the mountain to small village on a beach with coconut trees, fishing boats, and people in the distance dressed in colorful clothing. The music fades, and the deep, masculine voice of Morgan Freeman begins the narrative, "When I was a child in India in the tiny village of Harenmahkeester, I found a voice-over machine." As the vocal tones set the stage, the visual image of a sign with the village name and population is presented. In the forefront of the frame is Guru Pitka speaking into a microphone. As he is "caught" on camera using the voice-over machine, he stops and in a higher-pitched tone infused with giggles and an Indian accent says, "Oh hi, I am his Holiness the Guru Pitka." The multiple references in the visual and auditory frames at the beginning of the film reveal the lack of coherent direction in the film. For example, the voice-over machine that is mentioned at the beginning has the name "East India Voice-Over Machine" on the machine. This could be a reference to previous Orientalist narratives of India and the history of the British Raj that often dominate the representation of Indians. The use of the voice-over machine could be a literal reference to the fact that India's history has been "voiced over by others" with brown voice and other types of Indian accents. Both of these could be clever introductions to a story that is going to do something different from what has been previously portrayed. However, the direct reference to Freeman as a voice-over option (the choices are man, woman, and Freeman on the machine) seems to take this film in a very different direction.

On one hand, the reference to Freeman as an African American actor who played roles where he is the holder of American moral conscience, as in *Driving Miss Daisy* (1989) and *The Shawshank Redemption* (1984), introduces a black racial identity into the narrative of Indian spirituality. This could foreshadow that the film is about helping a black Canadian hockey player reunite with his wife and find his confidence so his team can win the Stanley Cup championship. The intersection of Indian spirituality and black racial history would be a novel idea to explore. But this does not happen in the film so the only other reason would be to characterize Morgan Freeman as a gendered alternative to woman and man and thus as a nonthreatening black man. Is that how Indian gurus and specifically Guru Pitka should be seen? Why is Myers including black-voice performance in his portrayal of an Indian-raised guru? This is one of the many out-of-place jokes in the film, and the result is confusion over where the parody and critique, if any, is directed.

The film is full of one-dimensional characters rather than one or two fully developed characters. Because everyone is seen as strange and exotic, there do not seem to be any norms or balances to contrast with Pitka or any of the other characters. In this film, Indian accents are the things that sound or look Indian to portray a foreign or different cultural norm and emphasize the silliness of Indian cultural ideas. The film tries to juxtapose the strange with the familiar in the opening credits when the music begins with a sitar track accompanied by images of the Los Angeles area, such as the beach and the Hollywood sign. However, the next frames are a series of sight and sound gags that feature Pitka riding an elephant in his opulent Ashram/palace while singing about his working life to the melody of "Nine to Five."

The film includes a cultural mishmash of musical numbers where Myers plays the sitar and sings American songs with an Indian accent. According to director Schnabel, the story is also about "re-creating Indian Bollywood musicals."[27] These scenes seem to be an attempt to cash in on the popularity of Bollywood musicals by trying to emulate the singing and dancing in popular Bollywood musicals by playing American music with Indian instruments. The songs that are played are the same tune, but there is no sense of American or Indian cultural context. Instead, the forced nature of pairing an American song with an Indian instrument only shows how unsuitable the pairing is and ends up highlighting the cultural disconnectedness of the music. The musical numbers become a bad translation of what the director and the writers think Bollywood film is and adds to the list of Orientalist films in which Americans are playing or acting what they think is Indian.

The last scene in the film is a parody of a Bollywood musical number that has all the cast members in Indian costumes in a nameless Indian village. In *The Love Guru*, most of the musical numbers are American songs that are played with traditional Indian instruments, such as the sitar, but held like a bass guitar. The film exaggerates Indian stereotypes through cultural things, such as the sitar and a village dance scene. The last scene has Alba dressed in a sari with a host of village girls lip-synching to a stylized Indian version of "The Joker" by the Steve Miller Band. But the masquerade exposes all the misunderstandings and shallowness of trying to portray Indians onscreen. The scene is another bad translation that highlights Indian culture as a series of objects and cultural moments and does not offer any new interpretations. It merely suggests that if one throws in a colorful dance sequence, then the film is suddenly a Bollywood musical. The end of the film is another consumer moment that implies if the film has an Indian setting, then it must include a song-and-dance number that is not central to the plot but offers a cultural accent.

The Love Guru, as a film, tries to do too much by including an origin story, a romance narrative, a sports drama, a spiritual transformation, and a rivalry for best guru. The film takes on the multiple representations of India and Indian spirituality, but the complexity associated with these portrayals is beyond the film's agenda. One of the reasons why the Austin Powers franchise is a successful comedy series is because the character is a lovable but bumbling goofball based on the James Bond brand of secret agents. He also has a recognizable foil and counterpart in the villain Dr. Evil. But in *The Love Guru*, all the characters are strange and foreign, and the plot is confusing. Because the main characters operate as accents, the result is a skewed vision of the dominant. Pitka does not find spiritual fulfillment in the narrative, but he does find true love. However, even his love interest is someone who has avidly consumed all of Guru Pitka's commercial products and consumer phrases. She is a fan from the beginning, and Pitka never has to change or transform himself in order to win her love. If everyone is "taken in" by Pitka's trademark phrases (including him), then there is no redeeming message about engaging in spirituality, and it makes fun of those who believe in spiritual practices rather than critiquing appropriations of spirituality.

Critics universally panned the film, including A. O. Scott of the *New York Times* who said, "The word 'unfunny' surely applies to Mr. Myers's obnoxious attempts to find mirth in physical and cultural differences but does not quite capture the strenuous unpleasantness of his performance. No, *The Love Guru* is downright anti-funny, an experience that makes you wonder if you will ever laugh again."[28] The film was a box-office bomb—it grossed $13.9 million on opening weekend and fell well short of its $62 million budget. The film won the three Razzies in 2009 for worst film, worst screenplay, and worst actor (Mike Myers). Owen Gleiberman in *Entertainment Weekly* comments, "Pitka performs a few songs on the sitar ('Nine to Five' and 'More Than This'), and he doles out words of wisdom in the form of dirty anagrams, but if you're in the mood for a delightful tweak of today's self-actualizing New Age gurus and their be-here-now snake oil, look elsewhere."[29] There could be many reasons why the film was deemed unfunny and a failure, but my speculation is that the overly exaggerated comedy about Indians that Myers offers seems more related to past narratives about Indians in the 1960s, such as *The Party*. The genre of comedy can take the threat out of something different and strange and make it accessible. *The Love Guru* only offers an exaggerated image of new-age spirituality, whereas *The Guru* offers a critique of the media-driven search for identity while also melding the story with realistic narratives of immigrant lives.

Personal Liberation and the American Dream in *The Guru*

The Guru is a variation on the American Dream, and unlike *The Love Guru*, which presents a cast of caricatures, *The Guru* focuses Indian immigrants (played by Indian actors) struggling to make a successful life in an America that tends to position them as Indian stereotypes. *The Guru* was written by Tracey Jackson. As a comedy, the film exaggerates the situation of Indian immigrants in New York City but also highlights how the expectations of the Indian immigrant do not always reflect reality. In this film, pop spirituality is also depicted as a lucrative capital enterprise, but the film does not only imitate the current obsession with new-age spirituality, it also examines through parody and satire, how the materiality of spirituality is disassociated from personal enlightenment. *The Guru* considers the tension between performing as an Indian cultural object, such as a guru, to achieve material success versus following an individual dream to become another kind of performer, a movie star.

The beginning and the end of *The Guru* are framed by three dance numbers: one that features the protagonist watching two separate musical scenes in a movie theater, one where he watches a television screen in which he inserts his own romantic dreams, and the third at the end where he is dancing with the love of his life, who is wearing a white wedding dress. The film opens with young Ramu Gupta (Douglas Dolan) watching a Hindi movie at a local Indian movie theater. When he becomes bored by the tame romantic song-and-dance numbers of the early Bollywood film, he sneaks out of one theater and finds he is inspired by the overt sexuality conveyed by dance in the American musical film *Grease*, directed by Randal Kleiser and starring John Travolta and Olivia Newton-John. All three numbers play the same two songs, the Hindi song "Chori Chori Hum Gori Se (Without letting anyone you know)" and *Grease*'s "You're the One That I Want." Ramu's narrative journey shows him participating in a song-and-dance ensemble that combines American and Hindi traditions into an integrated musical number. As an adult in India, Ramu (Jimi Mistry) is a dance instructor who teaches American popular dances, such as Michael Jackson's moonwalk and the macarena, to middle-class women. He finds joy and love in the expression of popular dance, but his real ambition is to utilize his skills as an actor on the big screen. The progression of the film song-and-dance numbers from two distinct cultural experiences at the beginning of the film into a seamless hybrid at the end when in which Ramu and Sharonna (Heather Graham) become the main characters in the scene that symbolizes the perfect happy ending to an American immigration story and the attainment of the American Dream.

The Guru features a Bollywood-inspired song-and-dance number with Graham, but her performance emphasizes the dance and song as a thematic part of the story that transcends cultural appropriation and instead effectively melds Bollywood with Hollywood. The premise of *The Guru* is that Ramu loves to dance, and so his first impromptu masquerade is based on a series of dance lessons. In India, he loves American musicals, and in the United States, he now dances to Hindi film songs, so it makes sense that the film features hybrid collaborations of Hindi and American music because he is also trying to find a way to reconcile his dreams with American expectations of Indian culture.[30] Ramu and Sharonna are in the same frame with the same dancers, but this time they are both actors playing out roles in an Indian film. Sharonna, dressed in a sari, imitates Bollywood dance moves and dances with Ramu, who plays the Indian romantic male lead singing to the woman he loves. The song then changes into English, and the ensemble cast breaks into the song from *Grease*, and both characters lip-synch to the lyrics and imitate the dance moves of that film. In this scene, Ramu's dreams of true love are framed within a television screen. His dreams of romance and success are mediated by popular culture, and he is trying to imagine a world where he can live without having to constantly perform. The final scene features Ramu in a Western suit and Sharonna in a white wedding dress, united in love, and reenacting the last scene from the film *Grease*, Ramu and Sharonna fly away in a red car into the sunset. The repetition of the song and the costume changes not only parody an American obsession with the movies and musicals but comment on how we are all consumers of mediated culture that involves cultural performances of all types. In these dance sequences, the Indian accents gesture towards a harmonious relationship between cultures. Indians are not only cultural things to be adapted to add an exotic element to a story but, in fact, are integrated with American life. This film examines how consumer practices related to spirituality and self-enlightenment cross racial and cultural boundaries.

One method to explore how culture is exchanged through mass media is to create new versions of familiar narratives in American film. The film repeatedly references American films, such as *The Graduate*, *42nd Street*, and *Grease*, but the situations involve Indian immigrants in the main roles. In their desire to make a "Bollywood-style American comedy," writer Jackson wanted to incorporate a story that was about other movies and how imported films are interpreted.[31] The film becomes a hybrid of Indian and American themes. Critics point out that the film "puts an Indian spin on a classic American tale of innocence lost and dollars gained."[32] The song-and-dance transcends imitation because it is not a number with Indian accents thrown in to fetishize difference but instead represents a hybrid that ties the film to the central theme of pursuing the American Dream. In the article "The Guru and the Cultural Politics of Placelessness," Sukhdev Sandhu comments that the film represents a collaboration of global effort on every scale of the film from production to plot but, most important, it is filmed in real locations in New York City.[33] Sandhu suggests that the on-the-street shots of Indians in various neighborhoods accentuates the idea of New York (along with Toronto and London) as "one of the hubs of the Brown Atlantic," and "this immersion in sidewalk solidarities means the film has more in common with Asian films from Britain that it does from those in the United States."[34] In other words, race and ethnic issues associated with American films play a secondary role to issues of class and territory that are often a focus in British films. While I agree that the film does concentrate on middle-class and working-class immigrant populations, I take issue with the claim that the film is more of a British narrative than an American one. In fact, Ramu gives up the celebrity and fame associated with upper echelons of American society to ride off into the sunset with his working-class girlfriend. He rejects commercial success in favor of true love and recoups the American Dream. This is about American individualism more than class solidarity. The end of the film is about exploring the frontier in the red convertible as he flies into the sky where there are no boundaries.

Despite his middle-class status and relatively secure position in India, Ramu Gupta wants to pursue his dream of acting in New York and Hollywood. The writers of the film are quick to point out that Ramu is leaving a loving, middle-class Indian family. He has a community to return to, so the narrative is not of an immigrant making a one-way journey but of a young man going to New York to follow his dream. His big plans are stifled by cultural bias and stereotypical ideas about how he can enter the acting business. It is not his Indian accent that prevents him from acting but his lack of experience. His forays into the acting world play more as a narrative of a naïve country bumpkin who becomes wise to the business of the acting industry rather than an immigrant story that emphasizes cultural differences between American and Indian culture. The film melds the class narrative of a middle-class man trying to make it big and the hardworking Indian immigrant story but with a comic spin.

The film confronts the realities of the new Indian immigrant in the late 1990s and 2000s. Scholar Inderpal Grewal claims that in contemporary times, the ideal of the American Dream was disseminated through a combination of technology and consumerism. The film supports this idea: Ramu has been inspired to immigrate to the United States because the film narratives he has watched have taught him that he can live his dream to be an actor in the United States. The American Dream, in Grewal's argument, allows for an attachment to new identities for Indian immigrants and the means to cross geographical, cultural, and national borders through the consumption of other cultures in the media or in fashion. Grewal reasons that there is a wide interest in consumer citizenship for migrants and immigrants where a "more heterogeneous group that passed as 'white'" could have access to the fruits of American culture without total assimilation of American national identity.[35] South Asian Americans, as a privileged minority with access to the English language, and middle-class status as professionals and producers and users of technology, are posed to be, if not already, a part of this group. Ramu, as a middle-class Indian consumer, could also be identified as a consumer citizen. The crossing of multiple borders also allows for an expansion of the definitions of national citizenship. Whereas American models of citizenship follow models of assimilation to the American norm, Grewal's idea posits that abandoning all cultural ties is no longer necessary to achieve success. Unlike earlier times when communications was limited, and travel back and forth to South Asian and other countries was cost prohibitive or not available, now immigrants no longer have to cast off their roots to be a viable and political force in America or India. The character of Ramu believes that he can reap the benefits of economic success in the United States without having to assimilate, but when he is faced with the financial reality of his everyday life, he is forced to play the stereotyped Indian roles that are dominant in American culture.

This film represents the realities of the Indian immigrant experience from a sympathetic point of view. While Ramu waits for his big break, he takes a job as a waiter with his Indian friend at an Indian restaurant and lives in one-room apartment with other Indians, including some undocumented workers. Although his first acting job is a part in an adult film with Sharonna, pornography films are neither the genre nor the kind of acting he envisions.[36] As his Indian friends point out, the only famous Indian in film and on TV (at this time) is Apu, and he's a cartoon. Ramu's friend Vijay (Marwa) says, "Do you know why they call it the American Dream? 'Cause it only happens when you are asleep." Through humor, Vijay suggests that for Indians in the United States, the American Dream is limited. Director Mayer utilizes comedy throughout the entire film to examine the stereotypes of Indian immigrants, spiritually empty Americans, and the American Dream. She commented, "If you can say something meaningful in a comedy context, it's much more powerful. When you go to a movie and you know you're getting a message, it's like you're taking your medicine."[37] But similarly, Ramu's understanding of American dance and culture is entirely through messages in media such as popular film and video.

Ramu's dream is not only limited because he is Indian but because he initially understands American culture only through popular film. He mimics dance scenes from his favorite movies and music videos but is not interested in modern American dance forms. His understanding of American culture is just as mediated as Americans' views of Indian spirituality. The film is pointing out that we are all influenced by media constructions of race, class, and nationality, and in essence all culture is performative.

Like Ramu, Alexandra Von Austerberg or Lexie (Marisa Tomei) is a young woman who has consumed multiple (rather than one) cultures in her own search for personal identity. However, unlike *The Love Guru*, this film makes fun of both Ramu's and Lexie's uncritical adoptions of American culture and Indian spirituality. The working-class world of Indian restaurants and adult film is contrasted in the film with the wealthy Upper East Side, and yet both Ramu and Lexie are enamored with the consumption of other cultures. Lexie is wealthy white woman who adopts and pays for the latest fads, including philosophies for achieving personal happiness and enlightenment. In her first glimpse of Swami Ramu, she interprets the dance movements of Ramu (dancing the macarena) as spiritual trance dance. She knows the names of Indian gods and goddesses and other cultures (Tibetan chants and Guatemalan music), but she does not know the meanings. She consumes items and dances that look exotic just because they represent a different culture on the surface level. She does not understand what she consumes and frequently misrepresents names and ideas. For example, she evokes the goddess Vishnu, but Ramu points out Vishnu is a man, and then when she says she is channeling Kali to calm herself, Ramu tells her that Kali is the goddess of death and destruction, and she might not be the best deity to call upon. The recitation and adoption of names and practices without meaning are indicative of the consumer spirituality that Americans have in relation to Indian culture. The film makes fun of her bad translations through contrast rather than affirming them as happens in *The Love Guru*. While the film does emphasize the commercial nature of spirituality, it also promotes that one of the central ideas of new-age spirituality and the American Dream—the power of people to transform their lives and situations by becoming self-aware instead of pretending to be someone they are not.

As it turns out, the only context in which Ramu can "make it" in America as an actor is in the role of a spiritual adviser, a guru. His first performance as a guru is exactly that, a performance in which he pretends to be a guru. During his impromptu charade at Lexie's birthday party, he applies his dance and movie-star philosophies, such as "Move your feet to the beat of your heart," to relax the guests. The result is a Bollywood-type musical number that is not a false imitation but an integrated part of the film. Class barriers break down when Ramu combines the dance moves of the macarena with his dance philosophy. This scene works well as a parody because it creates something new from stereotypical versions of spiritual seminars, which encourage "a little light chanting." Class barriers also break down as the wealthy socialites dance with the downstairs staff. There is an unusual mixing of the classes. Later, Mrs. Von Austerberg's (Christine Baranski) protests about Lexie going out with Ramu are not necessarily racialized but instead influenced by his class status. She does not think Lexie should date the "help." The film depicts a world where all of the wealthy white individuals have people of color working for them. Although Lexie tells her mother, "Not all people of color are here to serve you," Lexie has a Chinese acupuncture specialist and a Korean manicurist, and her mother has African American cooks in the kitchen. The film inserts some racial commentary but tends to veer away from any pointed criticism and instead promotes racial harmony.

The film is about the intersections among consumer quests for spirituality, the business of sex and pornography, and freedom of individual expression. Originally titled "The Guru of Sex," the writers and the studio shortened the title so they could appeal to a more general audience. Ramu borrows the marketing phrases he uses in his performance as the guru of sex from Sharonna's philosophy about sexuality through which she justifies her career as an actress in X-rated films. As the marketing agent in the film (played by Rob Morrow) says, "God is big. Paired with sex, this will be a big show." Unlike *The Love Guru*, which avoids a discussion of sex as a commodity, *The Guru* tackles this topic by depicting the main characters as adult movie actors who fall in love and, hence, contrasts the business of sex with the romantic nature of love. When Ramu decides to act the part of the guru of sex, he finds Sharonna's philosophy toward working in the porn industry one that he can use to advance his own self-interests. The philosophy of being comfortable in one's naked body and enjoying sex as God's creation references Bhagwan Shree Rajneesh's teachings about sex as one of the paths to personal enlightenment. But the film more explicitly links Ramu's work to the pornography industry. So as Sharonna instructs Ramu in acting in adult films, he becomes a guru who channels her lessons to a wider spiritual audience. She is teaching him to act, and his performance is another sort of pornography where sex sells, but it is under the guise of spiritual fulfillment.

As in *The Love Guru*, Swami Ramu has become the embodiment of "new Orientalism" and consumer spirituality, but *The Guru* reflects on how the role-playing and overt trappings of spirituality are questionable. Swami Ramu, the guru of sex, becomes a Westernized and modern incarnation of a celebrity Indian guru. He does not wear the traditional saffron robes or exotic cultural markers of a stereotypical guru but, instead, boasts a variety of outfits that include a simple white tunic and turban, jeans, leather jackets, and designer suits. Like Deepak Chopra, Swami Ramu is clean-shaven and wears Western clothing, but he is young and sexually desirable. Ramu's portrayal of a guru allows him to walk through the city streets of New York and blend in with American culture. His interest in playing the guru is for financial gain, and when he veers outside of this role, his manager, Vijay, constantly reminds him of where they used to be (working in an Indian restaurant) and emphasizes the material gains of the guru enterprise. The plans they make for merchandising and expansion of the brand of the guru of sex solidify Ramu's role as a guru as a business. The film offers a biting critique of the superficial understanding of spiritual fulfillment, especially at the end of the film when Ramu's masquerade as a swami is exposed to his followers.

While Ramu's fashion makeover into a modern guru includes trips to Barney's New York, a Mercedes convertible, and a downtown penthouse apartment, his disciple Lexie purges all of her material goods. She dresses in a plain Indian sari and gives up her wealth and reliance on material possessions. Lexie argues that the profits from the guru of sex shows should be donated to charity. At the moment Ramu is ready to go national with his guru-of-sex franchise on live television, he is exposed (by Sharonna) as a fake and a con man, and he does not deny this. He willingly hands his title and franchise to Lexie. He tells her, "The guru you saw in me is the guru you saw in you," and encourages her to spread her ideas to others. His advice sounds like a spiritual tagline that mirrors the slogans from *The Love Guru*. In finding "her own truth," Lexie had to give up everything she was (a reverse cultural assimilation), but at the end, she has found personal happiness. Lexie takes on the trappings of a new Orientalist spirituality and becomes another figure like Guru Pitka in *The Love Guru*. She is not upset that Ramu has duped her or his followers because she believes his teachings transcend him. "The guru" she sees in Ramu is the one who is a cultural object, and that she can so readily take his place in the business emphasizes that his role was a cultural performance more than teachings espoused by an individual. Lexie and other new-age followers still continue to make the brand a lucrative business. In one sense, the stereotype of an Indian guru has a life of its own that does not need an Indian figurehead, and the business can be lucrative with a white woman at the helm. When Sharonna identifies the business of spirituality as a con game, she forces Ramu to choose between his financial success and fame (which in his mind is based on a sham) or love.[38] Ramu decides to walks away from the manufactured image of the guru of sex to pursue his individual desire for true love, and together he and Sharonna fly off into a new frontier that promotes Indian and American hybridity rather than cultural objectification.

The Guru was shot in thirty-nine days in New York and New Delhi with a budget of $11 million. The film grossed $24 million and was a critical hit in the United States. Critics described the film as full of "buoyant spirit" and focused on the song-and-dance numbers.[39] The film also did well in England and India. Whereas the dismal reception of *The Love Guru* suggests that portrayals in which Indians are depicted as "cultural things" are hopefully in the past and on their way out, the success of *The Guru* shows another, more encouraging trend. Namely, that American audiences and critics have embraced a film that critiques the commodification of Indian spirituality and features an Indian actor in the central role.

Conclusion

This chapter discusses how the consumption and representation of Indian spiritual practices in Hollywood film are another way Indian accents are used as a means of personal and racialized transformation and assimilation. The representation and performance of Indian Americans as spiritual and wise gurus are the progression of the performance of brown voice out of animated portrayals into ethnic performances of Indians by white actors and also, I argue, Indian actors. The expression of accents does not only reside in vocal intonation but is also coupled with clothing and mannerisms that meld Indian cultural icons of the guru with the economic and consumer practices of Americans.

Mike Myers draws his inspiration of brownface performance from the narrative of Peter Sellers and *The Party*, but the retread of the 1960s vibe into a capitalistic-driven representation of Indian spirituality does not translate well in an era in which spirituality and yoga are an accepted norm in American cultural life. The transformative moment is that in modern times, there is no longer a need to go to India—cultural consumerism and spirituality, as depicted in *The Guru*, are now available in the United States. Indian immigrants and spiritual advisors are well versed in American culture and can rationalize the presence of spirituality and the rewards of material wealth to fit into our busy lives.

5

The (Asian) American Dream

Harold and Kumar Go to White Castle and the Pan-Ethnic Buddy Film

> This [journey to White Castle burgers] is about achieving what our parents set out for. This is about the pursuit of happiness. This night is about the American Dream.
>
> Kumar, *Harold and Kumar Go to White Castle* (2004)

The comedic pairing of the characters Harold Lee and Kumar Patel in the Harold and Kumar films places Asian American and, specifically, Indian accents at the center of American culture. While the previous chapters discuss brownface and brown-voice racial performances as the means to exoticize South Asians as cultural objects or assimilate South Asians as deracialized model minorities, the next two chapters delve into how American national and cultural identity is transformed when Asian Americans are the center of the narrative comedy. In the Harold and Kumar films, an Indian accent becomes associated with the larger racial landscape of the United States and responds to the changing nature of racial discourse in a post–9/11 America. The Harold and Kumar films make the performance of Indian accents (and Korean American accents) the center of an American Hollywood production. Harold and Kumar are the proactive subjects who frame the language and questions of the film, and everyone else stands in for the exotic other. As a result, these films reflect the changing representation of South Asian Americans in the United States, who are not only seen as foreign immigrants but also cultural Americans who define contemporary American life.

Harold and Kumar Go to White Castle, directed by Danny Leiner, was a sleeper hit of the summer of 2004 that drew the coveted seventeen-to-

twenty-four-year-old, white, male demographic but also was popular with
a wider audience, including Asian Americans. The film earned over $18 mil-
lion in U.S. box office and was even more successful on DVD.[1] The sequel
Harold and Kumar Escape from Guantanamo Bay, written and directed by
Jon Hurwitz and Hayden Schlossberg, premiered four years later and made
over $38 million.[2] The final film in the trilogy, *A Very Harold and Kumar 3D
Christmas* (2011), directed by Todd Strauss-Schulson, grossed $35 million in
three months. The financial success and widespread popularity of the Harold and Kumar films demonstrate that creating narratives that feature Asian
American and Indian American actors in multiple roles and situations is a
popular move. All three films use parody to create a fresh vision of American
buddy films and satire to challenge popular representations of Asian American and American identity. Asian Americans and South Asian Americans
no longer have a foreign accent and, instead, speak with American accents
that are normalized in relation to the people around them. However, as the
focus of the narrative, their racial position is not erased (as with Gandhi in
Clone High) but is emphasized as part of their everyday life. South Asian accents in the film are not just vocal or color caricatures but, instead, become
brownface performances that are complex images of cultural racialization
that includes accent (or no accent), class position, and cultural behavior.

The quotation in the epigraph occurs at the end of the first film and marks
how the protagonists of the film honor (in truth and with parody) the history
of their immigrant parents' journey to the United States. For the children of
immigrants (the second generation), the process of achieving the American
Dream is not just a physical feat of traversing adverse geography but is also
a psychological journey of risk taking to make dreams come true. And yet,
these words, combined with the image of a White Castle burger franchise as
the goal of their quest, also parody the conventions of the American Dream
because at journey's end, the ultimate source of happiness is the consumption
of American fast food. In *Harold and Kumar Go to White Castle*, the cultural
and national identity of Harold (John Cho) and Kumar (Kal Penn) is tied to
their quest for the quintessential expression of American male consumption,
the White Castle burger. In his review, film critic Roger Ebert says, "Many
comedies have the same starting place: A hero who *must* obtain his dream,
which should if possible be difficult, impractical, eccentric or immoral. As
he marches toward his goal, scattering conventional citizens behind him,
we laugh because of his selfishness, and because secretly that's how we'd like
to behave, if we thought we could get away with it."[3] To Ebert and the fans
of the film, Harold and Kumar are heroes whose journey to obtain White

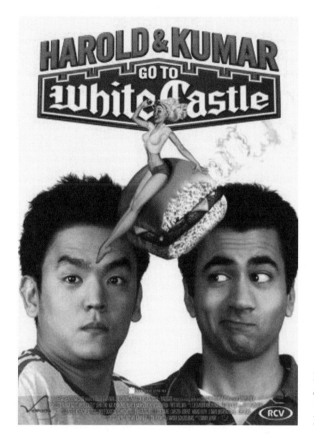

Film Poster, *Harold and Kumar Go to White Castle* (New Line Cinema, 2004)

Castle burgers exemplifies the American Dream. White Castle burgers are synonymous with American cultural identity because they are considered to be America's first ethnic food.[4] Moreover, as one of the first fast-food restaurants in the United States, the White Castle brand is nationally known and a part of American history.

The film redefines the concept of the "hero" and "conventional citizen" through the (comic) journey of two Asian American men and challenges American domestic racial stereotypes of Indian Americans and Korean Americans. The narrative journey shows the anxieties and pressures of young, educated, middle-class men trying to find their way in life. This film is an alternative to the immigrant journey often seen in American films in which the old country is full of hardships, and the new country of America offers freedom and opportunity. It also is a play on the spiritual quests associated with

Eastern religions. In the film, the cultural differences of East versus West are not at issue. Instead, the film explores the dichotomy between how Harold and Kumar define themselves and how others try to impose racial and cultural definitions on their actions. The quotation emphasizes that these characters embrace their identity as Asian Americans who are proud of their history, but what they offer is a new lens to view their journey and how to think about American cultural values.

Harold and Kumar Go to White Castle ends with a television news report featuring an all-points bulletin issued by the New Jersey Muckleburg County police regarding an escaped prisoner and his accomplice. The televised images are animated caricatures of Asians and Indians printed in nineteenth-century U.S. newspapers and magazines. But unlike the stereotypes that are reinforced with animated shows, such as *The Simpsons*, or with depictions of South Asians as racialized cultural objects, this chapter discusses how the first Harold and Kumar comedy film explodes those images and replaces caricatures with unique characters played by Asian American actors. As a comedy, the film's humor hinges on the contrast between the expectations of how Asian American characters have previously acted in mainstream films and the antics of Harold and Kumar witnessed on screen. Brownface and brown-voice performances are exposed as theatrical constructs that the main

Media images of an Asian and a Hindu from *Harold and Kumar Go to White Castle* (New Line Cinema, 2004)

characters encounter and contest in their everyday lives. The juxtaposition of what is expected and how the actors play against those expectations is the basis for a lot of the humor in the film. The film is a series of situations that feature minorities, but it's also a road trip that shows the evolution of Asian American and South Asian portrayals as more than the two-dimensional characters in prior racialized performances. Penn's and Cho's performances are contrasts to previous brownface, brown-voice, and yellowface depictions that were the norm in Hollywood productions.

Asian Americans on a Quest

In *Harold and Kumar Go to White Castle*, Kumar Patel is a recent Indian American college graduate who is taking time off (being financially supported by his father) to decide whether he wants to go to medical school like his father and brother or pursue an alternate career. His character is paired with his best friend and roommate, Harold Lee, a Korean American who is working as a junior analyst for an investment banking firm. One weeknight after work, both men get into Harold's car to fulfill their craving for the popular White Castle burgers, known as sliders. The film chronicles their adventures in New Jersey on their way to the burger place. When Harold and Kumar see the white towers (trimmed in blue) of their fast-food destination at the end of the film, they talk about their night of adventures as the journey that immigrants make to America. Driven by their hunger (both literal and figurative), they revel in the idea that being American earns them the right to be treated equally and eat burgers at White Castle. The film addresses domestic racial and ethnic stereotypes in the context of the American Dream.

Writers Hurwitz and Schlossberg remarked that they wanted to create "a new-generation Cheech and Chong" that featured Asians and Indians in the United States. They crafted their work as response to typical nineties youth comedies but choose to write about the story of the Asian American guy (they wrote the screenplay with the actor Cho in mind) who is usually a minor character in other Hollywood films. They both commented that their friends in college were a multiracial group but that they never saw stories with characters like them (the character Harold Lee is named after one of their friends in college).[5]

The film allows for a representation of what scholar Peter Feng has described as Asian American "identity in motion."[6] We not only see a performance of Asian American identity but also the motion or change in identity throughout the film. Not only do Harold and Kumar evolve during the narrative but the film also offers a comic commentary on representations of Asian Americans. The story presents multiple Asian American characters that are distinct from one another and the main characters, but unlike most other films with Asian Americans, their narrative journey takes place in an R-rated male-oriented comedy. Director Leiner commented, "Both Harold and Kumar go through this journey and confront issues in relation to their perception of self and how others perceive them."[7] Analyzing South Asian Americans and Asian Americans within the context of the genre of the stoner film offers an opportunity to satirize and reconfigure established stereotypes of Asian Americans as children of immigrants and model minorities.

Stoner Films and Ethnic Comedy

The Harold and Kumar films follow in the tradition of the racialized stoner films of Cheech Marin and Tommy Chong. As a genre, stoner films revolve around the use of marijuana. Although there are film lists that name *Reefer Madness* (1936), the historic antidrug film from the 1930s, as one of the origin films for cult enthusiasts, critic Marisa Meltzer identifies Cheech and Chong as the "spiritual fathers of the genre."[8] Popular films in the 1970s and 1980s included *Up in Smoke* (1978), *Cheech and Chong's Next Movie* (1980), *Cheech and Chong's Nice Dreams* (1981), and *Still Smoking* (1983). Written (and later films produced and directed) by Cheech and Chong, these films tackled racial and ethnic stereotypes on the California-Mexico border through comedy.[9] As a Mexican American who was partnered with Tommy Chong (mixed Chinese Irish), Marin routinely addressed issues related to immigration and Chicanos in the films. For example, in *Up in Smoke*, Cheech and Chong turn themselves to the Immigration and Naturalization Service (INS) as undocumented workers so they can get a free ride to Mexico for a family wedding. They turn an antagonistic relationship into a beneficial one and a comic moment. Other films that feature ethnic comedy, such as *Rush Hour* (1998) with Jackie Chan and Chris Tucker, also comment on race relations, but the genre of action-adventure drama follows a different narrative than the stoner films. Critics point to films such as *Half-Baked* (1998), directed by Tamra Davis, and *Friday* (1995), directed by F. Gary Gray, as stoner films that also feature racial diversity.[10]

Unlike the Cheech and Chong films, the writers of the Harold and Kumar films are two Jewish American men who grew up in New Jersey. The source material for their films originates from their friends, including Harold Lee, rather than a stand-up comic act or routine.[11] One key difference from the Cheech and Chong films is that the Harold and Kumar films feature Ivy League college graduates who embody middle-class and upper-class lifestyles. Their friends are all professionals or college graduates. "Stoner and slacker are usually used in the same sentence," explained Schlossberg. "We reject that stereotype. Harold has a great job; Kumar can be a top doctor in a second if he wants to. It's not marijuana that's holding them back."[12] Instead, the story is about deciding what kind of life they want to lead. In other words, one way to read this statement is that the stereotype of the slacker can be revitalized by the inclusion of another stereotype, that of the hard-working and intelligent middle-class Asian Americans. On a class level, the film implies that stoners can be professionals and occupy positions of power. Race and class are combined and embodied in the roles of Harold and Kumar, who are examples of what writer Benjamin Schwartz calls "well-educated articulate ethnic Americans."[13] They are financially successful or at least not in dire economic distress. Visually, they look ethnic, but they speak in an American accent that is clear, relaxed, and sometimes profane. Harold and Kumar are depicted as likable men who are good friends. They are able to navigate social and racial hierarchies in the United States because of their education, their college contacts, and their good-natured (though slightly neurotic) personalities.

Leiner, director of the first film, wanted *White Castle* to evoke the feelings of the Bob Hope and Bing Crosby road films, where two guys have comic adventures, and the actors ad-lib throughout the film.[14] Leiner, who directed the stoner film *Dude, Where's My Car* (2000) and television shows such as *The Gilmore Girls*, *Everwood*, and *Sports Night*, remarks in his DVD commentary session with Cho and Penn that he valued the improvisations the actors did. Leiner was interested in showing Harold and Kumar as "affable" guys, even in the sometimes-raunchy nature of some scenes.[15] The genre of road films emphasizes the physical journey of familiar comics in exotic locales and emphasized racial difference by embellishing cultural behaviors. Stoner films, like the road movies, feature two male friends who are on a particular mission or journey and also feature exaggerated cultural tropes as part of the comedy. However, stoner-film narratives focus on the escape from or avoidance of authority figures and emphasize the acquisition, possession, and smoking of weed.

The genre of stoner comedy film, particularly with regards to racial and ethnic humor in the United States, usually does not invite complex character development or psychological explorations of the immigration experience. Stoner films inspire a devoted cult following but are not mainstream films that appeal to a wide demographic or break box-office records. The narrative relies on the pursuit and consumption of illegal drugs, which is at odds with popular depictions of Asian American immigrant stories. The Cheech and Chong films, like the Harold and Kumar films, the Three Stooges films, or Sasha Baron Cohen's character skits with Ali G or Borat, emerge from a series of events built around an implausible premise. In the case of Harold and Kumar, the plot of the first film follows their night excursion to go out and get White Castle burgers. In the second film, through a comedy of errors, they are fugitives on the run from the U.S. Department of Homeland Security. The comedies are filled with slapstick humor that includes physical injuries, gastrointestinal excretions, exaggerated sexual metaphors, and visual gags. The violence mimics Warner Bros. cartoons in which Elmer Fudd and Wile E. Coyote may get into trouble, but no one ever really gets hurt. However, one of the reasons the Harold and Kumar films are unique is because the script introduces racial stereotypes into a new genre and transforms both the genre and how we approach multicultural issues. As reviewer Dennis Lim notes, "Cheech and Chong, notwithstanding, you don't go to a reefer horndog comedy for utopian multicultural ideals, but it's a nice surprise to find them there when the pot smoke clears."[16]

In the DVD commentary of *White Castle*, both actors remark on how the first film allowed them to directly address stereotypes and racial epithets that they grew up with or faced and still face in everyday life. They did not feel constrained by the limits of the genre. The films are a combination of parody, which is taking a recognizable genre and creating a new spin on the genre, and satire, which challenges the status quo. The Harold and Kumar films go beyond a mere imitation of the stoner film to create a unique Asian American narrative that challenges racial and ethnic stereotypes in the United States.

The *Clone High* animated series worked as a parody of high school narratives but failed as a satire with respect to the characterization of Gandhi. When it comes to matters of race and ethnicity, the animated show resorted to tired, old stereotypes for laughs rather than exposing racial and ethnic stereotypes in a new way. In the case of *The Love Guru*, the attempt at parody ended up being an imitation that reinforces existing stereotypes rather than changes them. *The Guru*, however, works as a parody of new-age spirituality but is less successful as a satire that challenges conventions of race and gender roles. What ethnic comedies such as the Cheech and Chong and Harold and Kumar films do is overlay exaggerated comic moments with an alternative way of reading ethnic stereotypes. In the article "Self-Directed Stereotyping in the Films of Cheech Marin," critic Christine List points out, "[I]f all characters in the film are exposed as having some sort of ethnicity which can be subject to equal ridicule the negative effects of stereotyping are altered."[17] She goes on to argue that all characters, specifically white characters, are "ethnicized" through exaggeration of speech, behavior, and clothing. These films resemble a modern minstrel show where all characters are ridiculed, and List says, "[I]n this context [of the comedy film] the Chicano stereotype is revealed to be as over-generalized as the Anglo type."[18] The performance of identity rather than the revelation of an authentic identity is the important comic element in a stoner film. On one hand, overgeneralizing all racial stereotypes only points out that whiteness is just as much a constructed category as other racial groups and in doing so denies racial hierarchies in the media. But, on the other hand, an argument could be put forward that the dominant narrative that underlies all the ethnic films is one of constant comparison to whiteness that challenges the boundaries of racial hierarchies and changes the way we look at race, ethnicity, and nationality. Film scholar Feng argues that Asian American cinematic identity is "produced by the friction between movies that arrest identity (essentialism) and Asian American movies that construct identity."[19] The Harold and Kumar films, though not written or directed by Asian Americans, do produce alternative performances of Asian American identities that challenge the portrayal of the Indian American medical student or the Korean American investment banker by showing the foibles and quirks of men who are more than their employment choices or racial categories.

Asian Americans at the Center of the Narrative

The beginning of the film does not open with Harold and Kumar but instead starts with a classic male narrative of two young, white investment bankers making their weekend plans. One man has just broken up with his girlfriend, and his coworker wants to take him out to live a little and "get laid" to help lift his friend's spirits. They foist their work on "the Asian guy" in the office, "who loves crunching numbers." The Asian guy is the minor character or the accent in the dominant white narrative. As the two men leave the company parking lot in a black convertible with the license plate "Lady's Man," an energetic rock song crescendos in the film soundtrack. This is a familiar story in Hollywood, and this plot device is characteristic of the "bromance," a variation on the male buddy film that focuses on an intimate but non-sexual relationship between two straight men.[20] *Harold and Kumar Go to White Castle* immediately departs from the familiar white-male narrative and instead through parody situates the accent character or "the Asian guy" at the center of the story. The Harold and Kumar films become an updated version of the genre, an ethnic bromance that features an intimate relationship between two Asian American men. This is a new narrative that has not been seen before in Hollywood.

The writers and the director refer to the first part of the film as the "fake out" that allows the audience to then settle in with the main characters. The fake-out is necessary to make the audience sympathize with Harold and learn to see the film from his point of view. As the two white men leave in the convertible, the camera pans back to Harold watching through the upper-story window and swearing in frustration. The depiction of visible anger and profanity in the "Asian" guy redirects the audience to see the events from Harold's point of view, and it is from this point that the film features first Harold and then introduces his friend Kumar. The Asian Americans are no longer sidekicks in the dominant white narrative. Harold is portrayed as a conscientious and hardworking employee who is the last one out of the office, but unlike the white guys in the convertible who are waved through security, he has to stop, and his identity has to be checked. As an Asian man, he is not individualized by the security in the same way as his colleagues. Instead, his identity is scrutinized, and his right to be in the building is questioned. This is an example of his everyday life. In a visual montage with a hip-hop musical soundtrack, the geography changes as Harold travels from a suburban office park past the skyline of Manhattan across the George Washington Bridge to Hoboken, New Jersey. The important part of this opening is that we are following him out of his stereotypical role as the hardworking Asian and into his individual life after work and into the world where he lives. For example, when he loses out on a prime parking spot to a hyped-up SUV filled with a jeering group of white youth known as the Extreme Punks, he becomes angry but then retreats rather than risk confrontation.[21] His journey in the film involves confronting and demanding respect from his coworkers and others who constantly deride him with racial assumptions and slurs. In addition, when he stands up for himself in front of his coworkers, he also works up the courage to speak to a girl he likes, Maria.

Harold has trouble expressing himself in his work environment and in his dating life. But he has no problem talking with his friend Kumar. The two Asian American men act as each other's sidekick, and their narrative revolves around the lives of young Asian American men. The film constantly plays with the image of how twenty-something Asian Americans should act by turning expectations on their head. For example, Harold tells Kumar he does not want to be associated with people he thinks are Asian American activists ("She calls me a Twinkie," Asian on the outside and white on the inside) or nerds, who, he believes, are only interested in their Asian culture clubs and what kinds of connections they can make for future jobs. Harold tries to avoid the college students at Princeton University, including his friend

Cindy Kim, who has a crush on him.[22] The narrative shows that Harold holds stereotypes about Asian Americans but also portrays how his assumptions are mistaken. As it turns out, the Asian American club party is full of dancing college kids who know how to enjoy life and be successful career-minded individuals. Asian Americans, in this context, are not portrayed as isolated, pathetic, or longing for male or female company.[23] The American Dream is about achieving professional success, but it does not make these characters robotic and one-dimensional. It is Harold who because of his assumptions ends up looking foolish and being alone in the middle of the film.

The other model-minority image that the film takes up is that of Indian American medical student. While Harold's opening montage features his relationship to work and women, Kumar is first shown in an interview with the dean of a medical school. The film flashes to a shot of an ivy-covered brick building on a green campus and moves to an interior shot in which Kumar is seated across from an older white man (Fred Willard) who is the dean. Kumar clearly has the intelligence and the grades to get into medical school (the dean notes this), but throughout the film, Kumar rebels against doing what he thinks his family and school officials expect of him.

The film depicts Kumar as knowledgeable, smart, and sensible. He speaks without any trace of a foreign accent and fulfills the image of a competent medical student and future physician. In his medical-school interview, the film parodies awkward moments that can happen in an interview, including inappropriate racial comments, the revelation of personal information in a professional situation, and ambivalence about the position. Kumar's racial position is immediately addressed as the dean struggles about how to use racial language and identity terms in his presence. At first, the dean talks about Kumar's father (who went to medical school with the dean) and then refers to how their science team was named after the Harlem Globetrotters, "the colored, I mean African American, I mean team of colors." Kumar receives this information in perplexed silence. On one hand, the dean is uncomfortable talking about racial identity, and he looks to Kumar's brown face for help in taking about racial issues, but Kumar is not part of the black-white racial narrative that the dean sets up. On the other hand, by bringing in racial identifications, the film draws attention to the racial narrative that is not black and white. The awkward silence between Kumar and the dean is interrupted by a phone call from Harold and emphasizes that the story is going to be about Harold and Kumar's Friday night plans.

Kumar's professional demeanor vanishes when he answers his cell phone in the interview (and humorously showing what not to do in an interview) and talks with Harold about "smoking weed." The dean is appalled by Kumar's language and his possession of weed and asks how he could ever admit Kumar after observing his behavior. Part of the stoner genre is to buck authority, and Kumar does not seem to care about making a good impression on the dean, but in a moment of earnest confession, Kumar reveals his reservations about going to medical school, even though the dean is amazed that Kumar with "his perfect MCAT scores" would want to do anything else. The dean only sees the numbers and the grades of a potential new candidate, and in a turn-around from the earlier awkward racial discourse, Kumar brings up how his racial identity is influencing his thinking. In his case, Kumar worries that he will be "just another Indian doctor," like his father, brother, and every other model-minority Indian American. Kumar's angst about his future reflects an important dilemma in the model-minority community because this is a crisis that we rarely see on film or television.

Kumar is struggling with the assumption that medical school, graduate school, or an MBA is what Indian American college graduates will pursue without question. While Harold has a lucrative and prestigious position at an investment bank, Kumar has been living off his father's handouts. The only constant is his life is his pursuit of marijuana (as seen in a riotous dream sequence in the film where he courts, marries, and lives the American Dream with a very large bag of weed). Kumar's father is a physician and expects him to go to medical school, but Kumar is not sure if he's doing it because he wants to or because it's what his parents want him to do. Kumar, like Harold, also holds certain stereotypes about South Asians, but his are related to family expectations, whereas Harold's views are about the Asian American college community. While the film challenges the Asian American college stereotypes, it confirms stereotypes of Indian families obsessed with medical school and becoming a doctor.

Later in the film, Kumar sees his father and his brother at a hospital. Kumar's father, Dr. Patel, speaks with a foreign accent that immediately identifies him as an immigrant. He also plays the role of the demanding father who expects Kumar to make a decision: "[I have put] too much time and energy into you" to throw it all away, and he threatens to cut Kumar's finances. While Kumar can talk to the dean about his hesitation, he does not seem able to talk with his father about his dilemma. The generational conflict between parents and children is a long-standing theme in Asian American narratives, but the conflict portrayed here is not about Kumar losing his Indian cultural roots or becoming too American. The emphasis is on his professional future and what kind of job he will have and his class status. The threat to cut Kumar's finances is a threat to reduce him to a different standard of living. An Indian accent in this film combines class status and profession with Indian American racial identity, and so part of Kumar's decision is rooted in whether he desires to maintain his class position or try something new.

Kumar is not the only one to face this decision. His brother, Saikat, is completing his residency as a physician. Dressed in his hospital scrubs, Saikat wears thick glasses and sports a receding hairline that represents a stereotype of competent Indian doctors who are smart but not physically attractive. He is in every way depicted as opposite to the hip vibe that is associated with Kumar (who has a full head of hair and has been shown to be sexually desirable to women).[24] Saikat fits into earlier stereotypes of Indian characters who are single minded and one dimensional. In front of their father, he admonishes Kumar to "stop this post-college rebel bullshit" and start medical school. Saikat is the son who has followed the expectations of his parents. To both Dr. Patel and Saikat, being a responsible Indian son and achieving the American Dream means becoming a physician.

The American Dream that is presented to Kumar is one of economic and professional status, and in the end, he decides to pursue that avenue because it's what he wants to do and not what is expected of him. At the conclusion of the film, Kumar says, "My whole life I've been scared of being one of those nerdy Indian guys turned doctor." He recognizes how the stereotype has inhibited him, and, yet, he realizes that there are "worse things in this world for being tapped for having a natural ability in medicine." In this case, ethnic humor does resonate and help reorient how to think about the model-minority stereotype. The image of being constrained by racial roles and stereotypes is particularly apt because Kumar releases himself from all the expectations and stereotypes. While it might have been an interesting script choice to have him take a year to try something else rather than go to medical school, the film does address the idea of doing something that one cares about rather than what one is good at, and for middle-class Indian Americans, this is not usually discussed in popular culture. In his case, the model-minority images are preventing him from seeing what his talents and role are for the future, rather than narrowing his possibilities.

The film specifically points out both Harold's and Kumar's racial positions in relation to Asian American middle-class model minorities. During the initial segment of their drive to White Castle in the suburbs, they accidentally take the turnpike exit into the dark streets of Newark. From the safety of their car, they see two Asian guys who, Kumar says "look just like us," walking down the street and then getting beaten up by a gang of young white men with baseball bats. The victims are a Korean American and an Indian American but ones who have not had the privilege of an Ivy League education. Harold and Kumar drive away from that sight and head to Princeton University, the exact opposite of working-class Newark. Their individual personalities, Harold as the conscientious but uptight man and Kumar as the carefree party persona, are negated in the face of the threat to them both as Asian Americans. Their awareness of the racial commonalities (privileges and threats) that bind them is the foundation of their friendship despite their separate professional paths.

The undermining of racial stereotypes is a common theme in the first two films. The writers and the director comment on black and white racial polemics, as well as Jewish and Asian American experiences. Leiner comments, "We're dealing with how perceptions of people are based on racial stereotypes. This movie both undercuts that and makes jokes about it at the same time, which to me, is the best way of dispelling myths about stereotypes and prejudice."[25] The films mercilessly portray the incompetence of established forms of law and order to understand racial difference. When Harold ends up in jail for jaywalking, the writers mock the racial profiling of African Americans by racist, white police officers (the same officers that identify Harold and Kumar as the caricatures shown earlier in this chapter). The police end up arresting the first man they find, an African American professor of social justice from Rutgers University, outside a Barnes & Noble bookstore in response to a report that a black man, many miles away in the city of Newark, was identified in robbing a store. Later, the police are shown rousing a black lawyer clad in pajamas out of his house. Like Harold and Kumar, both of these men are middle-class professionals with Ivy League credentials who are also subject to stereotypes of dangerous black men that are proven to be so ludicrous that they are laughable.[26]

One of the primary ways the film addresses Asian American stereotypes is to focus on how American identity is articulated in vocal accents and language. The film directly references the character of Apu from *The Simpsons* as an influential media stereotype that Kumar encounters in his daily life. One scene in the film features a convenience-store set where the man behind the counter is an older Indian American man with a heavy Indian accent. Instead of making fun of the accent, Kumar talks to the owner in Hindi and creates a relationship with the man. What is funny about this scene is the reversal of expectations, because we do not expect the owner to talk, but when he does, and it's in a different language, we do not expect Kumar to respond. The convenience-store owner is not a background fixture but someone who compliments Kumar on his knowledge of Hindi. In this case, unlike Apu, it is

THE (ASIAN) AMERICAN DREAM · 125

not his vocal accent or absence of vocal accent because the scene is not about marking a cultural difference. It's the fact that he is speaking a language that is perfectly understandable to one of the protagonists. The film reorients to whom we pay attention in the film. Like the opening scene when the camera switches to Harold, in this scene it is the working Indian man behind the counter who attracts interest because we are seeing the world through Kumar's eyes. He is not a cultural object but part of daily life. The film makes these adjustments with point of view throughout the story.

The scene changes when the disruptive extreme "white punk" gang (that reappears throughout the film) arrives to cause mischief at the convenience store. They lump Kumar and the store owner as indistinguishable and racialized immigrants and mock them by repeating the phrase, "Thank you, come again," with their brown-voice imitation of the character Apu's accent. This is also part of Kumar's daily life, in which he is the target of young men who want to racialize and marginalize him. By situating these two events side by side, the film shows how placing Kumar and Harold at the center of the narrative changes what events we find funny and what we do not. Later in the film, Kumar steals their car in angry retribution and offers that same phrase back to them in his performance of brown voice. When Kumar speaks, however, his intentionality in using the phrase and the accent is to take control of the situation rather than being made into the butt of the joke or being made to feel powerless or an outsider. The film addresses a variety of groups and portrays a comic vision of America that unites the audience in their understanding of common stereotypes and also portrays how these stereotypes do not fit what the audience is seeing on screen.

Harold and Kumar's Friday night escapade to White Castle is symbolic of "what [they] crave"—confidence for Harold and purpose for Kumar. The film is about hunger and desire wrapped up in the American Dream. Near the end of the film, Kumar makes the dramatic speech in the epigraph to convince Harold to take a chance in order to get what they desire.

> Our parents came to this country, escaping persecution, poverty, and hunger. Hunger, Harold. They were very, very hungry. They wanted to live in a land that treated them as equals, a land filled with hamburger stands. . . . That land was America. . . . Now, this is about achieving what our parents set out for. This is about the pursuit of happiness. This night . . . is about the American Dream.

The humor of this scene centers on the pairing of the drama of the immigrant journey with their decision to take the last steps to complete their desire to consume White Castle sliders. The music in the film swells as Kumar explicitly links the risk of getting into a hang glider to go to the White Castle burger franchise to the immigrant narratives of their parents and the duties of their children. For him, he is not only following in the footsteps of his parents' immigration journey but also finding happiness. To accomplish the American Dream, he must become a good consumer of America—whether eating fast food or making a lucrative career choice. In her work on food imagery in Asian American culture, Anita Mannur identifies this same scene of the film as the moment when South Asians (through their productions) no longer represent sites for food or exotic tourism for the mainstream but are now the consumers and shapers of American taste. As a result, the narrative of film helps to "re-frame which foods are deemed 'exotic,' un-American, and desirable."[27] White Castle burgers, an American success story, are made famous and slightly exotic by their inclusion in the film. What is considered American and what is a racialized cultural accent are transformed by Kumar and Harold's association with the burgers.

Conclusion

The story of the American Dream centers on the ability to achieve material success for both immigrants and their children. While the writers viciously parody youth-oriented advertising campaigns in the film, such as Extreme Sports, the idea that the consumption of White Castle burgers leads to a revelation of what one should do with one's life or gives one courage to stand up for oneself is more gently mocked because Harold and Kumar have fulfilled their quest. After the mass food orgy (shot in slow motion) of burgers, fries, and sodas, both Harold and Kumar are able to achieve a personal breakthrough and make a decision for their future. They have achieved a personal enlightenment that is not steeped in new-age spirituality but instead resides in the American value of consumption. Most important, they are in the central position of the narrative and frame the story, even though they do not control the events around them. This chapter shows how putting Asian Americans at the center of the narrative opens up how we see the racialized depiction of the American Dream. The second film, however, is about how their decisions and their future are not only a series of individual decisions but are influenced by a post–9/11 world with new American national security measures, federal policies, and international politics.

6

"Running from the Joint"

Harold and Kumar Escape from Guantanamo Bay and Comic Narrative after 9/11

> This is America, dude, and as long as I have my
> freedom of speech no one is going to shut me up.
>
> Kumar, *Harold and Kumar Escape*
> *from Guantanamo Bay* (2008)

Harold and Kumar Escape from Guantanamo Bay (2008), written and directed by Jon Hurwitz and Hayden Schlossberg, not only fits into the genre of stoner films but also is part of a growing body of films that chronicle the events and fallout of the 9/11 attacks in the United States. Hollywood and American television were initially cautious to develop programming and scripts that addressed topics related to the aftermath of September 11, 2001, including topics such as the wars in Afghanistan and Iraq, the prisoner abuses at Abu Ghraib, and the detentions at Guantánamo Bay. Popular comedians, such as David Letterman, Jay Leno, and Jon Stewart, struggled over how to address the situation in an era where every event, no matter how serious or tragic, was once thought to be fair game for parody. Paul Achter points out that after 9/11, then Mayor of New York Rudy Giuliani was asked to appear on the opening segment of *Saturday Night Live*, where producer Lorne Michaels asked him, "Is it OK to be funny again?" Giuliani's subsequent "benediction of comedy on SNL" was able to "mobilize a comic institution in the service of a country's need to laugh. Other commentators stated the mayor's point directly: comedy after 9/11 could be useful to audiences, and artists and comedians had a duty to provide it."[1] But while comedy was permitted, making comic narratives on the war on terror did not necessarily follow in mass media. Documentaries, such as *Fahrenheit 9/11* (2004), *The Ground*

Truth (2006), and *Standard Operating Procedure* (2008), delivered exposés of the attacks, the life of soldiers and veterans, and the abuses at detainment facilities. Hollywood dramas, to name a few, such as *Reign over Me* (2007), directed by Mike Binder; Oliver Stone's *World Trade Center* (2006); *United 93* (2006), directed by Paul Greengrass; and later, war dramas, such as *In the Valley of Elah* (2007), directed by Paul Haggis; *Lions for Lambs* (2007), directed by Robert Redford; *The Hurt Locker* (2008), directed by Kathryn Bigelow; and *Extremely Loud and Incredibly Close* (2011), directed by Stephen Daldry, portray narratives of the after-effects for Americans of 9/11 both at home and abroad. The film industry in India produced several narratives that addressed how the attacks impacted South Asians in the United States. Premier Indian actors starred in Bollywood films, such as *Kurbaan* (2009), directed by Renzil D'Silva; *New York* (2009), directed by Kabir Khan; and *My Name Is Khan* (2010), directed by Karan Johar. These films were seen in international venues all over the world and received both critical and popular attention in the United States and abroad. The number of narratives that addressed the war on terror proved that it was suitable subject for documentaries and dramas.

However, comic treatments of the repercussions of 9/11, aside from Albert Brooks's *Looking for Comedy in the Muslim World* (2005) and *Borat: Cultural Learnings of America for Make Benefit Glorious Nation of Kazakhstan* (2006), directed by Larry Charles, have been largely absent. *Harold and Kumar Escape from Guantanamo Bay* fills this void in an unexpected way.[2] The film, released in April 2008, was second at the box office (after Tina Fey's *Baby Mama*) on opening weekend. The second film in the Harold and Kumar franchise was one of industry's top-one-hundred highest- grossing films of the year, making over $30 million at the theaters. The film is a popular release on DVD and continues to appeal to a wide demographic that includes fans of the stoner genre, ethnic comedy, and the buddy film.

Harold and Kumar Escape from Guantanamo Bay is less about the immigrant story and more about the experiences of racial profiling and security for Asian Americans, particularly South Asian Americans during the George W. Bush era (2000–2008). Like the prior film, *Harold and Kumar Go to White Castle* (2004), this film has all the elements of a classic stoner film, which include the possession and consumption of marijuana, evading the law, outsmarting inept agents of national security and law enforcement, and narrative plot twists that descend into parody and slapstick. In his review of the film, Anthony Kaufmann interviews writer Jeremy Pikser, who claims that in the highly politicized environment regarding the war in Iraq and detentions at Guantánamo Bay, "[s]atire is the only way you can address this stuff and actually vent an appropriate level of anger. . . . If you get that angry without being funny, people just run in the other direction."[3] Comedy helps diffuse the anger and so allows for mainstream audience to confront issues that are not normally discussed.

However, the inclusion of Guantánamo Bay in the title of the sequel puts a seemingly innocuous comedy side by side with one of the most controversial places in post–9/11 culture. The subversive title raises issues of unlawful detainment and the suspension of civil liberties in a friendly stoner comedy. Even Amnesty International was put off by the title and announced on its Web site, "Guantanamo is no joke." Members were asked to attend screenings of the films to pass out information about alleged human-rights violations at Guantánamo.[4] "Guantánamo Bay" succinctly references the consequences of the war on terror for South Asians, in particular, and the inclusion of it in the film alerts us to how foreign policy and domestic issues racialize Harold and Kumar in different ways than the first film. The epigraph of this chapter signals that Kumar draws on his rights as an American to be vocal about whatever he wants, and yet the fact that he has to "escape" from Guantánamo also gestures to the realization that his rights as an American may be curtailed and questioned. What does it mean for Harold and Kumar *to escape* from Guantánamo Bay? Even though he does not exhibit the cultural signifiers of a brown-voice accent and an exaggerated brownface performance, Kumar continues to be differentiated from American cultural identity. Kumar is not simply an American (as he often claims)—he is also an Indian American— and the film chronicles his (and Harold's) experiences about what it means to be racialized Americans during heightened national security. The caption on the film poster reads: "This time they are running from the joint." Regardless of the double entendre that indicates this is a stoner film, the emphasis is that the duo are not going out for munchies but running away from the authorities. However, while the film's allegiance to the stoner genre works as both a means that allows the filmmakers to take narrative risks with the subject matter of Guantánamo, that very same devotion also limits the film from making an explicit critique of issues related to national security. The act of escape requires Kumar and Harold to be outside the law and fleeing from imprisonment. In order to avoid being caught requires them to be portrayed as patriots who do not protest but support the status quo.

This chapter addresses how the portrayal of Kumar's experiences reflect the aftermath of 9/11 for South Asians and also critiques a state policy that by 2008 had been deemed as going beyond the limits of national security. This is not just an alternative narrative but also one that reinvents the fear and terror embodied by brown and yellow bodies and through the use of comedy proves that brown and yellow bodies can be harmless, normal, and patriotic. Harold and Kumar become the characters that the audience roots for. As in the first film, an Indian accent is not a performative characteristic or object. What is notable is that Harold and Kumar are "accent-less," so their racial position does not define them. They do not act as cultural objects. In the world of the second film, however, government officials focus on what they look like—they are made hypervisible and seen only as a potential threat to the nation. In contrast to narrative of the paranoid security officials, the rest of the film minimizes their racial threat by having everyone else misrecognize them or surrounds them with exaggerated stereotypes that make Harold and Kumar normative and patriotic. The film allows Kumar, the victim of racial profiling, to protest his treatment and through humor diffuse some of the tension about issues related to detainment and racial profiling.

Racial Recognition and the Stoner Genre

The tension between the politics of racialized Asian American and Indian American bodies in the post–9/11 era of national security and the comic depictions in the stoner genre are at work throughout the film. In discussing the film, Schlossberg says, "We never thought of it as an educational film. But now we're starting to realize that most people—particularly young people—don't know about these things."[5] By focusing on Kumar's experiences as an Indian American and a U.S. citizen in a post–9/11 world, the film offers a central character that is particularly prone to racial profiling as a potential terrorist. In creating a comic narrative about a serious subject, the film diffuses the political protest and emotional responses and makes the topic readily available to a large audience. However, while the result may be showing that brown bodies and yellow bodies can be good American citizens, the film also diminishes what made the first Harold and Kumar film so innovative—representations of Indian American and Korean American that include their ethnic and cultural practices. The humor of this film depends upon how Kumar and Harold are consistently misread as a national security threats while emphasizing that they are patriotic American citizens. The early marketing material for the film has both the creators de-emphasizing Harold and Kumar's racial identity. While Hurwitz says, "These are Asian American characters that are just like the white character that you would see on the big screen," clearly, the incidents that happen to

Kumar and Harold would not happen to white people but to specific racial groups.[6] Schlossberg adds, "The culture and race of Harold and Kumar is incidental." This statement seems at odds with the storyline that seems to lose its energy after Harold and Kumar escape from Guantánamo Bay. Even the press release for the film downplays the political nature of the comedy by characterizing the story as being a "color-blind" and "agenda-less" political satire with no partisan bias. This retreat from the political aspect of the film after putting Guantánamo Bay in the title explains the mixed messages of the film that at times offers satiric critiques of national security practices and at other times offers up tired southern stereotypes that are not that funny. Perhaps the studio, the directors, and the producers were nervous about a potential political backlash in the media that could scare away audiences who were looking to see a humorous film. Clearly, there are some conflicted ideas about what the film is supposed to say. But this also returns back to the issue of what is allowed to be satirized post–9/11 and how not only comedians but mainstream media avoids certain political topics and privileges others on film and television. This can be seen in one

Kumar (Kal Penn) transformed into a terrorist in *Harold and Kumar Escape from Guantanamo Bay* (New Line Cinema, 2008)

of the most heavily previewed scenes in the film when Kumar and Harold get on a plane from New York/New Jersey to Amsterdam.

Visual profiling not only influences airport security procedures but also infects how the American public views South Asians. On the airplane, Kumar is magically transformed into a diabolical Osama bin Laden–like figure and labeled a terrorist in the imagination of an older white woman. Kumar is clean-shaven and dressed in jeans, and, yet, he becomes a stand-in for a much-older man in religious robes and a turban with a full-grown beard. The transformation is funny because from earlier experiences (his last movie), he is clearly not a terrorist. The real transformation that happens is among the viewers because we can laugh at this scene. The scene in the film contrasts Kumar's perspective with the senior woman. He smiles and sees her as a harmless old lady, but from her point of view, she can only see him as a terrorist. She is fearful of what he represents, but the film orients us to Kumar's point of view of what it is like to be looked at with suspicion and be part of a racially profiled group and distances us from her paranoid worldview. As the first film gives us a fake out to change our racial affiliations and point of view, so does this film also attempt to put the audience in Kumar's shoes. We do not see Kumar as a threat or an exotic figure but an all American (albeit brown) likable guy. Hence, the subsequent series of events that lead to detainment at Guantánamo Bay depicts Kumar as being misunderstood and misrecognized, because in the early part of the film, we have witnessed how he has been treated and sympathize with his character.

Despite the mixed messages from the directors, who say this is not a racial film, the representation of Kumar as a racial threat is the central narrative of the film and highlights the experiences of South Asians in relation to national security. The first part of the film is about establishing the culture of security, detainment, and interrogation that lead up to Harold and Kumar's incarceration and subsequent escape from Guantánamo Bay. The plot of the film focuses on what happens after Kumar's bong is mistaken for a bomb on their airplane flight to Amsterdam. Kumar's devotion to the possession of marijuana was established in the first film and is a vital element of the stoner genre. The changes in national security policy do not change his basic urges, but it does change the consequences and context of his act. Kumar is engaged in the illegal possession and transport of drugs and is subject to imprisonment. He is breaking the law in another war—the war on drugs. However, this infraction characterizes him as a normative and harmless young American male who is carrying some marijuana. Pot users are not usually deemed a national security threat. But by virtue of his skin color and the depiction of a paranoid government agency, he is detained as a terrorist.

Harold and Kumar are questioned by federal agents and then are sent by Homeland Security to Guantánamo Bay as potential threats to the United States. When they escape, their status as U.S. citizens and fugitives from the law drives the story as they make their journey through the American south. The second part of the film is a road narrative that focuses on Harold and Kumar's encounters with different racial groups and stereotypes in the American south that is similar to the narrative of the first film. There is a subsequent shift from international and national security to domestic race relations. Harold and Kumar are clearly outsiders in the southern states, and, yet, because they have been the victims of mistaken identity, the audience sympathizes with them. It is the people in the south who become "the other" in relation to Harold and Kumar. For example, everyone speaks with a regional accent except Harold and Kumar, so accents serve to embellish racial and class biases in the south. Accents in a post–9/11 world reflect the ambiguity of race relations and who is a "threat" and who is the outsider, depending on the relation to national security.

Kumar is the object and the subject of the film. The narrative follows his responses to racial profiling, but instead of being seen as a threat, he is first misread (also a characteristic of the stoner genre) as an international terrorist threat but then shown to be American. In the epigraph, Kumar verbalizes his rights to American citizenship in passionate and American-accented tones. In his mind, no one should be able to question his position or rights as an American. The film calms Kumar's outrage by mocking the security guards and the national security forces of the government who see Kumar as a threat. He expresses his anger, but he also serves as the comic vehicle to soothe fears about racial difference to mainstream audiences. The aftereffects of 9/11 upon South Asian communities have transformed former model-minority communities into potential terrorist threats and have led to divisions between those who encompass the stereotype and those who challenge that position.[7] Scholars Jasbir K. Puar and Amit Rai point out that the environment associated with national security "creates heightened public and political paranoia about those suspected to be linked to terrorist activities encompasses greater numbers of Muslims, Arab Americans, and South Asian Pakistanis, Bangladeshis, and Muslim Indians, we also see a retrenching and resolidification of the discourse of U.S. exceptionalism and growing conservatism of the model minorities emblematic of it."[8] Both Harold and Kumar vehemently insist and defend their rights as Americans and are symbolic of a conservative model minority that does not question U.S. policy of detainment and detention. This is particularly shown in a scene discussed later in which they are placed side by side with two "real" terrorists. During this scene and throughout their detainment, they emphatically and proudly proclaim their identity as Americans. The emphasis in the film is to transform the visible threat of a racialized Indian American into a citizen whose racial allegiances and stereotypes are sublimated by a patriotic American identity. Once they are established as American patriots, Kumar and Harold then can be depicted as domestic cultural and regional chameleons that travel through the south. What made them stand out as outsiders in the first part of the film is negated, and everyone else in the film becomes "the other" and an accent to their brand of racial and ethnic normalcy.

For South Asian Americans, the consequences of 9/11 have resulted in the changing representation of South Asians from the model minority to a possible terrorist (especially for Sikhs, Muslims, and brown men). Even if one does not identify with Harold and Kumar physically or racially as Asian Americans, verbally they express American sensibilities, accents, values, curse words, and current frustrations with airport security. On the one hand, national security officials identify them as terrorist threats based on their physical appearance, but, on the other hand, when they travel in the American south, they become the image of normative Americans in comparison to the "other" people they encounter. The second Harold and Kumar film portrays the changing nature of who is American or who "we" are by satirizing how Harold and Kumar are represented as both the image of the typical American and the potential terrorist/spy.

National Security and Foreign and Domestic Racial Profiling

While the 1990s racialization of South Asians was often related to the image of the model minority and the immigrant, since 2001 the racial position of "brown" has been complicated by national-security concerns. The increased fear of and hostility toward Muslims, Arab Americans, Sikhs, and others have made South Asians as a whole a more visible racial group in the United States. In the beginning of the film, the writers address how we visualize and recognize the racial difference of South Asian men as a potential terrorist threat in the era of national security when Kumar is pulled aside for a "random" security check at the airport by a Transportation Security Administration (TSA) guard. Harold is able to pass through security without being checked—his Asian racial characteristics do not make him a national threat. Kumar tells the guard that he knows he is being racially profiled and the guard is being racist. The guard responds, "What do you mean? I'm black." Kumar replies, "Please, I'm browner than you are." While Kumar questions the guard's "blackness," Harold seeks to mollify all the parties involved and affirms the guard's racial position. Harold does not challenge the racial assumptions or hierarchies that are in place. What this scene reveals is how blackness is inextricable from American national identity, whereas "brownness" is not only ambiguous but also potentially threatening to the nation. The scene at the airport is one in which Kumar is the object and then assumes control of the narrative at the expense of the black security guard.

The conundrum is where Kumar and (later) Harold fit in the racial picture in light of federal security categories after September 11, 2001. As cultural historian Jeffrey Melnick points out his book *9/11 Culture*, the events of September 11, 2001, have framed cultural, political, and rhetorical dialogue about American identity in complex ways that are still being explored and are constantly changing. South Asian Americans are a part of this dialogue. He describes the "tri-angulations of American, Middle Eastern, and South Asian" cultures that are occurring in hip-hop music among and between African American, Bollywood, British Indians, Arab Americans, and white Americans.[9] Prior to U.S. involvement in Afghanistan (not counting the Cold War support against the Union of Soviet Socialist Republics), the United States had not waged war on the South Asian subcontinent with other South Asians. Now, Afghanistan, Pakistan, and India are simultaneously involved in military decisions that include the United States.

This scene establishes a hierarchy of racial position among black, white, brown, and yellow. In the first film, Asian Americans are middle-class professionals who are doctors, investment bankers, and college students who confront racist attitudes but are rarely deemed threats to the community. However, at airport security in the second film, Kumar is physically viewed as a threat. The situation ends when an older, white, male supervisor, the symbol of the dominant authority who sets the standards, allows Kumar to pass on through rather than make a fuss. The black versus white racial categories are recognizable as American, but Kumar's brownness and Harold's yellowness register the problem with the binary understanding of racial categories. The scene invites a big laugh because in post–9/11 America, brown is perceived as a greater threat that any other race. The racial categories of who is most feared, "brown" or "black," have been exposed in the scene, but, ultimately,

Kumar (Kal Penn), Harold (John Cho), and guards at airport security in *Harold and Kumar Escape from Guantanamo Bay* (New Line Cinema, 2008)

to be "browner" or "blacker" is to be on the low end of the racial ladder in the United States. Two different racial groups are presented as being pitted against each other, and their argument is resolved by a dominant, white authority figure. Secondly, the scene also invites a nervous laugh because the process of racialization and who discriminates against whom are not limited to blacks and whites. The narrative casts Harold and Kumar as alternatives to the established American racial categories of black and white. When Kumar questions the black security officer's motives, he is pointing out that certain skin tones qualify as American, and others are seen as foreign.[10] As a brown person, he is categorized as a foreign threat that in situations of airport security trumps any other racial group.

Humor is used to diffuse an emotional situation but also to make a point that after 9/11, domestic racial and ethnic group identities, such as Asian American, African American, and South Asian American, fade in the era of national security. Instead, one is American, or one is foreign, and as the scene shows, the supervisors who make the decisions are white. Throughout the second film, both characters seem to go back and forth from being objects of humor to being producers of humor (and in control of the reception of the joke), but they are always the lenses through which the rest of action is being seen. While the scene at the airport highlights the different racial positions in the United States, the rest of the film muddies those categories by showing how difficult it is for others to racially identify the protagonists.

President George W. Bush appears as a character at the end of the film and "saves" Harold and Kumar from being sent back to Guantánamo Bay. Unlike the first film, it is not Harold's and Kumar's class mobility that gets them out of tight situations (though it still plays a factor) but their ability to interact with diverse groups in the United States. The narrative emphasizes how they are in situations that can cause them to be identified as foreign or American. However, the allusions to being Indian American or Korean American are absent from their interactions. It is their national identity as Americans and their knowledge of American tropes and stereotypes that helps them even as they are persistently seen as foreign by the federal government.

The film parodies the climate of fear associated with Bush-era politics. *New Yorker* film critic David Denby says of the second film, "Their skills are unreliable at best, but, willy-nilly, they've caught a significant demographic moment. The Harold and Kumar movies, in their slovenly and profane style, are about the transition to a post-racial society in which, as the *Salon* film critic Stephanie Zacharek puts it, 'no one in real life can say definitively what an American looks like.'"[11] Zacharek suggests that no can say what an American looks like, but the entire film is about how we do have common ideas of what and who Americans are and, as the airport scene shows, the racial hierarchies of differently racialized Americans. I also disagree that *Harold and Kumar Escape from Guantanamo Bay* is about a postracial society, although the film does try to normalize Harold and Kumar in the south. Instead, I believe the film exaggerates racial and regional and national stereotypes so that we cannot help but notice (and laugh) at how many racial and ethnic stereotypes still define the idea of who or what is an American.

The film emphasizes how visual racial profiling dominates national-security discourse and critiques the Bush-era neoliberal-conservative agenda that characterizes disagreement with American policies as un-American. In their pot-smoking scene with President Bush, the character Bush says, "You don't have to believe in your government to be American, just believe in your country." This statement seems to separate the system of politics and representation from the national ideals of the country. But Harold and Kumar are not just any two men; they are Asian American men constantly confronted with stereotypes and, thus, reveal how the definition of who is an American cannot be divested from politics and representation. Bush asks them to distinguish between the governing body of the state and cultural ideals of the country, but for Harold and Kumar, as Asian Americans, historically the rights of democracy and citizenship have always been intertwined. What happens to Harold and Kumar is because of the policies the government has instituted, and so to ask them not to have a political opinion or affiliation is to ask them to accept what the authority tells them to do, which runs counter to the tenets of a stoner film and their own interests as Asian Americans.

Racial Invisibility and Detainment

The juxtaposition of the stoners Harold and Kumar with the dark underbelly of U.S. national-security practices provides an opportunity to offer a political commentary on Guantánamo Bay and the position of the "enemy combat-ant." Guantánamo Bay has been a discursive site for multiple issues, includ-ing detention, immigration, and international human rights. Scholars, such as Amy Kaplan, Ann McClintock, and Rajini Srikanth, have framed their discussions of the camp to address U.S. imperialism. In geographical terms, Guantánamo Bay, Cuba, is a space that is outside of the United States but is U.S. territory. It is also a place where U.S. law can be suspended and where the exercise of power is not questioned. American Studies scholar Kaplan claims Guantánamo Bay portrays the United States as a "lawless zone" and one that "indefinitely detains, secretly transports, and tortures uncounted prisoners from all over the world."[12] While Harold and Kumar travel to a politically contentious space, they do not question any of the activities or events that happen there. The film, for example, gestures towards the 2004 prisoner abuses at Abu Ghraib by visually depicting Harold and Kumar in the same orange jumpsuits and black masks as the infamous photographs and subjecting them to sexually demeaning punishment by the guards. Guantá-namo Bay functions similar to a tourist site or an accent that contrasts the normalcy of Harold's and Kumar's previous lives with the time they spend at the prison. The line between comedy and the horror of prisoners giving the guards a "cockmeat" sandwich is thin in this case.[13] What Harold and Kumar are doing at Guantánamo Bay and how it works as part of a satire and a stoner film come into question. Schlossberg acknowledges, "While it's [the story] obviously absurd . . . there's an element of truth. There have been people thrown in Guantánamo who have done nothing. We like the idea of doing something about these subjects in a way that's not serious."[14] In this case, the point is that innocent people like Harold and Kumar have been mistakenly imprisoned in Guantánamo, but the film shies away from saying directly that there is a problem with the practices or policies associ-ated with Guantánamo Bay.

Film poster, *Harold and Kumar Escape from Guantanamo Bay* (New Line Cinema, 2008)

Harold and Kumar's incarceration at Guantánamo Bay is of short duration in the film (less than seven minutes), and their imprisonment involves distinguishing them from the "real terrorists." Exaggerating the sexual deviance and foreign nature of the inhabitants is the driving force behind the humor in the scenes at Guantánamo. This is particularly apparent when Harold and Kumar get into an argument with two "real terrorists," who are physically dressed just like them. However, the differences between them are immediately apparent. Despite similar clothing, the other two prisoners are brown skinned, have beards, and speak in a high-pitched, accented English associated with the Middle East. When they are confronted with foreign terrorists, the film contrasts Harold and Kumar as Americans in their speech (no foreign accent) and in their politics. Kumar verbally lashes out at the other prisoners, "You think you are heroes for killing innocent people?" Kumar, as the brown person, now can show his anger at the terrorist who is portrayed as the "real threat," whereas Kumar is the good, brown American. The film is interested in emphasizing their patriotism over any other allegiances. This is further seen when Harold yells at the terrorist, "It's because of assholes like you that we are even in this fucking place." When one terrorist criticizes American policy and says Harold and Kumar would fight if they "started realizing what your government is doing to the world," both of them vehemently defend their American (not Asian American) cultural identity (including the right to eat donuts) in the face of any threat. This scene emphasizes that Harold and Kumar have been imprisoned because they have the wrong designation—they have been misidentified as foreign threats, but they are really loyal and patriotic Americans. And in the era of post–9/11, in this part of the film there only seem to be two options: foreign or American. Penn confirms this, "Harold and Kumar are Americans first. Before they're guys, before they're New Jerseyians, and certainly before they're Asian or Indian. Before any of that they're American. Something you find in this movie is how much they love America and how ridiculous they find it when they run into people who are scared of them."[15] However, their affirmation as loyal Americans comes at the expense of the exaggerated foreignness of the other racialized terrorists. In her analysis of the film, Nina Seja comments that "comedy film . . . has the potential to test boundaries related to the status of the victim" in relationship to representations of Arabs or Muslims.[16] Because Harold and Kumar are misrecognized in the film as Arab rather than really being Arab, they are not punished when they escape.[17] However, the "authentic" incarcerated terrorist is punished by being portrayed as sexually deviant and later is electrocuted while trying to escape.[18] This, in turn, allows Harold and Kumar to escape, literally over the dead body of the nameless terrorist, and later allows them to be pardoned by President Bush. The film is not about questioning what/who American is but making sure one is not identified as Arab. On one hand, their escape is a comic moment, but the larger issues of Guantánamo Bay tend to rise up even in this rendition, and the ability of this stoner comedy to cross the political waters of Guantánamo Bay is dubious in this instant.[19]

Historically, Guantánamo Bay has been a site for detention for Haitian refugees and Cuban refugees trying to immigrate to the United States and now is a place for Arab and Muslim threats to the state. Amy Kaplan points out, "The image of the 'enemy combatant' is a racialized category" that conflates immigrants with terrorists.[20] This conflation is apparent in this scene because Harold and Kumar are distinguished through their accents and their politics as patriotic Americans. But they are also the children of immigrants. This combination of the two categories symbolically meets when Harold and Kumar escape from Guantánamo Bay. Their boat to the United States is filled with Cuban refugees, who desire to escape to pursue freedom and the American Dream in the United States. Harold and Kumar are literally in the same boat with the immigrants and refugees—they are entering the country as fugitives from the law. We also see this conflation later in the film when Homeland Security officials interrogate Harold's parents and Kumar's immigrant parents. Harold and Kumar are no longer depicted as terrorist threats (even though the government is after them), but they are undocumented and, hence, on the run from the law. Thus, in their escape from Guantánamo Bay, Harold and Kumar separate themselves from the category of foreign terrorist and return to the United States, where they are once again racially situated in the domestic discourse of the United States.

Accents in the Interrogation Room

The film mocks how visual racial identification is not an effective or accurate means of identification in a post–9/11 American world. Instead, difference is implied through vocal intonation that is perceived to be more accurate. At Guantánamo Bay, the real terrorists speak with a Middle Eastern accent, and the military guards talk with a regional southern accent. While the first film rarely discussed vocal accents, the second film depicts a variety of accents. On one hand, Harold and Kumar are considered foreigners and threats to American national security by Under Secretary Ron Fox (Rob Corddry) in Homeland Security, but, on the other hand, as the duo travels from Cuba through Miami, Alabama, and Texas, they model American identity through various regional clothing changes that include Miami prints, southern hunting gear, and Texas cowboy boots. Although their outfits change, their speech is always articulate and normalized as white American, whereas almost everyone else, including President Bush, is speaking with a regional American accent. The emphasis on accents to distinguish different communities in *Harold and Kumar Escape from Guantanamo Bay* shows how we are dependent upon vocal intonation as integral to our sense of identity because the reliance on physical identifications of racial and cultural difference often results in misunderstandings.

The premise and joke in the second film are that everyone in an authority position (except for the president) visually identifies Harold and Kumar as threats without either of them ever speaking a word. The interrogation of Harold and Kumar and, later, of their parents emphasizes that those in charge of national security judge everyone by physical features. For example, after seeing Kumar and Harold, they are immediately identified by Homeland security as part of a plot where al-Qaeda and North Korea are working together. Visually, racially brown and yellow skin tones could yield a number of nationalities, but Homeland Security categorizes Harold and Kumar as foreign threats to national security because they look different compared to a normative white racial standard. When he first meets Harold and Kumar in the holding cell, Under Secretary Fox comments on the shape of Harold's eyes, "What's wrong with your eyes—can't you see properly?" Earlier, he asks if there's a problem with Harold's eyes, "Is he handicapped?" The absence of the epicanthic fold in the eyelid is a common physical feature of those of East Asian heritage and not limited to Korean Americans. Although Harold is Korean American, Fox cannot distinguish one Asian nationality from another (he also calls Harold "Hello Kitty"), even though both Harold and Kumar insist in American accents that they are citizens of the United States. To Homeland Security, Asian Americans are first and foremost seen as foreign. Harold and Kumar not only articulate in what it sounds like to be American but also become the ears of the audience as we listen to them and then later to their parents. They speak nonaccented and easily understandable English when the government officials in charge seem to be driven by paranoia and are capable of only speaking nonsense.

While Harold and Kumar are racially identified by their physical looks, their parents offer a more complex depiction of racial stereotypes that combine physical and vocal profiling. The Department of Homeland Security question Harold's and Kumar's parents, the Lees and the Patels, respectively, after their sons' escape from the detainment facility at Guantánamo Bay. Although Kaplan's definition of enemy combatants as a "conflation" of immigrant and terrorist is meant to apply to prisoners, this conflation of categories also can be applied to how the Lees and the Patels are approached in their questioning. Their identity as "real" Americans is open to speculation because of their immigration status, and, thus, they are treated as potential threats. But in this case, the comments and questions given to them are not about physical differences from a normative white standard but instead focus on mixed meanings and interpretation of language. Srikanth describes Guantánamo Bay as a "zone of shifting meanings where language and law are protean and malleable."[21] The notion of language changing and having multiple meanings is particularly evident in the exchange between Dr. Patel

(Kumar's father, played by Errol Sitahal) and Fox and shows how the "zone" of Guantánamo Bay permeates their interaction. Meaning is obfuscated by ignorance and paranoia to the extent that the words exchanged lose any semblance of understanding. Those who are in positions of power mispronounce words, misinterpret words, and speak in gibberish with made-up words like "sublantics." There is a role reversal where the people who speak in incomprehensible English are visually normative white American authority figures and the people who are speaking in sensible and rational terms are South Asian and Korean Americans.

While Asian American narratives have often focused on generational rifts that pit Eastern cultural values versus American nationalism, *Harold and Kumar Escape from Guantanamo Bay* depicts Indian Americans and Korean Americans as citizens of the United States as well as parents who are concerned for their children. In the case of Dr. Patel, his racial identity, just like his son's (who is first identified as an al-Qaeda operative), is unable to be categorized by U.S. government officials. Indians Americans do not fit neatly into any of the U.S. racial categories. When Dr. Patel declares, "I am not *A-rab*. I am Indian," Secretary Fox from the Department of Homeland Security responds, "Look, Chief, I'm not here to argue *sublantics* with you, OK" (my emphasis). As in the Guantánamo Bay section, the narrative here emphatically distinguishes between Indian (good) and Arab (bad). The immigrant father proclaims his Indian heritage but as a means to avoid being associated with what he perceives as the more threatening stereotype—an Arab.[22] This is also one of the only times that the film allows for an expression of racial and ethnic identity. Kumar never says, "I'm Indian," in this film (he does in the previous film), and when his father does, it is to claim his difference from being seen as an Arab.

Secretary Fox's retort shows that he has no interest in ethnic, geographical, or historical categorizations of race. Because he is ignorant, he misinterprets what Dr. Patel says. He only sees someone who is different and a threat to the United States. Secretary Fox's malapropism of "sublantics" for the word "semantics" (the study of meaning) or "semiotics" (the study of signs and gestures in the system of communications) reveals one of the key questions in the film: How do Americans communicate about and with racialized others in a post–9/11 landscape? Contrary to the beliefs of Secretary Fox, it is important to discuss the semantics and semiotics of how we talk about race, ethnicity, and citizenship.

This moment is also characteristic of the stoner genre in that it exaggerates the incompetence of the authorities and Homeland Security. While

Dr. Patel does not celebrate or discuss his position in America as a citizen or model minority, he does mock the pronunciation of the government official before correcting the official about his mistake. In this exchange, the combination of the visual misidentification and the accentuated enunciation of an Arab identity represents Secretary Fox as an uneducated official who does not know the difference among Arab, Indian, and Native American cultural identities. In this film, it is not South Asian immigrants who are being laughed at but official government agents who are portrayed as incompetent because they cannot distinguish between different national and cultural identities.

In this scene, there is a clear difference in how the Lees are misrecognized and how the Patels are treated. With the Lees, the central concern is their citizenship status. When the Lees talk in American English (without a foreign accent) about being American citizens for forty years, Secretary Fox and the translator who supposedly speaks Korean cannot understand "their dialect." Indian Americans and Korean Americans, who have been stereotypically represented as foreigners who cannot speak English or who speak with an accent, suddenly exhibit culturally middle-class professional American qualities of higher education and perfectly articulated English. This exchange turns the idea of cultural markers on its head. The Lees and the Patels are not what they stereotypically and visually appear to be—they are part of American cultural identity even though their visual impressions (Asian and nonwhite) lead the government officials to see them as foreign. The authorities are limited by their reliance on visual identification of race and are unable to listen to what is being said.

When Mr. Lee (Clyde Kusatsu) asks in well-articulated English why his son Harold is being detained, the translator, Dr. Beecher (Roger Bart), says, "They are speaking some sort of dialect I've never heard before." Harold's parents do not speak with any accent and cannot understand the Korean (which is mostly nonsensical) that Dr. Beecher insists on speaking to them. The disconnect between what the translator expects and what comes out of Mr. Lee's mouth highlights how the visual difference overwhelms any sort of familiarity and becomes a threat to American national security. The non-accents for the Lees do not register with the agent, and the only way he can "hear" and "see" the Lees is through the lens of unintelligible language. Indian Americans, however, do not seem to have this problem. The notion of a "ching-chong" language is associated with Korean Americans and other East Asians, but Indian Americans are in a different position in relation to assimilation, model-minority politics, and American identity than most other Asian ethnicities. Indian Americans and Filipinos both have fluency in English. Korean Americans are treated as nonnative speakers and, hence, have the stereotype that they are unintelligible even though the Lees have no accent in the film and are native speakers. The Patels, on the other hand, have a distinct phonetic accent, but the presence or lack of a foreign accent does not change the suspicion of that they are a potential terrorist to the government officials.

In the era of national security, the film emphasizes that visual identification is the most important criteria in determining American citizenship and that the officials are in the wrong. The film allows us to see how the visual can overwhelm other forms of cultural communication and how mistaken this type of profiling can be because the individuals who are incarcerated are not only the most unlikely suspects but they are the heroes of the film. Harold and Kumar (and their parents) are the normative center of the film, and everyone else around them is characterized as the irrational "other."

The film undermines the idea of a postracial nation because everyone is hyperaware of his or her racial position. The second half of the film focuses on Harold's and Kumar's roles in the normative racial position in terms of regional identity rather than national security. During Harold and Kumar's road trip through the south, other characters cannot racially identity them and often misidentify them. No one sees them as a national security threat in the south. In fact, it is the other characters that possess accents, such as southern drawls or grammatically incorrect English. Kumar and Harold speak in a normative American accent. Most of the comic moments arise from jokes that juxtapose the normalcy of Harold and Kumar in the strange and threatening land of the south that includes avid hunters, inbred mutant children, African American basketball players, rich Texans, and the Ku Klux Klan. Although Texans and basketball players are not inherently abnormal, the film makes them out to be alien to Harold and Kumar. The revelation that these groups are just as misunderstood as Harold and Kumar drives the narrative of the rest of the film. Harold and Kumar are our tour guides to the strangeness of the people they encounter and in the course of the narrative become representative of American cultural identity.

The Racial Geographies of Southern Culture

When Harold and Kumar travel through the southern geographies of Florida, Alabama, and Texas in the second half of the film, the inability of the residents in the south in the film to racially pinpoint their identity is the basis for the comic situations. In this film, Harold and Kumar are on the run in the American south rather than in the middle-class suburban environment of hospitals, universities, or White Castle restaurants of New Jersey. They also are depicted as the only Asian Americans in the area despite the fact that the south (especially in Texas) has historically significant and vibrant Asian communities. They are invisible as a racial group, and as a result, this allows them to pass through the south in the garb of other racial and social stereotypes in the south. They become chameleons that take on the stereotypical clothing of the state in which they are traveling. Harold and Kumar seem to mirror the racial fears of whatever group they encounter. While in the first part of the film, they are misidentified as foreign terrorists by the federal government, in this section they are misidentified as domestic threats and challenge the mainstream definitions of racial groups such as Asian, Mexican, or white.

The film does not provide any answers on where Harold and Kumar should be placed in racial definitions, but there are reoccurring jokes about how Indian Americans and Korean Americans disrupt conventional racial stereotypes. Margaret Cho's ethnic stand-up routines about her experiences as a Korean American were made into a short-lived television situation comedy *All-American Girl* (1994–95). One of the reasons Cho believes the show was criticized and cancelled was because there was "an idea that there is one defining 'authentic' Asian-American experience that ignores the vast diversity of which we are capable. It discounts the facts that there can be many truths, and holds us [Asian Americans] in a racial spider web."[23]

The racial foreignness of Harold and Kumar is displaced by the regional stereotypes of the American south. As the duo travels through the south, they wear the sleek and simultaneously loud garb of *Miami Vice*, hunting vests and hats in Alabama, and even the robes of the KKK. Asian Americans engage in what American studies scholar Leslie Bow calls "racial interstiality," which is the in-between space of racial categorizations that "creates disorientation" of established categories.[24] For example, a violent rural southern hunter who kills a deer in front of their eyes transforms into an urbane and well-read local man who invites Harold and Kumar back to his modern and technologically progressive home in the backwoods. Their interaction provides an opportunity to show that the stereotypes that Harold and Kumar hold of the south might be just as problematic as the government officials have of them. These encounters tend to focus on how difference appears through accents associated with class and sexuality. Their experiences with African Americans are tangential as Harold and Kumar run away from (and don't even talk with) a group of black men they see. This is a missed opportunity, because they are traveling through Birmingham, Alabama—one of the central sites of the civil-rights movement and the legacy of Martin Luther King Jr. But instead of commenting on how civil-rights history might have connections to racial profiling and detainment at Guantánamo Bay, the film focuses on a more obvious and perhaps safe target of racism—the Ku Klux Klan.

The KKK is portrayed as a group of illiterate party boys who like to share their feelings around the campfire. When Harold and Kumar, who are wearing white hoods that disguise what they look like, are asked to share how they humiliated a minority, Harold talks about how he hit Kumar—a scene the audience just witnessed in the film. Kumar performs the role of a KKK stereotype by adopting the grammatically incorrect sentence structure and slow southern drawl to reveal what he did to a Korean. While the KKK members believe that Harold beat up someone because that person was a racial minority, the audience knows Harold and Kumar are best friends and can laugh at what they say about each other. But at the same time, both Harold and Kumar are minorities who have been the victims of racial discrimination. This scene creates multiple layers of how we think about, talk about, and see racial and ethnic stereotypes. When Harold and Kumar dress up in different clothes or create accents, these performances allow the audience to reaffirm Harold's and Kumar's national (albeit New Jersey) and masculine identities, just as everyone in the film doubts it because Harold and Kumar speak and act as American young men. However, being American does not mean denying their own knowledge about racial and ethnic experiences in the United States. This is particularly true when Harold and Kumar are the inadvertent participants in a KKK meeting. While they wear white hoods over their heads, they can speak to the other members of the Klan because their intonation does not have any recognizable or performed foreign accent, such as broken English or brown voice. Their American accents render them as normative American. When their faces are revealed, the KKK members scream, "Mexicans," and chase after them. They are misidentified as Mexicans (not black and not white and not as terrorists) because the KKK does not seem to recognize Asian Americans. Bow argues, "Asian 'foreign-ness' becomes the conduit to exposing the division not between white and black but between other lines that define superiority and inferiority, normativity and deviance."[25] Being Asian is not only about being a separate racial category but also about exposing hierarchies related to other cultural stereotypes. The KKK already have the cultural image of villains in narratives of the American south, but using Bow's idea, the Asian presence of Harold and Kumar also exposes how the KKK are depicted as inferior and pathetic compared to the other groups Harold and Kumar encounter in the film.

Similar to the first film, on this road trip, Harold and Kumar's class position as middle-class, Ivy league graduates ends up benefitting them, as their college connections become an important part of their racialized network. The early promise of a satirical critique of American national-security practices takes a back seat to the southern stereotypes and a farfetched, long-lost-love story of Kumar. Despite their romp in the unfamiliar south, Harold and Kumar keep on running into people that they know or met in college. When they first come to Miami after escaping from Cuba with Cuban refugees, they say, "Who do we know in Miami?" They contact their college friend Raza Syed, a wealthy Arab American Muslim man who invites Harold and Kumar to his party where he is trying to start a new "bottomless" trend. Raza's racial background does not come up in the film other than to note that he fled the country rather than face questioning by Homeland Security. In other words, the Arab American is erased from this narrative, and the film once again backs away from engaging how national-security policies have affected Muslims. Later, Harold and Kumar meet Neil Patrick Harris (from the first film) and call their friend Rosenberg in New Jersey en route to getting help from fellow alumnus Colton Graham, whose father is a friend of President Bush. The second film builds on the first film's attention to class position and professional status by showing Harold and Kumar as educated minorities who have connections at influential levels of American society.

The third film in the trilogy, *A Very Harold and Kumar 3D Christmas* (2011), once again cowritten by Hurwitz and Schlossberg, follows in the footsteps of the second half of the second film by focusing on how class, professional status, and domesticity have divided the Harold and Kumar couple. The ethnic narrative of model minority in the first film and the racial narrative of terrorist and domestic threat in the second film have been replaced by a color-blind narrative that seeks to breach the distance in Harold and Kumar's relationship and make them a couple again. Following the formula of the stoner genre, there are the traditional errors of mistaken identity, excessive pot smoking, slapstick comedy, and a Claymation sequence. As Roger Ebert notes in his review, "Ethnic jokes are cutting-edge among slack-jawed doper comedies, but sometimes (as in the first and still funny *Harold and Kumar Go to White Castle*), they had touches of wit and insight. Here the humor is intended to pound us over the head."[26] While the film is more a commentary on young professionals growing up and living a domestic life, it is also about bringing together a duo who have been separated. However, the barbed racial and ethnic commentaries that were in the first two films are missing. The main racial references in the film are stereotypes of Maria's large Latino family, who are in the film for a few minutes to tell Harold how he should celebrate a traditional Christmas with a specific type of Christmas tree and about a Christmas tree lot run by two black men. While in the other two films, there were other Asian American characters (students at Princeton, the parents), this film eliminates any mention of their Asian American racial and ethnic backgrounds. Kumar and Harold are whitewashed characters who have no connection to their racial and ethnic community. It is too much credit to give to the film that the driving narrative is to restore their relationship as an ethnic couple (this would be a clever plot) because there is no reference to it in the film.

In the third film, Harold is a successful Wall Street trader in Manhattan who lives in a beautiful house with his wife, Maria, and has given up weed. Kumar, on the other hand, is living in squalor in an empty bachelor apartment and is on a two-year hiatus from medical school after failing a drug test. He finds out that Vanessa, his ex-girlfriend, is pregnant with his child. They are visually racialized characters, but in every other way, they are white, middle-class men in their thirties. Reviewer Neil Genzlinger notes that "in this, their third feature film, they are upstaged by a baby."[27] The first two films reenergized the genre of the stoner comedy by introducing narratives about Asian Americans as the central subject and reorienting the comic commentaries about race. The genre of stoner films allows for risk taking in the name of comedy, and the first two films embraced taking on issues (sometimes with limited success), such as the American Dream, immigration, racial profiling, and detainment. But the last film pulls back to a more standard genre treatment that diminishes the novelty of the other films and reinforces narrative and racial conventions rather than testing them and making us laugh in the process.

Conclusion

While the Harold and Kumar films challenge the ideals of what a model minority is and what an American is, the satirical comedy is limited by its reliance on mostly male stereotypes for comedy and romance. The limitations of the stoner genre do not allow for alternative representations of women other than sexual or romantic objects. While both Harold and Kumar end up with romantic partners at the end of the film trilogy, their relationship to love and matrimony is secondary to the resistance to authority narrative in the stoner genre. And despite the tantalizing title of the second film, the film pulls back from a critique of the policies of national security regarding Guantánamo Bay. The press release for the second film states that the story is a "color-blind" and "agenda-less" political satire with no partisan bias.[28] The promise of the first two films, however, is that they are not "color-blind" and present new types of roles for Asian Americans and South Asian Americans that are not steeped in stereotypes. But the alternative to racial stereotyping does not mean creating "color-blind" roles that treat everyone as the same (as in the third film). Their cultural history and background influence their identity, but it need not be the defining characteristic of their identity or the way others treat them. This is the difference between being color-conscious and being color-blind. Instead, the hope is that Harold and Kumar represent an America that includes people with multiple cultural and ethnic backgrounds. This also includes creating Indian Americans without an accent. What the film shows is that even when Harold, Kumar, and their parents do not speak with accents, others will continue to hear them or see them as exotic others. While most of those who rely on stereotypes to determine their behavior are being mocked by the film, the fact that we recognize these racialized accents shows how embedded they are in American culture and how they continue to be repeated and used in television and film to the extent that they are virtually no other alternative representations. The first two Harold and Kumar films are the exception rather than the trend. Since the release of the first film in 2004, Hollywood has started to cast more South Asian Americans in key roles in film and television. The appeal of the Harold and Kumar films across a wide demographic will be difficult to replicate, but perhaps other writers and directors will be inspired to try cross-casting to reflect the changing nature of American identity.[29]

Epilogue

Well, here's the real America, son.
American tourist to Jamal,
Slumdog Millionaire

Indian Accents presents how racial performance of and by South Asians in American television and film acts as both an expression of privilege and difference with regards to racial identity. The progression of Indian accents, such as brownface and brown-voice performance, is not linear but, in fact, teleological as seen by the reappearance of racial stereotypes and the repetition of Indian vocal accents in different manifestations in film and television. Portrayals of South Asians and South Asian Americans fluctuate among British colonial narratives, Orientalist images, and American model-minority narratives. Contemporary stories have transformed former stereotypes of the native guide and the street-wise orphan into more-modern avatars, such as Apu, the wily immigrant, and Kumar, the patriotic model-minority stoner, who are well-known American cultural icons. In a post–9/11 world where South Asians and South Asian Americans are viewed as possible national-security threats, these racial performances continue to ease American anxieties about difference and promote the American Dream as one of the most valued tenets of American culture.

In the early twenty-first century, South Asians appear in more continuing roles in American television and film than ever before. All four networks as well as various cable stations, such as Bravo, HBO, SyFy Channel, and USA, boasted of Indian male and female characters playing South Asian roles.[1] The 2009 fall lineup on NBC, for example, included four television comedies— *Community* (2009–), *Parks and Recreation* (2008–), *The Office* (2005–), and *30 Rock* (2008–)—broadcast back to back that featured South Asian actors in the ensemble cast. Among South Asian American communities, Thursday night was jokingly referred to as "must see *desi* TV." Because now several depictions of South Asians are on television (film has followed a little more slowly), some diversity to the type of roles presented has come about. South Asians still play doctors, scientists, and reticent computer specialists, but they are also students, middle-class administrators, office workers, legal investigators, and administrative assistants.

Although there is the hope that these Indian characters will break out from the status of sidekick to white majority characters, the Indian characters are variations of the assimilated brownface character, such as Apu, or the suburban brownface teen, such as Gandhi. Characters, such as Kumar, who transgress stereotypical roles are rare. For the most part, these roles are supporting characters that oscillate between playing the assimilated model minority and the exotic colonial other. On television and film, South Asians Americans remain the sidekicks, and India (rather than Indians) is seen as a consumer and tourist destination—a place of material goods. India is seen as an influential economic and world power, and the continuing presence of India as a global power keeps the narratives about South Asians in the American mainstream. South Asians and South Asian Americans speak English, and South Asian culture has a proven market in the United States. South Asians represent a modern, hip, and post–civil rights example of American race relations in the domestic and global arenas. The daily news stories of Afghanistan and Pakistan emphasize the international and foreign aspect of South Asians, and film and television roles consistently reinforce Indians in the United States as immigrants. However, a new variation of brownface performance can be identified as a replacement for the colonial narrative and as a variation on the model-minority narrative that has Indians in India adopting American values and culture while retaining exotic cultural practices, such as dancing and singing.

This chapter's epigraph is from the Academy Award–winning best picture, *Slumdog Millionaire (2008)*, directed by Danny Boyle, set in modern-day India. The film follows the story of a slum-raised Muslim orphan boy in Mumbai who uses his life experiences to answer questions in a game show to win the monetary prize and find romance. The film projects a contemporary image of India and Indians engaged with American culture. Modern India is characterized by the presence of Bollywood film culture, American businesses represented by the call-center industry in India, and a reference (albeit brief and unexplained) to the Hindu-Muslim riots in Mumbai in 1992. Although the setting is in India, there are enough references to American capitalism and consumer practices, including the presence of

American tourists, to make the film both a familiar and exotic narrative. *Slumdog Millionaire* was made with a $15 million budget and opened on only ten screens in the United States in November 2008, but by the time the film left theaters in May 2009, it had grossed over $141 million in the United States and played to a maximum of three thousand screens across the country.[2] The popularity of *Slumdog Millionaire* is a testament to the prominence of American cultural values even though the film is about Indians set in India and, arguably, is a new variation of Indian racial performance. The film is indicative of how American mass media is intent on depicting Indians in a context that diffuses difference and makes Indians more like Americans.

In the scene that the epigraph comes from, teenage Jamal (Tanay Hemant Chheda) has been beaten up in front of the American tourists he is escorting who want to experience "the real India." To the Americans, Jamal plays the street-smart orphan boy straight from traditional British colonial narratives of India. He is a friendly and nonthreatening guide to the slightly dangerous and exotic places in India. However, in this narrative, the solicitous native is transformed into a frustrated individual who bitterly says, "You want to see the real India. Well, here it is." His experience with India is about the constant threat of being beaten and oppressed by those who are physically and economically more powerful. The American woman's response is to hand him American dollars and say, "Well, here's the real America, son." The Americans give him money (a $100 bill with the engraving of inventor Benjamin Franklin) as a means to solve Jamal's social problems. They offer him the promise of the American capital and hope it will work for him in India. However, despite Jamal's efforts at working at a steady job as a tea server in a call center, he cannot elevate his class position. It is the get-rich-quick mechanism of the consumer game show (based on *Who Wants to Be a Millionaire*, the American TV show adapted from the U.K. version) that is his path to advancement and the escape from a lower social-class position.

The audience and critical reception of *Slumdog Millionaire* in India were conflicted, as journalist Madhur Singh describes: "[M]any believe the reason that *Slumdog* has been raking in awards is simply that Western audiences haven't seen many films like it before."[3] Indian film critics gave positive reviews of the film but also predicted that the story appealed more to Western viewers than Indians. Indian author Vikas Swarup commented that his screenplay (the film is based on his 2005 novel *Q and A*) "might have 'fallen by the wayside if it had been made 20 years ago,'" and that at least part of the film's success is because "India is the flavor of the season. People want to know about this country of 9% growth and enormous variety. People want to see what makes India tick."[4] The post-Oscar coverage of the film's awards affirms this view that the popularity of India drives some of the hype around the film.[5] For example, several talk shows, including *Good Morning America*, featured segments on how to dance "Bollywood style" that emphasized the tourist appeal rather than the social message of the film. The film represented another "cultural thing" that could be consumed by Western audiences. This mirrors the history of the 1960s that ushered in Indian culture as a consumable item, but now it is Bollywood dance moves in addition to fashion that is popular with the modern-day youth and adults.[6]

The "real America" in the film is how consumerism and capitalism can pave the way for happiness and success in America and in India. However, *New York Times* critic Manohla Dargis comments that the modern-fairy-tale plot of the film "makes for a better viewing experience than it does for a reflective one. It's an undeniably attractive package, a seamless mixture of thrills and tears, armchair tourism (the Taj Mahal makes a guest appearance during a sprightly interlude) and crackerjack professionalism."[7] Dargis points out the tourist appeal of the film showcases India as an exotic destination. The addition of a Bollywood dance number at the end of the film seems woefully out of place to the rest of the narrative. *Slumdog Millionaire* was adapted for the screen by Simon Beaufoy and directed by Danny Boyle—two British white men.[8] Although the actors are Indian, British Indian, and Indian American, the story caters to Western notions of Indians and Indian culture. The American film industry, the British film industry, and the American public embraced this vision of modern India that cast Indians in familiar American style narratives.

The film also helped shed post–9/11 images of Muslims and brown men as inherently dangerous. Instead, the older Jamal (Dev Patel) was a likable Muslim Indian protagonist whom the audience could root for to succeed. As with *Harold and Kumar Escape from Guantanamo Bay*, this film also reinvents fear and terror embodied by brown bodies in a volatile situation but this time proves them to be self-sacrificing and heroic and safely in India. At the end of the film, Jamal is not immigrating to the United States (he cannot afford it), nor is he threatening American business interests or American culture. He displays no aggression toward the law or the established authority. He is trying to save his brother and the woman he loves—he is trying to restore his family. The drama depicts how traditional brownface narratives of British colonialism have been replaced by racial performances that reaffirm the ideals of the American Dream in India. Indians are becoming more American—they are contestants in American-like game shows, embrace the American ideals of capitalism, and long for a loving family (with a little dancing).

Even though *Slumdog Millionaire* appealed to American audiences and garnered numerous awards, it was not an American undertaking—it was British. After his role in the film, British Indian actor Patel acted in feature films as a middle-class Indian motel manager in British film *The Best Exotic Marigold Hotel* (2011), directed by John Madden, and as the villain Prince Zuko in the fantasy film *The Last Airbender* (2010), directed by M. Night Shyamalan. Patel is also on American television in the Aaron Sorkin's HBO drama *The Newsroom* (2012–), where he plays Neal Sampat, the technology expert who follows news trends on the internet and is the ghostwriter for the main character's blog. His roles follow the trajectory discussed in the introduction as he acts in American-produced stories. He is a science-fiction villain and then plays a variation of the computer nerd. In both cases, he is playing a variation of stereotypical brownface roles despite his breakout performance in his first film.

An attempt to break out of standard narratives and examine brownface and brown-voice racial performance appeared on American television with the development and broadcast of the comedy *Outsourced* (2010–11).[9] In the fall of 2010, NBC launched a situation comedy with five Indian characters in an Indian call center that was the first American television show set outside the United States since *MASH* (1972–83). The premise of the show follows a white, male manager's transfer to India when his company's business is outsourced from Kansas City to India. His job is to oversee the new operation and help train the Indian employees to sell American novelties, such as celebrity bobble-head dolls and yellow Cheeseheads. The series featured an ensemble cast with five South Asian and South Asian American (and Canadian) actors as well as South Asian and South Asian American writers. When it premiered, the show had mixed reviews from the critics, fans, and the South Asian American community.[10] As discussed previously, South Asians are racialized in the American media by their relationship to vocal communications or brown voice, and in the case of *Outsourced*, the call center's employees' ability to mimic American accents in the communications and technology industries is front and center. These portrayals are simultaneously comforting and threatening as South Asians are seen as assimilating in American culture because of their facility with language but also are shown to be an economic threat to national employment because they can also replace Americans (or take away American jobs) as global corporations retain their services instead of American workers.

However, the representation of call center in *Outsourced* takes a different approach than some of the single-Indian sidekick sitcoms because it shows the inconsistencies of American culture while in the process of training young (and somewhat innocent) middle-class Indians to follow American ideals. Instead of India and strange Indian customs being the sole source of humor in the show, the program also pokes fun at foibles and strange practices in American culture. While, on the one hand, this show can be seen as a progressive narrative to interrogate consumer Orientalism and Indian culture, on the other, the television format of the show collapses racial and cultural differences into an American middle-class narrative and thus participates in affirming the power of the nation state to make "everyone more like us," or American. The series was cancelled after one season, so it was not given the chance to develop the Indian characters, but the fact that the series included multiple South Asian and South Asian American writers does offer hope that more-complex stories will be written.

My study of Indian accents and racial performance does not end here but raises more questions and arenas for study. One area that deserves further exploration is how gender depictions change brownface performance. Most of the portrayals in television and film that discussed here are comic performances by men. How do women perform brownface and brown voice and challenge norms, such as marriage and sexuality? British Indian actress Archie Panjabi won an Emmy Award in 2010 for her supporting role as Indian American Kalinda Sharma in *The Good Wife* (2009–). As an investigator for the law firm in the show, Kalinda plays a vital role in the professional cases in the series. Her character exhibits a sultry sexuality that attracts both men and women in the show. She also harbors a mysterious background that includes her having changed her name. But besides her name, we do not get a sense of her as a racial being except through her sexuality. In other respects, she is a color-blind character. We do not see her family, hear her political views, or even see where she lives compared to the other supporting characters; however, this may change as the series progresses. Another popular TV character is physician assistant Divya Katdare, played by actress Reshma Shetty, on the USA drama *Royal Pains* (2009–). Divya is a smart medical professional who has been disowned by her parents after she broke off an arranged-marriage agreement. While her professional and personal lives mirror Indian stereotypes, she has been a breakout star on the show and has created an enthusiastic fan base in India as well as the United States. Outside of drama, one of the more well-known female Indian American comics is Mindy Kaling. As one of the original writers and a coexecutive producer,

Kaling costarred in the American version of *The Office*. She incorporates aspects of being Indian American in the show, such as in the "Diwali" episode, where the characters in the show attend an Indian party celebrating the Diwali holiday.[11] Others try to see her only in terms of media stereotypes of Indians but Kaling's character, Kelly Kapoor, defies conventional racial and gender stereotypes by admitting she doesn't know about Indian culture or by delivering misinformation about her heritage. Kalinda, Divya, and Kelly offer interesting examples to consider how Indian American sexuality and gender complicate Indian racial performance in a future study. Kaling will headline her own comedy on the Fox television network in the fall of 2012. For the first time since Margaret Cho's *All-American Girl* (1994–95) on ABC, an Asian American woman will star in and for the first time produce her own show on network television. Entitled *The Mindy Project*, Kaling plays a single, Indian American doctor who tries to balance her work life and her love life. Another area of inquiry that would be fruitful would be to examine cross-racial performances by actors and discuss the ramifications of multiracial and minority groups playing other minority groups, including probing into Asian-Latino crossovers and how accent is used to racialize Latinos/as, Asians, and South Asians.

Accent has become a central trope to discuss how South Asians are racialized beyond visual and physical descriptions and has become the means to comment on topics such as immigration, masculinity, racial profiling, consumer culture, and New Age spirituality. At the end of a project, one always thinks of new trends to add and other areas to discuss. New examples continue to accrue. Other scholars pursuing further investigations and conversations about racial performance and vocal accents are anticipated. My hope is that *Indian Accents* raises questions about the boundaries and categories used to frame racial performance and cultural nationalisms. Perhaps with new technologies in the entertainment industry, mainstream media will be pushed to challenge the established boundaries to encourage more conversations and alternative narratives of social and cultural identity.

Notes

Introduction. Rethinking Accents in America

1. The episode is Matt Groening's satire about the politics of California's Proposition 187, which was a 1994 statewide initiative to create a citizenship screening program. It also meant to bar undocumented immigrants from using state services, such as healthcare and public education. It passed, but the federal court deemed it unconstitutional. The episode portrays competing notions of citizenship and the social contracts of citizenship that bind the community together. According to *Animated TV* (about.com), this is Groening's third-favorite episode in his list of his top ten.

2. Raymond Williams, *Marxism and Literature* (London: Oxford University Press, 1977).

3. In the 1950s, philosopher Hannah Arendt used the term "audible minorities" to distinguish new immigrants from African American racial or "physical minorities." In her controversial piece "Reflections on Little Rock" (1959), she weighs in on segregation, education, and civil-rights protest. She argues that the manner of protest creates a class of nonwhite "audible minorities" (which includes Jewish immigrants) in contrast to physical minorities (African Americans) to cross into public and popular forums. She distinguishes the racialization of immigrants that includes "white ethnic groups" from the racial categorizations of African Americans grounded in the history of American slavery. Her use of "audible" is specifically related to organized political protest but could also be seen as identifying communication as a means of racial classification.

4. Stuart Hall, "New Ethnicities," in *Stuart Hall: Critical Dialogues in Cultural Studies*, edited by David Morley and Kuan-Hsing Chen (New York: Routledge, 1996), 446.

5. Ella Shohat and Robert Stam, *Unthinking Eurocentrism: Multiculturalism and the Media* (London: Routledge, 1994), 15.

6. Claire Jean Kim, "The Racial Triangulation of Asian Americans," in *Politics and Society* (Sage, 1999), 27:107.

7. Rosina Lippi-Green, *English with an Accent: Language, Ideology, and Discrimination in the United States* (New York: Routledge, 1997), 166.

8. To the American ear, the Midwestern newscaster American accent is ranked and trusted above a Texas drawl because it associated with an educated and standard model of speaking English. The most highly regarded foreign accent is a British accent.

9. Mari J. Matsuda, "Voices of America: Accent, Antidiscrimination Law, and a Jurisprudence for the Last Reconstruction," Centennial Issue, *Yale Law Journal* 100, no. 5 (1991), 1329–407, 1363.

10. See Ian Haney-Lopez, *White by Law* (New York: New York University Press, 1997). The 1923 *U.S. vs. Bhagat Singh Thind* case along with a series of prerequisite court cases (1878–1952) concerning naturalization became the center of debate about citizenship and race and the definition of "whiteness."

11. See Vijay Prasad, *The Karma of Brown Folk* (Minneapolis: University of Minnesota Press, 2000).

12. The English Only movements and American schools in the Philippines are only two possible examples of how language and accent are related to national origins.

13. See Mia Tuan, *Forever Foreigners or Honorary Whites? The Asian Ethnic Experience Today* (New Brunswick: Rutgers University Press, 1999), and Robert G. Lee, *Orientals: Asian Americans in Popular Culture* (Philadelphia: Temple University Press, 1999), for a larger discussion of the depiction of Asian Americans as perpetually foreign.

14. Mae Ngai, *Impossible Subjects: Illegal Aliens and the Making of Modern America* (Princeton, NJ: Princeton University Press, 2004), 37. See also Nazli Kabria's work on South Asian Americans including *Muslims in Motion: Islam and National Identity in the Bangladeshi Diaspora* (New Brunswick, NJ: Rutgers University Press, 2011). Historically, the first recorded presence of an Asian Indian (as Indian immigrants were initially categorized to distinguish them from American Indians and Native American populations) occurred in 1790. But even within the category of Asians, Indian immigrants (or "Hindoos" as this group was initially identified in the early twentieth century) did not fit into the racial definitions of the Chinese and Japanese, who were described by a combination of physical characteristics and country of origin.

15. There are useful studies of encounters between South Asians and populations of white persons, Africans, and Latinos and the process of racialization that occurs in these encounters. See the works of Neil Bhatia (2007), Vijay Prasad (2000), Karen Leonard (1992), and Shalini Shankar (2007).

16. See Haney-Lopez, *White by Law*.

17. Indian independence from Great Britain and Filipino independence from the United States were scheduled to happen in the following year, and so the United States was recognizing both new countries. The Philippines celebrated its independence in 1946, and India and Pakistan were independent nations in 1947. The changes first

began in 1946 when Congress approved the Luce-Celler Act, which granted natu-ralization rights to one hundred Asian Indians and Filipinos per year. The 1952 Mc-Carren Act eliminated all race-based exclusion, and quotas per individual country replaced it. In the 1965 Immigration Act, quotas from Eastern and Western Hemi-spheres replaced quotas by country and provided the foundation for contemporary immigration policies and debates.

18. The preferential order for immigration specified a partiality for adults, profes-sionals, artists, and those with needed skills before any other groups and also did not count immediate family as part of the quota allotment. The South Asian population went from less than 10,000 in 1965 to a recorded population of 525,000 in 1985 and 815,000 in 1990. By 2000, over 1.2 million South Asians were in the United States. Currently, South Asians are the third-largest U.S. Asian group with a population of almost 2 million in the United States, behind Chinese and Southeast Asians.

19. Many South Asians check the "Other" box rather Asian American because most South Asians identify themselves by national identity, such as Indian or Pakistani, and do not consider themselves "Asian" or from the Far East.

20. I first came across the term "privileged minority" when I was applying for fel-lowships in graduate school in 1992 at the University of Michigan. Although other racialized minority groups were eligible for minority merit fellowships, Indians were specifically determined ineligible because the administration deemed them a "privi-leged minority." In other words, because Indians were already represented enough in the graduate programs (particularly in the sciences), there was no need to recruit more. Other Asian ethnicities that are often barred from these fellowships, such as Chinese and Japanese, faced no such exclusion. I must point out that I was the only person of South Asian ethnic background in the English graduate program for five years, and on their books I did count as a minority. So I simultaneously was and wasn't a minority, and this experience was one that fueled my interest in Indians in America from a very early stage.

21. Eric Newburger and Thomas Gryn, *The Foreign-Born Labor Force in the United States: 2007*, American Community Survey Reports, U.S. Census Bureau, Econom-ics and Statistics Administration, U.S. Department of Commerce, December 2009, http://www.census.gov/prod/2009pubs/acs-10.pdf, 5–9, accessed January 15, 2010.

22. Ibid. The largest number of foreign-born residents of the United States comes from Mexico followed by China. The next two largest populations are from the Phil-ippines and India. If other South Asian groups are added to the Indian population, they are the third-largest immigrant population in the United States.

23. Ibid.

24. Many incidents of violence have occurred, but some of the most documented include the murder of Feroze Moody and the rise of the "Dot-Buster" gangs in the Northeast in the 1980s. Valerie Kaur's documentary *Divided We Fall* (2005) discusses the murder of a Sikh business owner just after 9/11.

25. See Shilpa Davé, Pawan Dhingra, Sunaina Maira, Partha Mazumdar, Lavina

Dhingra Shankar, Jaideep Singh, and Rajini Srikanth, "De-Privileging Positions: Indian Americans, South Asian Americans, and the Politics of Asian American Studies," *Journal of Asian American Studies* 3, no. 1 (2000): 67–100.

26. Rajini Srikanth, *The World Next Door: South Asian American Literature and the Idea of America* (Philadelphia: Temple University Press, 2006), 5.

27. For more information, see the anthologies *Alien Encounters: Popular Culture in Asian America*, ed. Mimi Thi Nguyen and Thuy Linh Nyguen Tu (Durham, NC: Duke University Press, 2007), and *East Main Street: Asian American Popular Culture*, ed. Shilpa Davé, LeiLani Nishime, and Tasha G. Oren (New York: New York University Press, 2005). In media studies, scholars Darrell Hamamoto, Peter Feng, and Gina Marchetti reiterate how Asian Americans continue to represent the exotic and the foreign in American film and television, but these scholars tend not to address South Asian Americans in their studies.

28. Scholars, such as Lisa Lowe, argue that the Orient and the Occident are not monolithic entities but are heterogeneous. Lowe explains that Asian Americans destabilize the monolithic notion of the Orient because of the contradictions of their subjectivity and cultural expressions within the complex systems of capitalism, patriarchy, and race relations that make up national identity. See Lowe, *Immigrant Acts: On Asian American Cultural Politics* (Durham, NC: Duke University Press, 1996). Lowe insists. "It is through the terrain of national culture that the individual subject is politically formed as the American citizen." 67.

29. Ibid.

30. David Palumbo-Liu, *Asian/American: Historical Crossings of a Racial Frontier* (Stanford, CA: Stanford University Press, 1999), 2.

31. Ibid., 1.

32. Ibid., 2.

33. Eric Lott, *Love and Theft: Blackface Minstrelsy and American Working Class* (New York: Oxford University Press, 1995), 4.

34. Michael Rogin, *Blackface, White Noise: Jewish Immigrants in the Hollywood Melting Pot* (Berkeley: University of California Press, 1998), 77.

35. Ibid.

36. Josephine D. Lee, *The Japan of Pure Invention: Gilbert & Sullivan's* The Mikado (Minneapolis: University of Minnesota Press, 2010), 93.

37. R. G. Lee, *Orientals: Asian Americans in Popular Culture* (Philadelphia: Temple University Press, 1999), 2.

38. Mary Beltrán, "Dolores Del Rio, the First 'Latin Invasion,' and Hollywood's Transitions to Sound," *Aztlán* 30, no. 1 (2005): 55–83.

39. Ibid., 66.

40. Ibid., 67.

41. R. G. Lee, *Orientals*, 37.

42. Angela C. Pao, "False Accents: Embodied Dialects and the Characterization of Ethnicity and Nationality," *Theater Topics* 14, no. 1 (2004): 353–72.

43. Ibid., 353. This quotation Pao uses is from Donald H. Molin, *Actor's Encyclopedia of Dialects*.

44. Comedy as a genre has been a medium for social and cultural critique. The work of Mikhail Bakhtin in *Rabelais and His World* (Bloomington: Indiana University Press, 1984) suggests elements of comedy cut across all social classes in his discussion of the carnival in the eighteenth century. The contrast between the grotesque and the real is the definition of exaggeration and offers a new way of thinking about what is real. Ethnic comedy in the United States has its roots in minstrelsy, the theater, and now stand-up, which the next chapter discusses further.

45. R. G. Lee, *Orientals*, 35.

46. Ibid.

47. Yen Espiritu's classic text *Asian American Women and Men: Labor, Laws, and Love* (Lanham, Md.: Rowman and Littlefield, 1997) discusses the effect of the racially specific immigration laws on family dynamics and gender dynamics of Asian Americans. Antimiscegenation policies effectively outlawed mixed marriages in many areas of the United States, and so Chinese immigrant men who remained in the United States and Asian communities in general (especially Chinese, Indian, and Filipino) had large bachelor communities without necessarily having the possibility to have a hetereonormative family life.

48. The Page Law was designed to stop Chinese prostitution in the West and reduce the number of Chinese women who were being brought over for the purposes of prostitution. The enforcement of the law tended to assume that all Asian women were prostitutes, and, hence, immigration of women (with the exception of merchant daughters and relatives of high officials) ceased. The Chinese Exclusion Act was the first time the United States barred immigration on the basis of race or nationality. The first act of ten years was extended another ten years and effectively reduced Chinese immigration until the act was lifted during World War II when China became an ally of the United States.

49. There is a long history of Asians in visual media from the yellow man in D. W. Griffith's 1919 *Broken Blossoms* to Long Duk Don in John Huston's 1984 film *Sixteen Candles*. Darrell Hamamoto's book *Monitored Peril: Asian Americans and the Politics of TV Representation* gives a solid history of Asians on television, and other books, such as Peter Feng's *Screening Asian Americans*, discuss both the representations and challenges to the stereotypes that appear in contemporary film.

50. Linda Hutcheon, *Irony's Edge: The Theory and Politics of Irony* (London: Routledge, 1994), 4, and *A Theory of Parody: The Teachings of Twentieth Century Art Forms* (Urbana: University of Illinois Press, 2000), 6.

51. Michael Ray Fitzgerald, "Evolutionary Stages of Minorities in the Mass Media: An Application to American Indian Television Representations," *Howard Journal of Communications* 21, no. 4 (2010): 367–84. Fitzgerald mentions communication studies scholar Cedric Clark's 1969 editorial in *Television Quarterly*, which first discussed these stages of representation.

Chapter 1. South Asians and the Hollywood Party

1. This is one of the first national representations of brownface performance with musical artist Korla Pandit, who had a national television show in San Francisco from the 1950s to the 1970s. He is seen as a precursor to Liberace. African American John Roland Redd developed the character Korla Pandit. There is not much information on him, and this would be a fascinating history to pursue.

2. Hank Azaria, "Azaria Has Hopes for 'Huff,'" interview by Terry Gross, *Fresh Air, National Public Radio*, podcast audio, December 6, 2004, http://www.npr.org/templates/rundowns/rundown.php?prgId=13&prgDate=12-6-2004, accessed August 15, 2007.

3. Mike Myers, "Myers' Path from Wayne to 'Love Guru,'" interview by Terry Gross, *Fresh Air, National Public Radio*, podcast audio, September 19, 2008, http://www.npr.org/templates/rundowns/rundown.php?prgId=13&prgDate=9-19-2008, accessed August 1, 2011.

4. As noted in the introduction, some South Asian diaspora scholars, such as Jigna Desai and Gayatri Gopinath, have discussed the representation of the South Asian diaspora in the United States in American, British, and South Asian films in important comparative studies, but they have not engaged directly with the ethnic representations and mainstream American media history.

5. Mandel Herbstman, review, *The Party, Motion Picture Daily*, March 22, 1968.

6. Gina Marchetti, *Romance and the Yellow Peril: Race, Sex, and Discursive Strategies in Hollywood Fiction* (Berkeley: University of California Press, 1993), 7.

7. Scholars James Chapman and Nicolas Cull, in their book *Projecting Empire: Imperialism and Popular Cinema* (New York: Tauris, 2009), note that the birth of cinema occurred at the "zenith of British imperialism and with the first stirrings of America as an imperial power." 1. Romantic stories and the products of British colonialism were already prominent in American popular culture through literature, consumer goods, and theater at the turn into the twentieth century, and with the advent of the motion picture, some of the earliest images continued to promote American and British presence in Asia, Africa, the Caribbean, and South America as heroic enterprises.

8. Dorothy B. Jones, *The Portrayal of China and India on the American Screen, 1896–1955* (Cambridge: MIT Press, 1955). Jones notes that most of the films made about Asia focused on China (5:1 ratio) over India, and before World War II, few films depicted a realistic picture of India, outside of the adventure stories of Kipling. She identifies thirty out of the sixty-six total films (which include features, documentaries, and short subjects from 1896 she catalogued about India) were produced between 1940 and 1954. 51, 52.

9. Homi K. Bhabha, *The Location of Culture* (New York: Routledge, 1994), 67.

10. Eric Lott, *Love and Theft: Black Minstrelsy and American Working Class* (New York: Oxford University Press, 1995).

11. D. B. Jones, *Portrayal of China and India*, 53.

12. Ibid., 55.

13. During the 1940s, one of the most well-known Indian actors onscreen was Sabu the Elephant Boy (Sabu Dastagir or Selar Shaik Sabu). British movie director Alexander Korda discovered him in South India at the age of twelve and sent him to England to learn English. Sabu eventually starred in twenty-three films, including *The Elephant Boy* (1937), *The Thief of Baghdad* (1940), and *Song of India* (1949). His image as the wily and mischievous native youth endures and is a role model for other portrayals of native or Indian youth, such as Kipling's famous character Mowgli in *The Jungle Book* (1942). In 1944, Sabu became a naturalized American citizen and continued to act until his death in 1963. Gary Brumburgh, "Sabu," IMDB Biography, imdb.com, http://www.imdb.com/name/nm0754942/bio, accessed March 2, 2010.

14. D. B. Jones, *Portrayal of China and India*, 55.

15. Christina Klein, *Cold War Orientalism: Asia in the Middlebrow Imagination, 1945–1961* (Berkeley: University of California Press, 2003), 5.

16. See Deborah Gee, *Slaying the Dragon* (1988).

17. Chapman and Cull, *Projecting Empire*, 67–86, 76, 77. Set in Ceylon (now Sri Lanka), which gained independence from the British in 1948, a newly married American bride (Elizabeth Taylor) arrives at her English husband's tea plantation to find that the "old" way of life of ruling the plantation and placating the natives no longer applies in the modern world. The plantation is run over and destroyed by elephants at the end of the film, forcing the couple to rebuild their house and their life in a new, decolonized world. But as the authors point out, the only protests to the remnants of imperialism in Ceylon are about the elephants, not the Ceylonese.

18. Jeffrey Melnick and Rachel Rubin, *Immigration and Popular Culture* (New York: New York University Press, 2008), 139.

19. The first film, *The Pink Panther* (1963), marked the beginning of a longtime collaboration between British director/writer Blake Edwards and British actor Peter Sellers.

20. Peter Sellers comments on his process of how he develops a character: "Well, having got to the stage where one sees a final script and has discussed the part with all concerned, I start with the voice. I find out how the character sounds. It's through the way he speaks that I find out the rest about him. I suppose that approach comes from having worked in radio for so long. After the voice comes the looks of the man. I do a lot of drawings of the character I play. Then I get together with the makeup man and we sort of transfer my drawings onto my face. An involved process." "Candid Conversation," interview, *Playboy Magazine* 9, October 1962. In *The Party*, Sellers rarely speaks so the emphasis is on his physical performance.

21. George Martin, who commissioned and produced the song, was the producer of Peter Sellers's comedy recording. It was a top-five British single in 1960 and helped to promote the film.

22. Andrew Sarris, review, *Village Voice*, March 1968.

23. *Indiana Jones and the Temple of Doom* also features the infamous scene where monkey brains were served as a delicacy to Indy and his friends in the rajah's palace. For an example of a review critical of this scene, see Vincent Canby, movie review, *Indiana Jones and the Temple of Doom*, *New York Times*, May 23, 1984, http://movies .nytimes.com/movie/review?res=9D06E5DF173BF930A15756C0A962948260.

24. R. G. Lee, *Orientals*, 190.

25. Stephen Hong Sohn, "Racialized Future," *MELUS* 33, no. 4 (2008): 5–22.

26. Jane Park, *Yellow Future: Oriental Style in Hollywood Cinema* (Minneapolis: University of Minnesota Press, 2010).

27. See David Morely and Kevin Robins, "Techno-Orientalism: Futures, Foreigners and Phobias," *New Formations* 16 (1992): 136–56, and Lisa Nakamura, *Cybertypes, Race, Ethnicity, and Identity on the Internet* (New York: Routledge, 2002), for discussions of how this term operates in popular culture and internet studies.

28. Jigna Desai, *Beyond Bollywood: The Cultural Politics of South Asian Diasporic Film* (New Brunswick, NJ: Rutgers University Press, 2004).

29. British Indian director Gurinder Chadha has been one of the few filmmakers who make dramatic comedies. Commercially successful films, such as *Bhaji on the Beach* (1993), *Bend It like Beckham* (2002), and *Bride and Prejudice* (2004), all include elements of satire of American, British, and Indian culture.

Chapter 2. Apu's Brown Voice

1. I have previously defined "cultural citizenship" as being seen as a permanent part of the popular imagination of a specific nation or culture. See Shilpa Davé, "'Community Beauty': Transnational Embodiments and Cultural Citizenship in 'Miss India Georgia,'" *Lit: Literature Interpretation Theory* 12, no. 3 (2001): 335–58. This is distinct from a political citizenship that promises equal rights under the law. Cultural citizenship is associated with quintessentially American images, such as cowboys, baseball, and American accents.

2. Carole A. Stabile and Mark Harrison's collection *Prime Time Animation: Television Animation and American Culture* (New York: Routledge, 2003), features historical and critical analysis of televised animated shows in relation to American cultural life but does not address the racial politics of performance. Michelle Hilmes discusses the concept of the voice and accents in her study on radio drama, but virtually no work has been done on the voices behind the animated scripts that have been generated since the 1930s.

3. See Kaja Silverman, *The Acoustic Mirror* (Bloomington: Indiana University Press, 1988). Also thanks to David Eng for pointing out the resonance of queer theory with this work.

4. D. L. Rubin's 1992 study of the effects of accent and ethnicity between undergraduates and nonnative teaching assistants is cited in Rosina Lippi-Green, *English with an Accent*, 127.

5. Films such as Joel Schumacher's *Falling Down* (1993) and Spike Lee's *Do the Right Thing* (1989) show how the black community is frustrated with the Korean grocery-store owner. Lee's films *The 25th Hour* (2002) and *Do the Right Thing* also include a series of "rants" about different ethnic and racial communities.

6. Lippi-Green, *English with an Accent*, 64.

7. Legal Scholar Mari Matsuda presents several legal cases that detail how accent discrimination is routinely neglected under the employment discrimination clause of the 1964 Civil Rights Act. Accent is seen as related to "not being understood" rather than outright racial discrimination in the workplace and so not a clear-cut violation of the law. Matsuda argues that even though the courts and the Equal Employment Opportunity Commission (EEOC) have stated that discriminating against accents associated with foreign birth is discrimination by national origin and a violation of Title VII of the 1964 Civil Rights Act, plaintiffs do not win accent discrimination cases. See Matsuda, "Voices of America: Accent, Antidiscrimination Law, and a Jurisprudence from the Last Reconstruction," *Yale Law Journal* 100 (1991), 1329–467.

8. Rosina Lippi-Green, "Accent, Standard Language Ideology, and Discriminatory Pretext in the Courts," *Language in Society* 23, no. 2 (1994): 163–98.

9. Ibid., 165.

10. In G. N. Trenité's speech exercise book *Drop Your Foreign Accent* (Haarlem: H. D. Tjeenk Willink and Zoon, 1944), the author declares in his preface: "Your most distinguished speaker, wonderful though his fluency may be, correct his grammar and admirable his choice of words, is the awkward man as long as he has not dropped his foreign accent. . . . He irritates. There is a distinct element of courtesy in the foreigner's correct pronunciation—the thought: I have deemed it worth my while to grapple with the difficulties of your language, till I have overcome them. This pleases as much as slovenly pronunciation displeases. It is an open letter of recommendation, like a clear handwriting, a neat dress or a handsome face" (7). In other words, good pronunciation reflects proper respect and manners for the dominant culture, and, hence, if one can practice them, one, too, can become a good citizen. But of particular interest is the idea of "irritation," because essentially what the book is preaching is the idea of a unified and homogenous nationalism and the fact that different races and social classes arise is contrary to that ideal.

11. "Broken English" is an interesting phrase—to break English is to shake up the unified notion of what is national identity, an identity people cling to that is not rooted in experience of immigration but instead in the process of the way in which they culturally express themselves such as the American accent.

12. See Morris Young, "Whose Paradise? Hawai'i, Desire, and the Global-Local Tensions of Popular Culture," *in East Main Street: Asian American Popular Culture*, ed. Shilpa Davé, LeiLani Nishime, and Tasha Oren (New York: New York University, 2005), 183–203.

13. Michele Hilmes, *Radio Voices* (Minneapolis: University of Minnesota Press, 1997), 13.

14. See Anonymous, "Moreover: Broadcasting to the Nation," *Economist*, March 27, 1999, 86.

15. Hilmes, *Radio Voices*, 89.

16. Ibid.

17. The 1930s radio program *Amos 'n' Andy* was one of the first radio dramas that featured black characters (voiced by white men) and also the most popular radio drama of its time.

18. See Stabile and Harrison, *Prime Time Animation*.

19. The most recent count is fourteen awards for voice over performances. "ASCAP Film and Television Music Awards," "Awards for The Simpsons," imdb.com, http://www.imdb.com/title/tt0096697/awards, accessed July 1, 2012.

20. As Wendy Hilton-Morrow and David T. McMahan note in their chapter "*The Flintstones* to *Futurama*: Networks and Prime Time Animation" in Stabile and Harrison, *Prime Time Animation*, the first prime-time animated drama to deliver social commentary and satire was *The Flintstones*, which first aired on ABC in 1961 until it went off the air in 1966 and then reappeared in syndication on Saturday mornings in the 1970s.

21. In May 2012, the marketing firm for Popchips pulled an advertisement from the internet that featured actor Ashton Kutcher in brownface performing brown voice, due to large-scale protests online about racial and racist representations of Indians and Indian Americans. Sara Khan, "Do We Amuse You?" India Ink, global edition: India, *New York Times*, May 14, 2012, http://nyti.ms/L2rXT0.

22. The most notable exception, as my colleague Lisa Nakamura pointed out to me, is Jar-Jar Binks from the *Star Wars* films. Not only did his accent irritate but it also inflamed talk about racial representations and computer-graphic characters. Interestingly enough, there are Web sites from which one can download the latest films where fans have eliminated the character Jar-Jar from the narrative.

23. Disney began this practice after the success of Robin Williams as the genie in the animated feature *Aladdin* (1992). This is now common practice for animated feature films.

24. Eric Garrison, "The Simpsons: A Reflection of Society and a Message on Family," November 12, 2001, *The Simpsons Archive*, http://www.snpp.com/other/papers/eg.paper.html, accessed March 2003.

25. Kristal Brent Zook, *Color by Fox: The Revolution in Black Television* (London: Oxford University Press, 1999), 4.

26. Ibid., 5.

27. Daniel Kimmel, *The Fourth Network: How Fox Broke the Rules and Invented Television* (Lanham, MD: Ivan R. Dee, 2004), 97.

28. Dean Kuipers, "'3rd Degree: Harry Shearer,'" *Los Angeles: CityBeat*, April 15, 2004, http://www.lacitybeat.com/cms/story/detail/?id=568&IssueNum=32, accessed November 3, 2009.

29. Anita C. Ramdharry, "Ay Carumba: *The Simpsons*: A Transnational Text to a Transnational Audience" (master's thesis, University of North Dakota, 2001), 144.

30. As my colleagues Grace Hong and Victor Bascara have observed to me, Apu is a part of Homer's bowling team rather than a member of "The Stereotypes" team in the episode "Pin Pals."

31. "Lisa the Vegetarian," season 7, episode 5, *The Simpsons: The Complete Seventh Season*, 1995 (Twentieth Century Fox, 2005), DVD.

32. Nancy Basile, "The Simpsons Characters: Homer Simpson and the Rest of Springfield," *Animated TV*, about.com, http://animatedtv.about.com/od/lists/tp/sicharacters.htm, accessed February 12, 2003.

33. See Amit Rai, "The World according to Apu: A Look at Network Television's Only Regular South Asian Character," *India Currents* 7, no. 12 (1994): 7. Rai mentions that the character of Apu is depicted as a greedy storekeeper. Actually, this character trait is one that reoccurs from colonial narratives that feature the greedy native that can be bribed but ultimately is killed by his greed. Variations on this theme are seen from the Indiana Jones films to *The Mummy* films.

34. *The Guru*, directed by Daisy von Scherler Mayer (2003; DVD Universal Studios), DVD.

35. Robert Lee asserts that Asians fall into two categories: the alien and/or the foreigner. The alien is considered an ever-present pollutant, whereas the foreigner is considered a sojourner or traveler who will eventually go away. Both labels imply a distance from the community. Lee contends "Orientals" have been produced by popular culture to fit these categories. Apu, however, is seen as part of the Springfield community, but his alien-ness is magnified when the show focuses on him. *Orientals: Asian American Popular Culture* (Philadelphia: Temple University Press, 2000), 5.

36. In the same first season, George Takei is the guest voice of Akira, a waiter at a Japanese sushi restaurant, and Sab Shimono does the voiceover of the Master Chef. So Asian Americans are brought in to do voiceovers but not characters.

37. Joe Rhodes, "Flash! 24 Simpsons Stars Reveal Themselves," *TV Guide*, October 21, 2000.

38. In an article written on the widely popular Web site *The Simpsons Archive*, Eric Garrison reflects on the cultural messages of the show: "Already, the show had a few stereotypes, or portraits of the modern American family. The first few seasons of *The Simpsons* pointed fun at many American issues and provided their own ethical solutions to many moral dilemmas. In the seasons to come, more characters would enter the show, and the show itself would grow from a small cast, to a cast of hundreds. One of the main issues that some of the public would begin hold to against the show was stereotyping." Garrison, "Simpsons."

39. S. Ali, "Will the Real Apu Please Stand Up?" *India Abroad* 33, no. 10 (2001): M5.

40. Garrison, "Simpsons."

41. Similarly, Indian American director M. Night Shyamalan often introduces a

secondary character played by an Indian or minority character (usually himself) in his films who by his or her very presence visually confirms the diverse world by showing brown people who are doctors, art consumers, potential drug dealers, and engaged couples without marking them as "foreign" or "strange." He highlights the presence of Indian Americans without stereotyping what they are by accent or race or religion but rather locating Indian Americans as an everyday part of American cultural geography.

42. Paul Cantor, "The Simpsons' America," *Wilson Quarterly* 25, no. 3 (2001): 33, and Cantor, "Atomistic Politics and the Nuclear Family," *Political Theory* 27, no. 6 (1999): 734–49. Political scientist Cantor convincingly applies this statement to the show's tendency to lampoon both the right and left wings of government and portray the lack of trust of those in power, especially those who are not local community members.

43. One of the earliest cartoon depictions of a reoccurring Indian character was Hadji (voiced by Michael Bravo), the sidekick of adventure boy/ sleuth Johnny Quest in *The Adventures of Johnny Quest*. I vividly remember watching this show in syndication in the 1970s and being very pleased to see an Indian boy on television. Some of the episodes were set in India so I saw some Indian girls, too. Interestingly enough, it was initially aired as a prime-time animated series on ABC. Produced in 1964 by Hanna-Barbera Productions, Hadji was the turban-clad boy who had "magic" or mystical powers that usually went wrong and made the situation worse for the boys. A 1990s update of the show presents Hadji as the now-adopted son of Dr. Quest (now Johnny's brother). Hadji is particularly adept in the sciences and with computer technology.

44. T. B. Macaulay, "Minute on Education," in *Sources of Indian Tradition*, vol. 2, Modern India and Pakistan, ed. Stephen Hay (New York: Columbia University Press, 1958), 49.

45. In his groundbreaking work, *Orientalism*, Edward Said enumerates the many ways in which Europe has constructed a tangible other, the East, in order to reinforce its own identity as a masterful civilized power. In essence, colonial holdings, such as India, were conceptualized as "a locale requiring Western attention, reconstruction, even redemption. The Orient existed as a place isolated from the mainstream of European progress in the sciences, arts, and commerce." *Orientalism* (New York: Vintage, 1978), 206.

46. Homi K. Bhabha, "Of Mimicry and Man: The Ambivalence of Colonial Discourse," in *The Location of Culture*, ed. Homi Bhabha (New York: Routledge, 1994), 86.

47. The amalgamation of Hindi and English, Hinglish, is common in Bollywood film as well as in Indian immigrant communities.

Chapter 3. Animating Gandhi

1. A series of cartoon ads featured Gandhi being beaten up by and at the mercy of a muscular, blond, white man in the February 2003 issues of the men's magazine *Maxim*. The magazine, an international men's publication based in Great Britain, has

special editions for several countries, including India. The editors issued an apology on January 30, 2003, the anniversary of Gandhi's death and four days after India issued a protest, which started on January 26, 2003, India's Republic Day.

2. "MTV Ridicules Gandhi Using 'Clone,'" *The Hindu*, January 30, 2003, http://hindu.com/2003/01/30/stories/2003013001751200.html, accessed October 22, 2005.

3. Ashok Sharma, "MTV's Gandhi 'Insult' Outrages Indian MPs," *The Guardian*, January 31, 2003, http://www.guardian.co.uk/media/2003/jan/31/pressandpublishing.india?INTCMP=SRCH.

4. *Clone High* was created by Phil Lord, Christopher Miller, and Bill Lawrence (also creator of the NBC situation comedy *Scrubs*). The series, coproduced by Nelvana (Canada) and MTV, was shown in both Canada and the United States, but the full run of episodes was only broadcast in Canada. The show is a parody of the teen dramas of the 1990s such as *Saved by the Bell*, *Beverly Hills 90210*, and *Dawson's Creek*.

5. The *Jyllands Posten*–Muhammad controversy happened in September 2005 after the Danish newspaper *Jyllands Posten* on September 30, 2005, published twelve political editorial cartoons that depicted the Islamic prophet Muhammad. Muslins first held protests in Denmark, and then protests occurred all over the world.

6. Kal Penn, commentary, on the convenience-store scene, special features, *Harold and Kumar Go to White Castle*, directed by Danny Leiner (2004; unrated extended edition, New Line Home Video, December 2005), DVD.

7. Richard Fung, "Looking for My Penis: The Eroticized Asian in Gay Video Porn," in *How Do I Look: Queer Film and Video*, ed. Bad Object-Choices (Seattle: Bay Press, 1991), 148.

8. MTV India has its central office in Mumbai, India, and is a subsidiary of MTV Networks (owned by Viacom), which has headquarters in New York City. It is the most popular music channel in India and has spawned many Indian channels that have copied its format. MTV (the original U.S.-based channel) was first was broadcast in India in 1991 and with the launch of regional MTV India in 1996 has created a blockbuster business that has outgrown global stations such as CNN.

9. "MTV Apologizes for Show's Gandhi Lampoon," Entertainment Television and Culture, Associated Press Online, Lexus Nexus, January 31, 2003, accessed August 31, 2007, my emphasis.

10. Maxim's apology statement from editor-in-chief Keith Blanchard to India also takes a similar tone where he justifies the representation of Gandhi being shown kicked and beaten by a white bodybuilder ("Maxim's Kick-Ass Workout") by saying it was intended as ironic humor. The statement, in Maxim's May 2003 issue, reads: "We apologize if our cartoon depicting Mahatma Gandhi in the February 2003 issue of Maxim was interpreted as offensive. An edgy sense of humor, laced with irony, has always been a central element of Maxim's editorial. For some people, this piece may have gone one step too far. We at Maxim do, in fact, believe in Gandhi's teachings of peace. *In fact, we chose Gandhi as the subject of our workout cartoon specifically*

because he is the least likely target of aggression imaginable. No offense was intended to anyone" (my italics). The historical ignorance associated with this statement and the lack of understanding of how Asian men are seen in a post–9/11 world seem to have eluded the editor.

11. Phil Lord, quoted in Josh Grossberg, "MTV Apologizes for Gandhi Goofing," *E! Online*, January 31, 2003, http://www.eonline.com/print/index.jsp?uuid=c520a80c -f8ba-4e92–9355-cbbf7c15647a&contentType=newsStory.

12. The show creators did not select any black figures as central characters in the show such as Martin Luther King Jr. or Malcolm X perhaps because to parody these men would have probably caused them and MTV problems with African American groups in the United States. The only black figure on the show is inventor George Washington Carver, whom most people associate with the peanut. However, the show still needed someone to represent minority interests. Although there were several people to choose from, such as Mao Tse-tung, Golda Meir, Indira Gandhi, Cesar Chavez, or Che Guevara, among others, the creators chose Mohandas Gandhi.

13. Tom Lowry, "Can MTV Stay Cool?" *Business Week*, February 20, 2006.

14. Kobena Mercer, "Monster Metaphors: Notes on Michael Jackson's 'Thriller,'" *Screen* 27, no. 1 (1986): 26–43.

15. Andrew Goodwin, "Fatal Distractions: MTV Meets Postmodern Theory," in *Sound and Vision: The Music Video Reader*, ed. Simon Frith, Andrew Goodwin, and Lawrence Grossberg (New York: Routledge, 1992), 52–65.

16. John Kraszewski, "'I Don't Know Who You Are': Multiracialism, *The Real World*, and MTV's New Brand," presentation, 2008 Annual Meeting for Society of Cinema and Media Studies, Philadelphia, Pennsylvania, March 8, 2008.

17. Kraszewski draws heavily from an April 4, 2004, *Village Voice* article, "Rage against the Machine," pointing out that Rowe was charged with replacing the liberal nature of programming to a nonpartisan stance that included conservative and liberal viewpoints. For the first time, the Republican National Committee appeared on the channel, and MTV reality celebrities with conservative values promoted registering to vote.

18. R. Anderson Sutton. "Local, Global, or National? Popular Music on Indonesian Television," in *Planet TV: A Global Television Reader*, ed. Lisa Parks and Shanti Kumar (New York: New York University Press, 2003), 320–40.

19. Currently, there are specialized MTV channels for particular countries in Asia, including MTV Korea, MTV Japan, MTV Pakistan, MTV Philippines, and MTV Indonesia.

20. Kraszewski, "'I Don't Know Who You Are.'"

21. A number of studies and articles discuss the representation of Asian American masculinity and femininity. For more on the history of Asian American masculinity, see David Eng, *Racial Castration: Managing Masculinity in Asian American* (Durham, NC: Duke University Press, 2001), and Martin Manalansan, *Global Divas: Filipino Gay Men in the Diaspora* (Durham, NC: Duke University Press, 2003). For work on rep-

resentations of Asian American women, see Deborah Gee's documentary *Slaying the Dragon* (1988), Elaine Kim's documentary *Slaying the Dragon: Reloaded: Asian Women in Hollywood and Beyond* (2011), and Laura Hyun Yi Kang, *Compositional Subjects: Enfiguring Asian/American Women* (Durham, NC: Duke University Press, 2002).

22. Robert Lee discusses these images in *Orientals: Asians in American Popular Culture*, and Darrell Hamamoto in history of Asian Americans on television from the 1950s to the 1980s details the specific roles Asians were allowed to play in *Monitored Peril*.

23. William Peterson, "Success Story, Japanese-American Style," *New York Times Magazine*, January 9, 1966, 20–21, 33, 36, 38, 40–41, 43; "Success Story of One Minority in the U.S.," *U.S. News and World Report*, December 26, 1966, 73–78.

24. Keith Osajima quoted in "Success Story," 75.

25. The creators of the show, David Guarascio and Moses Port, wanted to use the character to explore issues of faith and spirituality, but "when they finally settled on Raja because of the topical possibilities the character would create, he [Guarascio] knew little about Muslims and had to do research." Mrinalini Reddy, "Muslims on TV, No Terror in Sight," *New York Times*, November 11, 2007, 30.

26. When Mr. Tolchuck loses his job, Raja gets a job at a convenience store to help out. Raja's religious practices shame the Tolchucks into going to church. In the last episode, Raja does start to date a young Muslim girl when he meets one of the only other Muslim families in town.

27. Although the film was the star vehicle for actor Ryan Reynolds (as the title character) and actress Tara Reid, it was Kal Penn in the role of Taj who eventually starred in the sequel set in Britain.

28. In one instance, Taj's parents and his sister are called a racial epithet with Indian and Pakistani overtones, but the film avoids racial conflicts and instead situates Taj in a class conflict with the established and overprivileged aristocratic English against Taj's team of misfits, which includes a nerd, a heavy-drinking Irishman, and a shy genius.

29. Shalini Shankar, *Desiland: Teen Culture, Class, and Success in Silicon Valley* (Durham, NC: Duke University Press, 2003), 3.

30. Sunaina Maira, *Desis in the House: Indian American Youth Culture in New York City* (Philadelphia: Temple University Press, 2002).

31. I remember that a special screening was held in my hometown for the Indian community. Many second-generation Indians confessed that they felt a pride in their Indian background that they never had before they saw the film. It opened up a new way of relating to India.

32. The other film of note that was made about Gandhi was *Nine Hours to Rama*, directed by Mark Robson and released in 1963. The film was about Naturam Godse, the man who assassinated Gandhi.

33. Jack Kroll, "A Magnificent Life of Gandhi," *Newsweek*, December 13, 1982, 60.

34. Stuart Auerbach, "Trouble Shooting: The Gandhi Controversy: Indians Protest the Filming of Gandhi's Life," *Washington Post*, November 28, 1980, Style C1.

35. Kroll, "Magnificent Life," 60.

36. William K. Stevens, "For India's Young, 'Gandhi' Brings Gandhi to Life," special, *New York Times*, April 13, 1983, sec. A, 2. In the article, Stevens talks about how the film inspires young Indians who did not know about Gandhi outside of school history books: "The movie has been overwhelmingly praised since its premiere here in November and since its long-term run, at a tax-free price amounting to half the usual admission, started in January. Some critics have quarreled with some omissions of historical fact, but many more Indians would probably agree with the magazine *India Today*, which said that in terms of cinematic art, Sir Richard [Attenborough] 'has taken the best of both worlds, East and West, and merged them to produce an epic that should become required viewing in all schools and colleges.'"

37. Vincent Canby, "Ben Kingsley in Panoramic Gandhi," *New York Times*, December 8, 1982, sec. C, 21.

38. The Bollywood film *Lage Raho Munnabhai* (Carry On, Munnabhai), directed by Rajkumar Hirani, was released in September 2006. The film included the ghost of Gandhi, who reappeared in modern times to advise some of the main characters, and was one of the most popular Bollywood releases in Great Britain and the United States as well as India. The film *Gandhi, My Father*, directed by Feroz Abbas Khan and released in 2007, is an independent British film that focuses on the conflict between Gandhi and his eldest son Harilal (whom he disowned).

39. Gandhi was a spokesperson for religious tolerance and supported all forms of worship. A Hindu fundamentalist faction that believed he was too lenient toward Muslims during and after Indian and Pakistani Independence assassinated him.

40. Vijay Prasad, *The Karma of Brown Folk* (Minneapolis: University of Minnesota Press, 2000), viii. Prasad is responding to W. E .B. Du Bois's classic text *The Souls of Black Folk*, which comments on race relations at the turn of twentieth century, when Du Bois asks how it feels for black Americans to be seen as a problem. Prasad's book discusses how South Asians are often used as a model minority and compared to black Americans.

41. Laurie Ouellette and James Hay, "Makeover TV: Labors of Reinvention," in *Better Living through Reality TV: Television and Post-Welfare Citizenship* (Malden, MA: Blackwell, 2008), 99–133.

42. Jacobson says, "If Kennedy's ascendance to the White House seemed to denote the absolute assimilation of the Irish in American life, his sentimental journey [back to Ireland] in the summer of 1963 suggested that perhaps 'assimilation' itself was more complicated than many had assumed." *Roots Too: White Ethnic Revival in Post–Civil Rights America* (Cambridge: Harvard University Press, 2006), 12. Kennedy began the idea that all Americans (specifically European Americans) should embrace their immigrant ancestors because that history constitutes one of the defining aspects of national identity. He also touches on the circumstance that assimilation does not mean that immigrants are completely subsumed into the dominant culture without a past. What is important is through the influence and representation of Kennedy's

relation to his past that the national ideals about immigration and assimilation enter the popular imaginary. The irony is that his character in the series is the one who eases Gandhi's assimilation into American masculinity by teaching him to speak with an accent.

43. Eng, *Racial Castration*, 3.

44. Ouellette and Hay, "Makeover TV," 100.

45. One can't help but draw parallels to the appeal of Barack Obama in the 2008 election.

46. Interestingly, the Bollywood film industry has responded to this portrayal with a series of films that promote Gandhian behavior to the contemporary generation. For example, in the Bollywood hit film *Lage Raho Munnabhai*, the ghost of Gandhi appears to a Bombay thief and his friends to teach them how his principles can help them in their everyday life and even in romance. Gandhi, portrayed as humorous and practical, also discusses the discipline of nonviolence and how one person can "be the change" even in the modern era. Instead of using himself or invoking his name, Gandhi tells the main characters to act on his principles. In the first ten days, the film made 1.05 billion rupees (£12 million or US$18.8 million) at the Indian box office. For additional information, see Jeremy Page, "Play It Again, Mahatma, But This Time with a Lesson in Laughs," *London Times*, September 12, 2006, 39.

Chapter 4. Indian Gurus in the American Marketplace

1. Jane Naomi Iwamura, *Virtual Orientalism: Asian Religion and American Popular Culture* (New York: Oxford University Press, 2011), 4, 6.

2. Deborah Solomon, "Questions for Deepak Chopra: Imagining the Prophet," *New York Times Magazine*, September 5, 2010, 15.

3. Deepak Chopra, who today is a household name, has recently been involved with Virgin Comics to present a new line of graphic novels entitled *India Authentic*, which features reinterpretations of Indian religion.

4. Prasad, *Karma of Brown Folk*, 48.

5. Spirituality has been increasingly talked about and discussed in contemporary culture. A 2004 *Time* cover asks, "How Spiritual Are You?" and the magazine printed a twenty-question quiz that measures spiritual awareness. Questions evaluate individual connection to emotions, people, nature, the world, and extrasensory perception. *Newsweek* magazine's 2005 cover story on "Spirituality in America" highlights a poll that proclaims that 79 percent of readers describe themselves as "spiritual." And while the institutionalized idea of religion is a global practice, the notion of spirituality is often defined as an individual connection to a higher being and has commonly been associated with Asian religions and Asian cultures in China and India.

6. In 2008, Deepak Chopra published the book *Why Is God Laughing? The Path to Joy and Spiritual Optimism*. The book is a fictional account of a Los Angeles comedian who struggles to find humor and happiness after his father's death. The book

includes a foreword by comedian Mike Myers, who had recently lost his father and became good friends with Chopra.

7. For more on the representation of the Asian monk, see Iwamura's *Virtual Orientalism*.

8. Rachel Rubin and Jeffrey Melnick, *Immigration and Popular Culture* (New York: New York University, 2007), 129–75. Jeffrey Melnick discusses how Indian "gurus" (including musician Ravi Shankar) appeared at U.S. rock festivals, such as Woodstock. Hippie culture embraced Indian things, including religion and music.

9. Kimberly J. Lau, *New Age Capitalism: Making Money East of Eden* (Philadelphia: University of Pennsylvania Press, 2000), 23, 32.

10. While the independent-film scene has developed a variety of South Asian American projects, Hollywood films that have been featured in the 1990s and post-2000 era have mostly been comedies featuring South Asian American sidekicks, such as Taj from *National Lampoon's Van Wilder* (2002) and *National Lampoon's Van Wilder 2: The Rise of Taj* (2006). Some notable exceptions have been the drama *The Namesake* (2006) and the comic Harold and Kumar films (2004, 2008). The prominent Indian American actor in all these films is Kal Penn.

11. Sunaina Maira, "Trance-formations: Orientalism and Cosmopolitanism in Youth Culture," in Davé, Nishime, and Oren, *East Main Street*, 27.

12. Prasad, *Karma of Brown Folk*, 35.

13. Iwamura, *Virtual Orientalism*, 69.

14. Hugh Urban, "Zorba the Buddha: Capitalism, Charisma, and the Cult of Bhagwan Shree Rajneesh," *Religion* 26 (1996): 162.

15. Prasad, *Karma of Brown Folk*, 63.

16. Lau, *New Age Capitalism*, 17.

17. Lisa Duggan, *The Twilight of Equality? Neoliberalism, Cultural Politics, and the Attack on Democracy* (Boston: Beacon, 2003), xii.

18. Movements in the 1960s (civil rights, gay rights, third-world movements, and women's rights) recognized the connections and relations between economic flows and cultural moments. Lisa Duggan identifies the 1980s as the moment when the discourse of culture was divided from economics.

19. Paramount Pictures held a special screening before the general release of the film in order to quell any concern among Hindu and Sikh communities in the case of objectionable stereotypes. There was no offense except, perhaps, that the film was so bad.

20. Jeffrey Melnick and Rachel Rubin, *Immigration and American Popular Culture* (New York: New York University Press, 2007), 159.

21. Commentary, *The Love Guru* (2008), Paramount Pictures, DVD.

22. Digital press kit, *The Love Guru* (2008), Margaret Herrick Academy for Motion Picture Library, accessed June 2011.

23. The name of Pitka's assistant, Rajneesh, is a reference to Bhagwan Shree Rajneesh, who was also known as the "sex guru" because he preached that human beings

should celebrate the human body and that sex was divine and would lead to spiritual enlightenment. The narrative focuses on the love story in which Guru Pitka is a sexual innocent who is looking for love and helps others find romantic love.

24. Digital press kit, *Love Guru*.

25. Myers, "Myers' Path" (see chap. 1 n3).

26. Mike Myers, DVD interview, "The Making of The Love Guru," *Love Guru*.

27. Marco Schnabel, DVD commentary, *Love Guru*.

28. A. O. Scott, "Just Say 'Mariska Hargitay' and Snicker," *New York Times*, June 20, 2008, newyorktimes.com, accessed August 7, 2009.

29. Owen Gleiberman, review, *The Love Guru*, ew.com, June 20, 2008, accessed August 7, 2009.

30. One American Bollywood film crossover was *Marigold* (2007), directed by Willard Carroll. The plot revolves around an American actress (Ali Larter) who gets stranded in India and makes a Bollywood film with a major Indian star (Salman Khan) who is also a prince. The film was made in India. Danny Boyle's *Slumdog Millionaire* (2007) also featured a dance number in the train station at the end of the drama, even though the dance did not fit into the narrative. It signaled a happy ending and followed some of the conventions that British Indian director Gurinder Chadha used at the end of *Beck It like Beckham* (2002) and *Bride and Prejudice* (2004).

31. Daisy von Scherler Mayer and Tracey Jackson, commentary, *The Guru* (2004), DVD.

32. Sorina Diaconescu, "Slipping Insights In with Laughs," *Los Angeles Times*, January 31, 2003, 40, also available at http://articles.latimes.com/2003/jan/31/entertainment/et-diaconescu31, accessed July 15 2012.

33. Sukhdev Sandhu, "The Guru and the Cultural Politics of Placelessness," in *Alien Encounters: Popular Culture in Asian America*, ed. Mimi Thi Nguyen and Thuy Linh Nguyen Tu (Durham, NC: Duke University Press, 2007), 161–75.

34. Ibid., 170.

35. Inderpal Grewal, *Transnational America: Feminisms, Diasporas, Neoliberalisms* (Durham, NC: Duke University Press, 2005), 7.

36. His first acting audition is for an adult movie (although he does not realize this) when he dances the famous Tom-Cruise-dancing-in-his-underwear scene from the film *Risky Business* (1983), directed by Paul Brickman.

37. Diaconescu, "Slipping Insights," 40.

38. Sharonna says, "I made it [the philosophy] up to make it seem like I was doing something important and respectable." She is a porn star, and he is a spiritual star, but in attaining their dreams, they both have to act and so cannot be themselves except with each other. In the romantic subplot, Sharonna is pretending to be a schoolteacher and sexual innocent for her New York–fireman boyfriend fiancé. At the end, it turns out that he is also acting—he is love with his male partner fireman.

39. Brent Simon, "Mind, Body and Spirit," *Entertainment Today*, January 31–February 6, 2003, in digital press file, *The Guru*.

Chapter 5. The (Asian) American Dream

1. *Harold and Kumar Go to White Castle*, bringing in $18 million, was the 110th highest-grossing film of 2004, with the top honors going to *Shrek 2* ($441 million) and *Spider-Man 2* ($373.5 million). Of course, the budgets for the latter two films were each ten times the $9 million budget allocated to the first Harold and Kumar film, which has grossed more than $60 million in DVD rentals and sales. "2004 Domestic Gross," *Box Office Mojo*, boxofficemojo.com, accessed July 1, 2010.

2. *Harold and Kumar Escape from Guantanamo Bay* was the seventy-fifth-highest-grossing film of 2008, with $38 million in box office that year. "2008 Domestic Gross," *Box Office Mojo*, boxofficemojo.com, accessed July 1, 2010.

3. Roger Ebert, review of *Harold and Kumar Go to White Castle, Chicago Sun Times,* rogerebert.com, July 30, 2004.

4. David Gerard Hogan, *Selling Them by the Sack: White Castle and the Creation of American Food* (New York: New York University, 1997), 6.

5. "Commentary," special features, *Harold and Kumar Go to White Castle.*

6. Peter Feng, *Identities in Motion: Asian American Film and Video* (Durham, NC: Duke University Press, 2002), 2.

7. Digital press kit, *Harold and Kumar Go to White Castle*, July 30, 2004, Margaret Herrick Library, Academy of Motion Picture Arts and Sciences, accessed June 2011.

8. Marisa Meltzer, "Leisure and Innocence: The Eternal Appeal of the Stoner Movie," *Slate*, June 26, 2007, www.slate.com, accessed July 11, 2010.

9. Cheech Marin and Tommy Chong had a stand-up routine and worked as partners on the comedy circuit before they started making films.

10. Chris Tucker and Ice Cube were in a series of films known as the *Friday* films: *Friday* (1995), *Next Friday* (2000), and *Friday after Next* (2005). Dave Chappelle starred in *Half-Baked* and was a cowriter.

11. The real Harold Lee participates in the DVD commentary for the first film.

12. Shirley Halperin, "Going to Pot," *Entertainment Weekly*, April 18, 2008, 38–41.

13. Benjamin Schwartz, "The Devil's in the Details: What's Wrong and What's Gloriously Right with *Mad Men*," *Atlantic Monthly*, November 2009, 98.

14. A series of seven MGM films (1940 to 1962) starring Bing Crosby and Bob Hope were action-adventure comedies and musicals. Most of the films included scenes that were improvisations and ad-libbing by the actors. The first one was *The Road to Singapore*. It is in *The Road to Hong Kong* (1962) that Crosby and Hope first encounter Peter Sellers, in brownface performance, playing an Indian doctor with an accent.

15. Commentary, *Harold and Kumar Go to White Castle.*

16. Dennis Lim, "The Wild Munch," *Village Voice*, July 20, 2004, accessed online July 15, 2011.

17. Christine List, "Self-Directed Stereotyping in the Films of Cheech Marin," in *Chicanos and Film: Essays on Chicano Representation and Resistance*, ed. Chon Noriega (New York: Garland, 1992), 209.

18. Ibid.

19. Feng, *Identities in Motion*, 4.

20. Modern-day bromances include films such as *I Love You Man* and *Superbad*. The bromance can be traced back to early films, such as *Butch Cassidy and the Sundance Kid*, *Brian's Song*, *Rush Hour*, and *The Great Escape*, that fall into this category although most of the narratives are dramas or action adventure that may have some elements of comedy.

21. The Extreme Punks resemble disgruntled New Jersey youth who dress in sports gear and jeer, "Better luck tomorrow." This is an in-joke to audience members who might be familiar with John Cho's work in Justin Lin's feature film *Better Luck Tomorrow* (2002). The film chronicles the exploits of Asian American overachievers and model minorities who become small-time criminals.

22. The romance in these films does not delve into serious relationships or lead to marriage. Harold's and Kumar's (particularly Kumar) interest is in the pursuit of and relationship with marijuana.

23. Even Kumar admits that they may have made a mistake in not going to the party. For Harold, his transformation is personal confidence that allows him to stand up for what he believes rather than try to appease those around him. He steals the truck of the white gang who stole his parking spot, beat up the Asian guys, and called him "Mr. Miyagi" from the film *The Karate Kid*, and he kisses Maria at the end of the film. Just as in Harold's dream sequence where he envisions himself as a masked hero who picks up a gun and then fights off the bad guys to rescue Maria, he musters the will to act heroic in his everyday life.

24. Kumar, as a South Asian, is treated as a sexualized exotic object. Two British coeds at the college and an old white man who strokes his hand in the hospital waiting room ogle him. When Kumar is performing an emergency surgery, a white surgical resident mops Kumar's brow and admires his "soft chocolate lips." His skin color and racial difference make him desirable because he is a cultural accent rather than an individual. The film mocks the sexualization of Indian American men in contrast to the sexual reticence of Korean American men. Kumar is not distracted by love or sexual desire for people (only marijuana) because he is trying to decide what his future professional life should be—should he go to medical school or not?

25. Digital press kit, *Harold and Kumar Go to White Castle*.

26. In the movie, the professor, reading his book of essays on civil disobedience, says that he's in jail "for being black." Harold later listens to the professor's advice about not letting others "rile him up because the universe" will eventually even everything up. This philosophy echoes Martin Luther King Jr. and Gandhi and it is no coincidence that it is discussed in a jail.

27. Anita Mannur, *Culinary Fictions: Food in South Asian Diasporic Culture* (Philadelphia: Temple University Press, 2010), 173.

Chapter 6. "Running from the Joint"

1. Paul Achter, "Comedy in Unfunny Times: News Parody and Carnival after 9/11," *Critical Studies in Media Communication* 25, no. 3 (2008): 275.

2. The sequel *Harold and Kumar Escape from Guantanamo Bay* had a budget of $12 million and grossed over $38 million at the box office in 2008, making it one of the top-seventy-five highest-grossing films of the year.

3. Anthony Kaufman, "Absurdistan," *Village Voice*, April 16–22, 2008, 60.

4. Amnesty International, quoted in "Trivia," *Harold and Kumar Escape from Guantanamo Bay*, imdb.com, http://www.imdb.com/title/tt0481536/trivia, accessed June 15, 2011.

5. Kaufman, "Absurdistan," 60.

6. Press kit, *Harold and Kumar Escape from Guantanamo Bay*, Margaret Herrick Library of Academy Motion Pictures, accessed June 2011.

7. Jasbir K. Puar and Amit Rai, "The Remaking of a Model Minority: Perverse Projectiles under the Spectre of (Counter)Terrorism," *Social Text* 80, 22, no. 3 (2004): 81.

8. Ibid.

9. Jeffrey Melnick, *9/11 Culture: America under Construction* (Malden: Wiley–Blackwell, 2009), 112.

10. This scene mirrors one of the exchanges between an African American police detective played by Denzel Washington and a potential Sikh American suspect played by Waris Ahluwalia in Spike Lee's post–9/11 New York action film *Inside Man* (2006). When Ahluwalia's character complains that no one respects his rights anymore, Washington's character jokes, "Well, at least you can get a cab." This references the discrimination that black men have experienced in trying to hail a cab driven by South Asian cab drivers. In Lori Harrison-Kahan's thought-provoking analysis of the film, she points out, "Lee reveals that he improvised the dialogue by telling Ahluwalia to 'think of all the times since September 11 where you've been suspected of being bin Laden's brother and the treatment that you received. 'Cause that's what this script is about.' The scene has drawn attention as an example of blatantly political content in *Inside Man*, content deemed marginal to the film's overall project, but the dialogue—improvised by two actors of color who are drawing on their personal experiences—also points us in the direction of Lee's masked political agenda." In this drama, Lee uses humor to show the irony of racial identity. It's a memorable scene because it's also one of the only ones that address black–South Asian relations. Lori Harrison-Kahan, "Inside *Inside Man*: Spike Lee and Post-9/11 Entertainment," *Cinema Journal* 50, no. 1 (2010): 40.

11. David Denby, "The Current Cinema: The Unquiet Life," *New Yorker*, May 19, 2008, accessed online July 15, 2011.

12. Amy Kaplan, "Where Is Guantánamo?" *American Quarterly* 57, no. 3 (2005): 831.

13. In her book *Terrorist Assemblages: Homonationalism in Queer Times* (2007), Jasbir K. Puar introduces the idea of the "sexuality of terrorism" in which she discusses how narratives of hetero- and homosexuality are utilized to create clear differences

between Arab/Muslim identity/sexuality as masculine and overtly patriarchal versus American sexuality as inclusive and gay friendly. The discussion of gay sexuality and the cockmeat sandwich that occurs among the imprisoned terrorists, the American guards, and Harold and Kumar would support her argument and serves as another way to portray Harold and Kumar as heteronormative Americans.

14. Kaufman, "Absurdistan," 60.

15. Press kit, *Harold and Kumar Escape from Guantanamo Bay*.

16. Nina Seja, "No Laughing Matter? Comedy and the Politics of the Terrorist/Victim," *Continuum* 25, no. 2 (2011): 234.

17. Ibid., 233.

18. Ibid.

19. Rajini Srikanth, *Constructing the Enemy: Empathy/Antipathy in U.S. Literature and Law* (Philadelphia: Temple University Press, 2012). Srikanth points out in an early version of her argument that "the detainees' (whether domestic or on Guantánamo Bay) experience is not recognized as trauma; even when their body is present in the unmistakable and ultimate sign of trauma—the corpse of suicide—that body is read as something commodified, as tawdry signifier, as propaganda." In the film, the body of a terrorist is both a comic vehicle and a means to highlight Harold's and Kumar's patriotism and, hence, fits Srikanth's definition.

20. Kaplan, "Where Is Guantánamo?" 840.

21. Srikanth, *Constructing the Enemy*, 156.

22. The only Arab American in the film is Harold and Kumar's college friend Raza Syed, who lives in Miami. He eventually flees the country when Homeland Security tries to contact him.

23. Margaret Cho, *I'm the One That I Want* (New York: Ballantine, 2001), 140.

24. Leslie Bow, *Partly Colored: Asian Americans and Racial Anomaly in the Segregated South* (New York: New York University Press, 2010), 12.

25. Ibid., 166.

26. Roger Ebert, "A Very Harold and Kumar 3D Christmas," RogerEbert.com, November 2, 2011.

27. Neil Genzlinger, "A Holiday Up in Smoke," *New York Times*, November 3, 2011, accessed online January 15, 2012.

28. Press kit, *Harold and Kumar Escape from Guantanamo Bay*.

29. Speaking up brought Kumar trouble in the film, but it brought actor Kal Penn fame, fortune, and multiple opportunities both in and out of Hollywood. He starred in the critical drama *The Namesake* (2006), directed by Mira Nair, and was offered more roles in Hollywood as one of the most recognizable South Asian American actors. In 2009, he took the opportunity to "speak up" as Kumar could not by joining the Barack Obama administration for two years as an associate director in the White House Office of Public Engagement in the West Wing. Lately, he has returned to Hollywood to pursue his acting career but continues to be involved in politics and government service.

Epilogue

1. These include shows such as Bravo's *Top Chef* with host Padma Lakshmi, *Battlestar Galactica*'s Rekha Sharma, HBO's *In Treatment* with Irrfan Khan, and *Royal Pains*' Reshma Shetty.

2. *Slumdog Millionaire*, imdb.com. The film also did extremely well in Great Britain, grossing $50 million. In India, the film was not as popular; although it did well for an American film release in India, it was far behind the numbers generated by the Indian film industry.

3. Madhur Singh, "*Slumdog Millionaire*, an Oscar Favorite, Is No Hit in India," time.com, January 26, 2009, accessed June 15, 2010.

4. Ibid.

5. While the film was lauded as a cinematic success, the reality and consequences of filming a production in India had some unforeseen consequences. The success of the movie represented a slightly different picture for the young Indian actors who were "discovered" in the film. Upon their triumphant return to India as stars in an Academy Award–winning movie, one of the boys was slapped on camera by his father for not performing for the press (jeopardizing his income for the family). Caitlin Millat, "Slumdog Millionaire Child Star Azharuddin Allegedly Beaten by Father Days after Oscar Win," *New York Daily News*, February 27, 2009.

6. However, Swarup also points to the economic growth in India that offers a slightly modified vision of Indians not only as cultural things but also as competitors to the American economy. This threat of competition is diffused through the emphasis on Indian culture as a consumable good and also by depicting Indians as fitting into American culture.

7. Manohla Dargis, "Orphan's Lifeline Out of Hell Could Be a Game Show in Mumbai," *New York Times*, November 12, 2008, http://www.nytimes.com/, accessed April 19, 2009.

8. Boyle also credits casting director Loveleen Tanda with a codirecting nod for the portion filmed in India.

9. This show is based on the independent film *Outsourced* (2006), directed by John Jeffcoat.

10. The *New York Times* liked it, and *Entertainment Weekly* thought it was inoffensive. The comments to both online columns show how the discussion focused on whether or not the show was funny or racist. On the blog *Sepia Mutiny*, the South Asian community complained about the "inauthentic" Indian customs or accents, which has been an ongoing criticism. "Outsourced . . . It Was OK," *Sepia Mutiny*, September 24, 2010, www.sepiamutiny.com/sepia/archives/006330.html.

11. "Diwali," *The Office*, season 3, episode 34, written by Mindy Kaling and directed by Miguel Arteta, aired November 2, 2006, NBC, television.

Index

accents: belonging and, 1–2, 4, 6, 40–41, 46–50; brownface performances and, 13, 99; characteristics of, 30–32, 45; as cultural objects, 2, 97–102; definitions of, 2–4, 98, 130, 159n3; discrimination and, 4; immigrant status and, 122–23, 125, 142–45; John Wayne's idiosyncrasy and, 1–2, 5, 15; Midwestern, 5, 160n8; mystic stereotypes and, 85–86; othering and, 85–86, 100, 133–34, 138–41; parody and, 14–15, 111–12; post-9/11 era and, 141–45; privilege and, 8, 40–41, 44; racialization processes and, 43–44, 46–50, 65, 155, 157, 166n1, 167n7; racial or ethnic performativity and, 3, 6, 13; self-fashioning narratives and, 77–84; Southerners and, 133, 141, 145–48; voice acting and, 40–43; whiteness and, 78–84
Actor's Studio, The, 58
Adventures of Johnny Quest (series), 170n43
Afghanistan, 8, 127, 135, 152
African Americans: minstrel shows and, 11–12; racial performance and, 7, 47–48, 124, 134–35, 146; stereotypical roles for, 69, 100, 107, 147, 149; television programming and, 50–51, 66–67, 83, 171n12
Aliens in America (series), 70–71
All-American Girl (Cho), 146, 157
American Dream, 3, 72, 77–84, 91–92, 102–27, 141, 151–53. *See also* United States
Amnesty International, 129

Amritraj, Vijay, 32
animated cartoons: model minority tropes in, 76–84; racialization's inflections in, 48–49, 61–62, 92, 166n1; voice acting in, 41–43, 47–50. *See also specific series*
animatedtv.com (Web site), 53
Apu (*Simpsons* character). *See* Nahasapeemapetilon, Apu
Arab Americans, 134–35, 140, 143–44, 148
Arendt, Hannah, 159n3
Asian Americans: foreignness tropes and, 120, 148–49; *Harold and Kumar* films and, 4, 17, 112, 115–16; misrecognition of, 138–45; model minority trope and, 4, 34–35, 67–73, 85–86, 116–27, 145; Orientalism and, 10–14, 36; patriotism tropes and, 138–41; racialization of, 5, 11, 62, 115–16, 130–34; spirituality stereotypes and, 85–86; whitewashing and, 49–50
Asian Indians. *See* Indian Americans
Asian Pacific American (racial category), 7
assimilation processes, 12, 15, 40–41, 57–73, 77–84, 105–10, 152, 174n42
Attenborough, Richard, 73, 74
Austin Powers (films), 93
Azaria, Hank, 19, 30–31, 49–50, 54, 55, 58, 90

Bakhtin, Mikhail, 163n44
Bakshi, Hrundi V. (character), 19–39, 42, 49
Bangladesh, 7–8
Baranski, Christine, 91, 107

Tahir, Faran, 37
Tandan, Loveleen, 38
Taylor, Elizabeth, 27
Teahouse of the August Moon, The (film), 27
television: American Dream representations
on, 3, 9–10, 65–66; citizenship discourses
and, 1–3, 151; counterprogramming and,
50–52; 9/11 attacks and, 127, 131; Orientalist discourses in, 10–14, 18; racial performativity and, 7–8, 52–56, 62, 67–73;
sidekick characters in, 1–2, 67–73; voice
acting and, 40–41, 47–50. *See also specific
series and shows*
10 Things I Hate about You (film), 81
Tomei, Marisa, 91, 106
Tracey Ullman Show, The, 51
Transcendental Movement, 87, 94
Travolta, John, 92, 103
Tucker, Chris, 116
"Two Mrs. Nahasapeemapetilons, The"
(*Simpsons* episode), 53

Ullman, Tracey, 51
United 93 (Greengrass), 128
United States: American Dream representations in, 3, 72, 77–84, 91–92, 102–27, 141,
151; as capitalism's center, 25, 94–102, 152–
55; citizenship practices of, 1–4, 8–9, 29–
32, 53, 58–59, 94–110, 120; colonial narratives and, 19–27, 58; consumerism in, 15,
39, 80, 82, 94–102, 152–53; exceptionalism
and, 132–33; geopolitical allegiances of,
27–28, 30; identity formation in, 9–10,
26; immigration laws of, 5–7, 9, 15, 20,
29–32, 58–59, 69, 88, 106, 160n17, 161n18,
163n48; India's revolution and, 24–25,
67–69; masculinity representations in, 42,
61–73, 100, 123, 147–48, 157, 179n24; mimicry concept, 57–58, 77–78, 80–81, 118,
155; neoliberal globalization and, 32, 34,
65–66, 82, 85–86, 137; 9/11 responses and,
127–29, 134–41; Orientalism and, 10–14;
othering practices and, 5; parodic views

of, 134–50, 156; racial hierarchies in, 4–7,
11–15, 21, 23–24, 37–39, 53, 58, 67, 69–70,
79, 83–84, 121, 123–24, 135–36, 143, 147–48,
159n3, 163n47, 167n5; security and terrorism discourses in, 17; Southern culture
within, 145–48; spiritualism movements
in, 85–102, 175n3, 176n8
United States v. Bhagat Singh Thind, 6
Up in Smoke (film), 116
Urban, Hugh, 95

Valentino, Rudolph, 24
Van Wilder (films), 35, 62, 71–72
Very Harold and Kumar 3D Christmas, A
(Strauss-Schulson), 112, 148
Vietnam War, 15, 26, 29–30, 37
Vivekananda, Swami, 94
voice acting and actors, 47–50

Washington, Denzel, 37, 180n10
Wayans, Keenan Ivory, 51
Wayne, John, 1–2, 5, 15, 78
West, Kanye, 98
What a Girl Wants (Gordon), 90
whiteness, 5–18, 47–48, 58–66, 79–81, 105,
118–20, 124–27, 130–31. *See also* ethnicity;
racialization; United States
Who Wants to Be a Millionaire (show), 153
Willard, Fred, 121
Williams, Raymond, 3
Williams, Robin, 168n23
World Parliament of Religions, 94
World Trade Center (Stone), 128
World War II, 6, 15, 27, 34, 163n48

yellowface, 7, 12–13, 50, 115
Yellow Peril trope, 15, 34–35
Young Raja, The (Paramount), 24
"You're the One That I Want" (song), 103

Zip Coon (character), 11
Zook, Kristal Brent, 50–51

SHILPA S. DAVÉ is an assistant professor of American studies at Brandeis University and the coeditor of *East Main Street: Asian American Popular Culture.*

THE ASIAN AMERICAN EXPERIENCE

The University of Illinois Press
is a founding member of the
Association of American University Presses.

Composed in 10.5/13 Minion Pro
with Lucida Sans display
by Celia Shapland
at the University of Illinois Press
Manufactured by Thomson-Shore, Inc.

University of Illinois Press
1325 South Oak Street
Champaign, IL 61820-6903
www.press.uillinois.edu